D0327036

EDUCATING THE EXPERT SOCIETY

Chandler Publications in
ANTHROPOLOGY AND SOCIOLOGY
Leonard Broom, *Editor*

EDUCATING THE EXPERT SOCIETY

BY BURTON R. CLARK

CENTER FOR THE STUDY OF HIGHER EDUCATION
UNIVERSITY OF CALIFORNIA, BERKELEY

CHANDLER PUBLISHING COMPANY

124 SPEAR STREET SAN FRANCISCO, CALIFORNIA 94105

Library of Congress Catalog Card No. 62-10868
Printed in the United States of America

To Adele

Preface

THIS BOOK is a study in the sociology of education, an attempt to educate myself as well as others about some connections between education and society and the nature of the educational institution today. Long an almost dormant field of study in the United States, the sociology of education has recently come alive. Much promising research and speculation is now underway, making this an opportune time to sense the scope of the field, report its findings, speculate about its ideas, and point its future. Any one of these activities is sufficient cause to commit a book.

I wish to thank Howard S. Becker and Leonard Broom for critical review of this book in manuscript; William D. Johnson for helping in many ways; and Martin A. Trow for contributing to my understanding of education and society. I am also indebted to the Center for the Study of Higher Education, Berkeley, and its director, T. R. McConnell, for financial and secretarial assistance and the opportunity to inquire firsthand and full-time into educational affairs.

B. R. C.

Contents

Tables

Charts

EDUCATING THE EXPERT SOCIETY

Introduction

Education in the Technological Age

In the middle of the twentieth century, education in the United States without doubt has become a problem of national scope. A sense of crisis is shaped by the convergence of three great phenomena: rapid change in modern science and technology, a high birth rate at home, and the expanding thrust of totalitarianism abroad. The atomic age presses against education at a time when the number of students is doubling and tripling and the nation is committed to the winning of a cold war. With this convergence, many citizens and officials feel that educational inadequacies are enormously detrimental, that conceivably they may cost our freedom or even our lives.

More than before, the strengthening of schools and colleges is seen as a means of solving national problems, of securing the national welfare, and there is every sign this concern will increase in the decades to come. We see this interest exemplified in the case of a former president of Harvard University, later United States ambassador to West Germany, studying high schools in the United States and suggesting universal standards. There is a growing interest in federal legislation on education, and the federal government is supporting research and reform in education through the United States Office of Education, the National Science Foundation, and other channels. Nearly every civic club, professional association, and academic discipline, it sometimes seems, is out to "save education." This public sense of education's importance in society—a sense growing in all modern countries and in many underdeveloped countries—infuses the study of educational institutions with new meaning.

The growing concern reaffirms the need, long understood by some observers, to comprehend education as a social institution, examining how it is shaped by society and how it in turn influences other institutions. In brief form, this book attempts such a task. I intend here especially to emphasize the distinctive impact of modern conditions upon education and thereby to extend and sharpen discussion of certain topics traditional to the sociology of education. I mean also to introduce some new issues and uncommon perspectives that, however slightly, may serve to broaden systematic study and illumine the popular understanding.

One modern condition of great moment is the harnessing of society to a technology, already huge, that expands at an accelerating pace. Modern man is clearly in a second scientific revolution. The first revolution centered on the steam engine and the spinning machine, and put machines in place of muscle. The second scientific revolution (occurring in the last forty years and especially since 1945) centers on atomic energy, automation, computers, and chemical materials. It greatly magnifies technically produced energy, changes processing methods, alters the materials on which men and machines work, and often substitutes machines for human thought and control. Although we have been sliding into a technological age on the basis of accumulated techniques produced by the first scientific revolution, we are now in for technology with a vengeance. Through its ramifying effects—for example, on transportation, communications, and the distribution of goods—technology alters nearly all institutions.

Not the least of the alterations is seen in technology's effect on the role of education. Our age demands army upon army of skilled technicians and professional experts, and to the task of preparing these men the educational system is increasingly dedicated. The ideal of the expert ascends over the ideal of the cultivated man, in the general society and in education itself. Some forty years ago the German sociologist Max Weber observed:[1]

> Behind all the present discussions of the foundations of the educational system, the struggle of the "specialist type of man" against the older type of "cultivated man" is hidden at some decisive point. This fight is determined by the irresistibly expanding bureaucratization of all public and private relations of authority and by the ever-increasing importance of expert and specialized knowledge. This fight intrudes into all intimate cultural questions.

These comments are no less relevant in America in the 1960's. The expert versus the cultivated man, the specialist versus the generalist, the scientist versus the humanist, these are themes running through modern debate over education and intellectual life. The effect of technological advance is to increase the pre-eminence and power of the expert, and with this, to increase the commitment of education to technical and professional preparation. We will return frequently to this theme in the chapters to follow.

Even in an advanced stage of industrialism, science and technology are not the only engines of change. Population expansion is a primary determinant of change in society;

[1] H. H. Gerth and C. Wright Mills (eds.), *From Max Weber: Essays in Sociology* (New York: Oxford University Press, 1946), p. 243.

and the high birth rate sustained in the United States since 1945 is causing a series of alterations—for our purposes, notably in the magnitude of the educational task and in the diversity and scope of the agencies formed to fulfill it. Everywhere, too, in modern institutions organizations become larger and more impersonal, under impulses aside from population growth, and the requirements of complex organization affect education from outside and from within. Administration is increasingly administration by experts, and would-be experts need training and diplomas. Education is altered from within by bureaucratic requirements as specialization proceeds and the staff proliferates. To speak of the technological society is to speak of mass population and complex organization as well as of science and technology. These are the broad social factors to which we refer repeatedly in this book.

The following chapters, in their sequence of topics, move from the outside to the inside of the educational institution, and somewhat from the general to the specific.

We first consider the cultural roles of education. As education becomes a separate institution, set off principally in the school and the college, it becomes society's main vehicle of cultural indoctrination. Society expects education to do its bidding, transmitting a heritage and preparing the next generation in approved ways. But the transmission of the culture and the preparation of the young are no simple tasks in a complex society; the volume of knowledge is large, groups differ over what should be taught, and the general values of society contain many contradictions. Significantly, education in a technological society becomes itself an active force, one of the important institutions in innovation and in changing what men think. In emphasizing its growing influence, we will be extending, even seriously modifying, the traditional conception of how education relates to the culture. But, both as passive instrument and as active force, education connects the culture of the past and future, and in Chapter 1 its cultural roles are discussed.

As a training ground, increasingly related to the world of work, formal education also becomes the primary means of betterment for individuals, social classes, and minority groups. Education is now the main avenue for achieving the rewards of higher occupational and social status; the connections between social origin, education, and career loom ever larger. The contribution of education to the aspirations and destinies of minorities is, of course, now a major issue in America. Many persons see equal access to schools and colleges, along with voting and job rights, to be at the core of the democratic struggle. These concerns of class, occupation, and race, or what might be called the social roles of education, constitute the subject matter of Chapters 2 and 3.

When education is set aside in a special establishment and there given basic societal tasks, its control is an important matter. Who will determine what shall be done—what to teach, who shall be educated, the direction of change? In a complex society, various groups—economic, social, religious, political—have different interests and ideas on this matter. The form of control helps to determine the character and capability of a school or college, and as education becomes more important, the nature of its control demands greater understanding. Accordingly, we need to examine, as best we can, the structures of influence that surround and pervade schools and colleges, though little has been neatly determined and most of what we need to know remains in the shadows of political maneuver and informal pressure. Chapter 4 is a brief essay in political sociology, examining community influences, the trend toward centralization, and the types of authority that compete in American education.

In considering who runs educational agencies, we naturally move inside to look at the school or college as an administrative system. Education has been caught up in the growing bureaucratization of human activity, notably in higher education, where major campuses have reached the size of small cities. This trend affects the participation of students, as will be noted especially in Chapter 6. It alters the role of board members, administrators, and teachers. It makes more complex the arrangements of work and people, and leads to the emergence of new specialties, counseling for example. But there is much variation, and Chapter 5 grapples with the internal structure and administrative tendencies of small and large educational systems.

Educational agencies also contain subcultures and subsocieties that influence what they are able to do. Chapters 6 and 7 take up the manners and mores of students, first in college and then in high school. Students are frequently a strange tribe, ill-understood by their elders and able to defeat their superiors despite their formally inferior position and status. The instruction of students, which is largely what education is all about, is conditioned by diverse student orientations which have their own tradition and their own continuing supports in society and in the school. Some students in high school are oriented primarily to study, others to play, others to delinquency. Colleges contain vocational and bohemian subcultures, the serious student and Joe College. These two chapters attempt to explain why student enclaves take the form they do, and to offer an estimate of the directions in which they are changing. It will appear that the situation in high school is diverse and confusing, while in college there is diversity but also a pronounced strengthening of the vocational orientation.

In Chapter 8, a short concluding chapter, some materials of the first seven chapters are reorganized and summarized and a last look is taken at things to come. In the advanced industrial society of the mid-twentieth century, we know that education will grow ever more complex, with larger and more differentiated staffs and student bodies. Where will this trend lead? Prediction is hazardous, for we know little about the outcomes of formal schooling in the past and present, and education in the future will have unique aspects. Clearly, the tension—between quality and quantity, between selection and open door, between the preparation of leaders and the education of the masses—will continue, perhaps becoming greater than ever before. That the schools will offer universal training and broad opportunity is hardly in doubt. Unclear, however, are the social and cultural consequences of mass education—the results for the quality of human interaction, the strength of traditional values, the integration of society. Chapter 8 extends several ideas that pervade earlier sections of the book and raises new issues that appear as concomitants of continued growth in a technological society.

A word needs to be said about the question of quality or excellence in education, for this matter, now so widely discussed, intrudes into our discussion; no effort has been made to exclude it simply because it seems to depend on value judgments. There are, of course, no absolute standards of quality in such a broad matter as education; one man's quality in education is another man's nonsense; liberal-arts professors and small shopkeepers may differ profoundly on what is educational quality. But neither is quality completely relative. There are major pockets of social agreement, and an observer can roughly assess quality in education on the basis of its appropriateness for the requirements of adulthood. In the technological age, schools must perform more than a custodial function; for, more than ever, the young need a technical and cultural competence if they are to perform adult tasks—and, more than ever, as the schools take over the training function, personal capabilities must be developed through the school. Thus the attitude of delinquents in high school is hardly supportive of quality. So, too, an emphasis on fun in college detracts from rather than contributes to a quality education.

In this book I attempt to edge toward a "clinical" judgment of quality, on the basis of how adequately education prepares the young for adult life. In doing this, it is not necessary to identify quality with the humanities and the fine arts, even though the higher levels of cultural competence include humanistic learning. But the grounds of competence are being defined more specifically and clearly. The schools in previous eras might merely keep the kids off the streets and yet their graduates might function adequately in adult society. College might merely be a place for collegiate play and the graduate of the college might even so be prepared for a place in business. But not today. The technological society makes the appropriateness of preparation less a relative matter of differing perspective. Below certain levels of literacy lies a deep and lifelong cultural incompetence. Below certain levels of skill lies the probability of unemployment and part-time work; there used to be a large number of jobs for unskilled laborers, but now a low-grade vocational education does not lead anywhere. Without long systematic preparation, the higher occupations are generally not open. Without a broad education in the sciences and the humanities, public and business leaders are without the perspectives and understandings they need. Believing that modern society tends in these directions, I shall attempt to discuss quality in education without, be it hoped, reducing the matter to a set of personal preferences.

This short book, of course, is not exhaustive either of the topics covered or of the many subjects that could properly be included. Major systems of education, for example, now exist outside of schools and colleges: in industry, in religion, and in the military establishment. But because little is known and space is limited, these systems are not examined, despite their growing importance and their implication for the diffusion of education into other institutions. Also, the topic of teaching as a profession is barely broached, being touched upon only here and there in an offhand fashion. Further, little is said about socialization, the process that many sociologists consider central to any treatment of education and society. We subsume it under the transmitting of culture from one generation to the next and largely bypass the question of *how* culture becomes instilled in the minds of the young.

In its subject matter, this book differs from most textbooks in educational sociology that attempt to cover much of the ground of general sociology. Failure to impose boundaries has caused books in the sociology of education to wander far afield, with chapters in "social structure," "the social basis of human development," "the family," and "community institutions." The sociology of education, upon taking its conceptual leads from sociology, needs to limit attention to matters educational, exploring topics such as race, family, and population only as they *importantly* bear on education. Without such delimitation, all social phenomena become grist for the mill, since the whole world is interrelated in some degree and everything bears on everything else. This brief review attempts to stay close to the educational institution in each chapter, centering on a few subjects rather than many. At the same time, the book highlights several subjects that have received little attention in most texts: the structure of educational control, the formal organization of the school and college, student culture in college as well as in the high school. Additionally, higher education and the public schools are integrated in a general treatment that cuts across educational lines.

It should also be clear that this book does not purport to

examine educational theories or to recommend education practices. A sociology is not an essay on what ought to be, nor a tract on what constitutes effective procedure. Rather it is an examination from a particular perspective of what *is*—in this case, the social aspects of educational structures and processes, their social causes and consequences. The attempt made here to peer into educational affairs through sociological glasses differs sharply from efforts to plead a cause or push a theory or promote an educational method, and it is best that this difference be clearly realized in the beginning.

A treatment of education, as a social institution, that hopes to be reasonably objective and restrained in value judgment may well seem distant and cold from the standpoint of those who must decide, or wish to know, what should be done in education here and now. But observation in a broad perspective may reveal findings that otherwise are obscured and may develop interpretations that otherwise might be overlooked. The long view in this book has the side virtue of covering terrain that is largely apart from the tangled web of educational theory, the thicket of charges and countercharges of the modern debate between educationists and their critics. There is a proverb, not yet completely out of date, which holds that a man should never run after a bus, a woman, or an educational theory—another one will be along very soon. This book will have little to say about educational theories, unless they help toward an understanding of the connections between society and education and of the nature of education as an institution.

Chapter I

Education as a Cultural Agent

THE TRANSMISSION OF CULTURE

EDUCATION HAS long been viewed as playing a decisive role in the historical continuity of culture, in maintaining man's heritage of knowledge, beliefs, customs, and skills. Education transmits a common cultural fund to the next generation and in the process helps to bring hordes of young barbarians to adult ways that are continuous with the past. In a sense, the school acts as an agent of the whole society, conserving and controlling in its image. Some educational institutions function similarly for smaller enclaves that want to perpetuate their own heritage. A parochial school attempts to instill the religious beliefs of its parent church, as well as to inculcate basic precepts of the nation. Thus schools preserve and transmit culture, general and specific, for different groups. This historic role of education is a significant topic with which to begin an examination of educational institutions, for when we talk about culture we touch upon the values we live by, the definitions of the desirable and the right that give meaning to human existence. Cultural transmission is a fundamental link between educational institutions and the general society.

Of course, schools and colleges as we know them did not always exist but emerged as education became a distinct function. Education is now a quite visible thing because much of it takes place in a separate establishment; educational work is concentrated in certain places, some adults specialize in it, and the young go off to the detached setting that is called a school. But cultural transmission and socialization of the young have always taken place, only in less obvious ways in earlier and simpler societies. In preliterate societies, education was (and is) concentrated in the family, the tribe, and the other social groupings within which the young were raised.[1] The earliest "educational systems" were no more than a woman instructing a daughter or a man and a boy walking, talking, and working together. In the Stone Age, we may bet, there were no elementary classes in flint chipping; a boy learned to chip flints by watching adults. Where there was little lore and skill to transmit, and the life of the society was lived out before a child's eyes, education was blended with other activities.

The basic historical trend has been for the blended to become unblended. As some societies grew in size and complexity, and as their cultural heritage extended and deepened, education became a separate, visible sphere. Stepping back only for a moment into the quiet cloisters of history, we may say that this evolution was quite slow up to the last three centuries; throughout most of recorded history, organized education—formal instruction—generally touched only a few. The mass of men from the dawn of history to

[1] For a clear description of the education of children in a preliterate society where adults in the family and tribe teach the young—and the young teach the very young—see Margaret Mead, *Coming of Age in Samoa* (New York: Wm. Morrow & Company, 1928; also New York: The New American Library, Mentor Books, 1949), Chapter 3, "The Education of the Samoan Child."

the Industrial Revolution remained untutored and illiterate, while a "high culture" arose gradually in society after society. A small body of kings, nobles, priests, and functionnaries came to possess special knowledge and lore and cultivated taste. In the middle ages there existed an almost precious world of art, music, history, and literature—and political intrigue—centered in the courts and the cathedrals. This esoteric culture was transmitted by the education of a few, through schools in the monasteries and the cathedrals, and through the private tutor in the courts and the independent master who would hang out a shingle and hope that a few students would appear and stay. The ruling groups largely monopolized knowledge, and the limitation of education to a relative few was, of course, a part of their self-perpetuation as ruling groups.

However limited, this systematic transmission functioned to conserve and perpetuate the gradually accumulating wisdom of man. Many ideas in science and in political thought that had been patiently developed by the Greeks and the Romans were carried through the middle ages by very small bands of men, often scholarly monks sequestered in monasteries, who would zealously guard a parchment or laboriously copy over its contents. Such scholars knew Aristotle and more Aristotle. At the same time, the great mass of men, largely illiterate peasants, received the general "low" culture through the home, church, estate, or community. There was neither time nor reason for the classroom. A boy of eight in medieval times was a breadwinner, helping the father in the fields.[2] Found throughout much of man's recorded history, the pattern of formally educated elites and informally educated or uneducated masses was

[2] See Eileen Power's description of the life of the peasant in France during the ninth century, in her *Medieval People* (London: 1924; also Garden City, N.Y.: Doubleday & Company, Inc. [Anchor Books], 1954), Chapter 1.

appropriate to a world of circumscribed knowledge, unskilled labor, and stable, integrated relationships. Even at the time of the first colonial settlements in America, formal education still played a very limited role. As one historian has described it:[3]

> Family, community, and church together accounted for the greater part of the mechanism by which English culture transferred itself across the generations. The instruments of deliberate pedagogy, of explicit, literate education, accounted for a smaller, though indispensable, portion of the process. For all the interest in formal instruction shown in the century after the Reformation in England, and for all the extension of explicitly educational agencies, the span of pedagogy in the entire spectrum of education remained small.

This pattern changed radically when science and technology burst open the bounds of knowledge and changed the nature of work. Dating from roughly the seventeenth century, rapidly expanding knowledge has required more scholars and scientists to conserve and produce it, men committed to a life of the mind and trained through prolonged education. Too, any one adult, increasingly, could acquaint himself with only a small part of all knowledge and more specialists in knowledge were required for its effective transmission. More important yet, work itself became complicated and specialized under the impulse of advancing techniques of production and distribution, and with this the "educational threshold" of employment was progressively raised. The worker, as well as the ruler and the scholar, needed longer, systematic instruction, although at first this amounted for most only to reading, writing, and arithmetic of the simplest kind. In recent decades, those trained in the more advanced techniques had need of pro-

[3] Bernard Bailyn, *Education in the Forming of American Society* (Chapel Hill: The University of North Carolina Press, 1960), pp. 18–19.

longed instruction, topped by schooling with expert practitioners and specialists. Then, too, as the Industrial Revolution concentrated the means of production in factories, family breadwinners increasingly worked away from home; being out of sight, they could not initiate the young into adult work nor could the young learn by sheer observation—other than in the case of child labor in the factory. In any event, men's jobs became radically different from one another, and the observation of adult activities could no longer provide a common schooling. Besides, in large societies, the young are so numerous that it is "efficient" to bunch them, to educate them in batches.

In brief, formal schooling became a necessity as the home and the community became ineffectual, even incompetent, in training the young for adulthood through informal contact. A new class of cultural agents—the teachers of the commoners—grew up. The changing nature of knowledge and work brought the children of the common man into the schoolhouse and gave to the schools a greatly broadened and deepened role in cultural transmission and continuity. This basic trend of industrial society promises to continue without limit, for knowledge constantly expands, production techniques grow more complex, and the educational requirements of work steadily rise. (See Chapter 2.) To the education of elites as the organized means of cultural transmission there has been permanently added the education of the masses. These two streams of education now mix and contend with one another.

The culture that the school and the teacher in most American communities are now asked to transmit to the next generation is an enormously complex web of values, norms, and knowledge. It includes political ideals, such as belief in democratic government and national loyalty; economic conceptions, such as free enterprise; social practices, from telling time to monogamous marriage; and even implicit religious understandings, such as the premise that society is based on a single God. With every set of general values there are scores of specific directives that teachers need to instill, deliberately or unconsciously, directly or indirectly. Consider what it means for the schools to transfer belief in democracy. Abstract statements about democratic society are short on meaning unless they are spelled out in connected assertions about how to act democratically, and are exemplified in models, living or dead, of democratic action. The "rules" of democracy are as general as broad clauses about freedom of speech in a constitution or as specific as the norms that the good citizen does not stuff the ballot box nor the political candidate assassinate his opponents. The events and behaviors taught to inhere in democracy may range all the way from the conditions under which revolution is justifiable to the ways of voting for a school board.

A general value has been transmitted securely when its traditional meanings for action, written or unwritten, rigidly prescribed or flexibly adaptive, have been made clear to the next generation. Without a content of behavioral precepts, general values become empty and precarious, honored in the breach and easily pushed aside. We may note the precariousness of democratic ideals in new nations where the vocabulary of democracy is understood but related behavior and necessary supporting conditions are not —where, for example, the defeated politician offers not a handshake but the threat of a coup or revolution. In stable, integrated societies, broad values are almost unconsciously transmitted in all their supporting detail by the informal instruction of the family and other institutions. But where we expect the schools to carry much of the load of educating and training the great mass of men, then the fate of many core values depends in part upon how well teachers understand and interpret the numerous sets of values, often vague and conflicting, that the adult society lives by. As societies grow more complex, the formal task of culture transmission grows ever more difficult and problematic.

In fact, it sometimes seems in doubt whether a society as heterogeneous as the United States in the middle of the twentieth century has any shared cultural understandings to which nearly all of the young are exposed, since there are so many variations among regions, towns and cities, religious schools and public schools, the lower class and the middle class. But some shared understandings seem to obtain still, although persons located in different parts of society differ in exposure and commitment to them. For example, achievement through individual effort is widely applauded in this country; it is taught in the schools as a general value and is buttressed with many specific practices and models, such as looking with pride upon the graduates of the school who achieve eminence. For a specific example of common culture, we may point to the American understanding of the causes, events, and outcomes of the Revolutionary War—a heritage reflected in the history books of American secondary schools. The contrast with the legends of the British about the same war—transmitted as part of *their* common schooling—is amusingly shown in the following comparison (on page 18) of American and British textbooks (pre-1938).[4]

These different interpretations of historical events have been perpetuated in England and the United States as part of the national legends that contribute to the respective national identities. We Americans have had a national consensus on this and similar matters, and schools throughout the country have almost uniformly transmitted these under-

[4] Bernard Berelson, *Content Analysis* (Glencoe, Illinois: The Free Press, 1952), pp. 36–37; summarized by Berelson from Arthur Walworth, *School Histories at War* (Cambridge: Harvard University Press, 1938), pp. 3–20.

UNITED STATES TEXTBOOKS	BRITISH TEXTBOOKS
King George III was a blundering bigot, obstinate and narrow-minded.	King George was a man of moderate ability with a firm will, real courage, and a high sense of royal obligation to the public.
America had contributed to British prosperity.	The colonies were a liability rather than an asset to the British Empire.
The "Intolerable Acts" passed by the British Parliament were the beginning of hostilities.	Acts of violence committed by the radical element in the colonies made military action necessary.
The Colonies were fighting the cause of traditional English liberty by their actions.	[omitted]
[omitted]	King George made a last attempt at reconciliation.
[With reference to the rout of the Hessians at Trenton] This brilliant exploit, at a time when all seemed lost, put new life into the patriot cause.	Though Washington achieved a brilliant little success [sic] by surprising a detached force of Hessians at Trenton, his position was extremely difficult.
The American defeat at Bunker Hill was a moral victory, for it showed that the raw Colonial troops could face the regulars without flinching.	The small English army suffered as heavy losses with as steady courage as has ever been shown on prouder fields of honour.

standings to the next generation, modified gradually as historians have offered new interpretations.

Education's role in transmitting cultural premises is under constantly increasing strain, however, in considerable part because expanding knowledge fragments the common culture and leads to diverse interpretations on what is essential. No man knows more than a segment of the basic knowledge and even the broadest philosopher is a specialist. At the same time, the average adult needs to know more about more matters to function as worker, citizen, and cultivated man. Longer, more intensive preparation for work means that the time given to vocational training competes with general studies. The conflict in American secondary schools between vocational training and general education is rooted in the tendency of formal education to be swamped by the task of cultural transmission. There is not enough time in the school day to do all the things asked, and time is more squeezed as the cultural burden grows heavier.

An allied source of strain upon the school's transmission of culture is the high speed of social change. With rapid change, the schools become less sure that what was right for the last generation is right for the next. In stable societies, this difficulty exists in minor degree if at all: preliterate societies may go virtually unchanged for centuries; on the feudal estates of medieval Europe, the adult way of life changed quite slowly. But in modern society, the new generation faces technological and social tasks that never existed before its time, with the future promising additional changes of unknown nature. Rapid change heightens the need to educate for adaptability,[5] often at the expense of imparting the cultural heritage. Schools become impatient with the work of instilling a knowledge of history and

[5] Karl Mannheim, *Freedom, Power and Democratic Planning* (London: Routledge & Kegan Paul, Ltd., 1951), pp. 248–250; David Riesman, *The Lonely Crowd* (New Haven: Yale University Press, 1950), Chapter II.

literature, for example, knowledge that often appears irrelevant in the light of the demands made by current affairs. Preparing youth for a dynamic society pulls the attention of parents and educators alike to the future: What are the challenges that Junior will have to cope with later in life? How can he be best prepared for these challenges and others that are unknown? Scholars may answer: Acquaint him with the best thought of mankind. But this has not been the answer emanating from the neighborhood and the school in the last half-century.

The following excerpt from the work of David Riesman dramatizes changes that have taken place in some elementary classrooms, where the emphasis has shifted from knowledge to group relations. Riesman suggests that the American elementary school is now less concerned with the transmission of a cultural heritage—Caesar and Pompeii—and more committed to the molding of adaptable personalities. He describes specific changes in the teacher's orientation and in classroom arrangements and practices, changes generally associated in this country with the progressive-education movement.

FROM KNOWLEDGE TO GROUP RELATIONS [6]

Progressive education began as a movement to liberate children from the crushing of talent and breaking of will that was the fate of many. . . . Its aim, and to a very considerable degree, its achievement, was to develop the individuality of the child; and its method was to focus the teacher's attention on more facets of the child than his intellectual abilities. Today, however, progressive education is often no longer progressive; as people have become more other-directed, educational methods that were once liberating may even tend to thwart individuality rather than advance and protect it. The story can be quickly told.

[6] David Riesman, *The Lonely Crowd* (New Haven: Yale University Press, 1950), pp. 60–64.

Progressive schools have helped lower the age of school entry; the two- to five-year-old groups learn to associate school not with forbidding adults and dreary subjects but with play and understanding adults. The latter are, increasingly, young college graduates who have been taught to be more concerned with the child's social and psychological adjustment than with his academic progress—indeed, to scan the intellectual performance for signs of social maladjustment. These new teachers are more specialized. They don't claim to "understand children" but to have studied under Gesell on the "fives" or the "nines"; and this greater knowledge not only prevents the children from uniting in a wall of distrust or conspiracy against the school but also permits the teacher to take a greater hand in the socialization of spheres—consumption, friendship, fantasy—which the older-type teacher, whatever her personal desires, could not touch. Our wealthier society can afford this amount of individuation and "unnecessary" schooling.

Here also physical arrangements—in seating, age grading, decoration—symbolize the changes in the teacher's function. The sexes are mixed. Seating is arranged "informally." That is, *alphabetic* forms disappear, often to be replaced by *sociometric* forms that bring together compeers. This often means that where to sit becomes problematical—a clue to one's location on the friendship chart. Gesell grading is as severe as intellectual grading was in the earlier era; whatever their intellectual gifts, children stay with their presumed social peers. The desks change their form, too; they are more apt to be movable tables with open shelves than places where one may hide things. The teacher no longer sits on a dais or struts before a blackboard but joins the family circle.

Above all, the walls change their look. The walls of the modern grade school are decorated with the paintings of the children or their montages from the class in social studies. Thus the competitive and contemporary problems of the children look down on them from walls which, like the teacher herself, are no longer impersonal. This looks progressive, looks like a salute to creativeness and individuality; but again we meet paradox. While the school de-emphasizes grades and report cards, the displays seem almost to ask the children: "Mirror, mirror on the wall, who is fairest of us all?"

What is perhaps most important, while the children's paintings and montages show considerable imaginative gift in the pre-adolescent period, the school itself is still one of the agencies for the destruction of fantasy, as it was in the preceding era. Imagination withers in most of the children by adolescence. What survives is neither artistic craft nor artistic fantasy but the socialization of taste and interest that can already be seen in process in the stylization of perception in the children's paintings and stories. The stories of the later progressive grades are apt to be characterized by "realism." This realism is subtly influenced by the ideals of the progressive movement. Caesar and Pompeii are replaced by visits to stores and dairies, by maps from *Life,* and by *The Weekly Reader;* and fairy tales are replaced by stories about trains, telephones, and grocery stores, and, later, by material on race relations or the United Nations or "our Latin American neighbors."

These changes in arrangement and topic assist the breakdown of walls between student and student, permitting that rapid circulation of tastes which is a prelude to other-directed socialization. Whereas the inner-directed school child might well have hidden his stories and paintings under his bed . . . the other-directed child reads his stories to the group and puts his paintings on the wall. Play, which in the earlier epoch is often an extra-curricular and private hobby, shared at most with a small group, now becomes part of the school enterprise itself, serving a "realistic" purpose.

The teacher's role in this situation is often that of opinion leader. She is the spreader of the messages concerning taste that come from the progressive urban centers. She conveys to the children that what matters is not their industry or learning as such but their adjustment in the group, their cooperation, their (carefully stylized and limited) initiative and leadership.

Especially important is the fact that the cooperation and leadership that are inculcated in and expected of the children are frequently contentless. In nursery school it is not important whether Johnny plays with a truck or in the sandbox, but it matters very much whether he involves himself with Bill—via any object at all. To be sure, there are a few, a very few, truly progressive schools where the children operating on the Dalton plan and similar plans exercise genuine choice of their program, move at their own pace, and use the teacher as a friendly reference library; here cooperation is necessary and meaningful in actual work on serious projects. Far more frequently, however, the teacher continues to hold the reins of authority in her hands, hiding her authority, like her compeer, the other-directed parent, under the cloak of "reasoning" and manipulation. She determines the program and its pace—indeed, often holding the children back because she fails to realize that children, left to themselves, are capable of curiosity about highly abstract matters. She may delay them by making arithmetic "realistic" and languages fun—as well as by substituting social studies for history. In extreme forms of this situation there is nothing on which the children have to cooperate in order to get it done. The teacher will do it for them anyway. Hence when she asks that they be cooperative she is really asking simply that they be nice.

However, though the request seems simple, it is not casually made: the teacher is very tense about it. Deprived of older methods of discipline, she is, if anything, even more helpless than the parents who can always fall back on those methods in a pinch, though guiltily and rather ineffectively. The teacher neither dares to nor cares to; she has been taught that bad behavior on the children's part implies poor management on her part. Moreover, she herself is not interested in the intellectual content of what is taught, nor is this content apt to come up in a staff meeting or PTA discussion. These adult groups are often concerned with teaching tolerance, both ethnic and economic; and the emphasis on social studies that results means that intellectual content and skill become still more attenuated. Consequently, the teacher's emotional energies are channeled into the area of group relations. Her social skills develop; she may be sensitive to cliques based on "mere friendship" and seek to break them up lest any be left out. Correspondingly, her love for certain specific children may be trained out of her. All the more, she needs the general cooperation of all the children to assure herself that she is doing her job. Her surface amiability and friendliness, coupled with this underlying anxiety concerning the children's response, must be very confusing to the children who will probably conclude that to be uncooperative is about the worst thing one can be.

Of course the teacher will see to it that the children practice cooperation in small matters; in deciding whether to study the Peruvians or the Colombians, in nominating class officers for early practice in the great contemporary rituals of electioneering and parliamenteering, and in organizing contributions for the Red Cross or a Tag Day. Thus the children are supposed to learn democracy by underplaying the skills of intellect and overplaying the skills of gregariousness and amiability—skill democracy, in fact, based on respect for ability to do something, tends to survive only in athletics.

There is, therefore, a curious resemblance between the role of the teacher in the small-class modern school—a role that has spread from the progressive private schools to some of the public schools—and the role of the industrial-relations department in a modern factory. The latter is also increasingly concerned with cooperation between men and men and between men and management, as technical skill becomes less and less of a major concern. In a few of the more advanced plants there is even a pattern of democratic decision on moot matters—occasionally important because it affects piecework rates and seniority rules, but usually as trivial as the similar decisions of grammar-school government. Thus the other-directed child is taught at school to take his place in a society where the concern of the group is less with what it produces than with its internal group relations, its morale.

It is difficult to tell what lasting effects such changes in the elementary school have on the personality of the young; this would require long, painstaking analysis. It is also hard to know whether apparent changes are short-run zigs and zags or long-run shifts. Since the writing of *The Lonely Crowd,* there has been a new emphasis in American education on hard subjects and basic knowledge—more English, arithmetic, science, and foreign languages, even in the lower grades. Was the progressive education era of which Riesman writes a short-term deviation or part of a basic trend? Or is the new "hard" emphasis the passing thing, temporarily excited by shocks and strains of international tension? Probably, the heyday of progressive education is behind us, but many of its concerns will remain. Cooperation and morale are important aspects of modern organized activity; these aspects demand attention to human relations—sociability—and preparatory agencies are oriented to such considerations as well as to the traditional culture. The schools of the foreseeable future, it is certain, will not return to a single-minded transmission of knowledge; the question is how far the schools will move away from this function, largely unknowingly, as they turn to other tasks.

EDUCATION AS AN ACTIVE AGENT

The role of the school in transmitting culture and socializing the young[7] has led many observers to view education as largely a passive, dependent institution. If the school passes on a heritage to succeeding generations, it conserves existing society; if it forms the young in the image of previous generations, then traditional patterns of behavior are perpetuated. The school does society's bidding, and is indeed then largely a passive agent.

Sociologists have also long stressed that social institutions are interdependent and social change largely unplanned and evolutionary, a perspective that sees education as a dependent element in a slowly evolving web of institutions. This conception is best expressed in the statement by Emile

[7] The individual is socialized through learning group-defined ways of acting, feeling, and thinking, internalizing the norms of the culture. Socialization takes place primarily in the family, the school, and the peer groups of the young; it also occurs in the learning of skills and in the performing of adult roles.

Durkheim, the great French sociologist, that education is "a collection of practices and institutions that have been organized slowly in the course of time, which are comparable with all the other social institutions and which express them, and which, therefore, can no more be changed at will than the structure of the society itself."[8]

In this view, the school has little independence, little room to maneuver or innovate. Its teachers, administrators, and controlling boards cannot cause or "will" basic changes, but rather are themselves steered by the mores of the larger society and the nature of other institutions. Systems of education "depend upon religion, political organization, the degree of development of science, the state of industry, etc."[9] Society dictates to the school, the school cannot dictate to society.

This "conservative" view of the cultural role of education needs re-evaluation: Is it appropriate and adequate for advanced industrial societies in the middle of the twentieth century? We have already suggested that cultural transmission may be a weakening function, a theme to which we shall return later in the book. Here we will supplement the traditional perspective with a second view that the educational institution is now a prime contributor to change in society. Education is not purely dependent, always following the lead of other dominant institutions, for schools and colleges change society in a number of ways. These ways, at least in democratic societies, are not a result of the efforts of planners and reformers; deliberate attempts to use the schools for social transformation have made little headway. Rather, education is becoming an active center of cultural and social change as it grows in size and com-

[8] Emile Durkheim, *Education and Sociology,* translated by Sherwood D. Fox (Glencoe, Illinois: The Free Press, 1956), p. 65. (Originally published in 1922.)

[9] Durkheim, *Education and Sociology,* p. 66.

plexity and takes on new tasks. Its relation to other institutions as well as its own character changes as the technological society assigns it an increasingly important place. Much of its new significance stems from a vast broadening of its cultural role.

Education Produces New Culture

Education is portrayed as largely a conservator of society when it is seen as an enterprise devoted to preserving and transmitting the learnings of the past. This conception is still appropriate for elementary and secondary education, despite the innovations of progressive education, for these lower echelons remain a teaching establishment; but it is only part of the picture of higher education in modern society. True, colleges and universities still serve as custodians of the intellectual capital of mankind; but "they also serve as centers of innovation and change, of investigation of the application of knowledge to current needs, and of re-examination and criticism of society."[10]

The traditional conception of education particularly overlooks the increasingly large role of the university as an inventor of knowledge and technique.[11] While the university in this country engages in undergraduate education, it is, as elsewhere, centrally the home of graduate work and the professional school, of research and scholarship. Research is institutionalized in the American university, even massively bureaucratized there according to some critics.[12] The amount of research done within universities has increased enormously since the beginning of World War II. The

10 *The Price of Excellence,* Problems and Policies Committee, American Council on Education (Washington, D.C.: October, 1960), p. 1.

11 A. H. Halsey, "The Changing Functions of Universities in Advanced Industrial Societies," *Harvard Educational Review,* Vol. 30 (Spring, 1960), pp. 118–127.

12 William H. Whyte, Jr., *The Organization Man* (Garden City, New York: Doubleday & Co., Inc., 1957), Chapter 17.

amount spent on research in all American universities rose more than 2,600 per cent between 1939–40 and 1957–58, from $27,000,000 to $734,000,000. The Harvard Medical School alone, in 1959, had a research budget of over $5,000,000, compared to approximately $220,000 twenty-five years before.[13] The fruits of all this research—some bitter, some sweet—touch all institutions and lives. Research in physics and chemistry alters our technology which in turn affects the structure of industry, the distribution of population, the status of occupations, and even the tenor of international relations. Atomic research, of course, has been a prime mover in society since 1945, one that has worked out of the Universities of Chicago and California as well as such firms as General Electric. Polio vaccine and long-staple cotton, as examples, also have come out of the work of the university. Along with the research of physical and biological science, scholars in the humanities and the social sciences contribute new findings and perspectives to the understanding of history and the conditions of modern man. The *conservation* of knowledge has intermittently throughout the history of higher education led in modest degree to its *development;* in modern times, the point is, many more scholars spend much more time in the deliberate development of knowledge than ever before. Out of the old-time scholar emerges the likes of the researcher in linguistics, public administration, or food technology. Such latter-day academic specialists are primary producers of man's expanding supply of basic knowledge.

The university is not only a research center but also the place that trains the men who do the research wherever it is located. Of the highly trained men "produced" by the university, some remain in its own laboratories; but others in increasing number go out to staff the rapidly growing re-

[13] Nathan M. Pusey, "The American University Today," *School and Society,* Vol. 89 (Feb. 11, 1961), p. 49.

search facilities of industry and government. (See Chapter 2.)

The educational institution also provides some separation and protection for men devoted to critical assessment and innovation. Despite its ties to economic and political institutions, ties which in some respects grow ever tighter, education offers a base of operations in which men may be relatively independent. Some academic researchers and scholars remain *relatively* detached from the mores of the general culture, their freedom exceeded only by that of the few intellectuals who are detached from all establishments. Oriented to critical thought and set apart from many pressures of the market place, academic men can and do become free intellectuals, critical and innovating.[14] With the major, especially the best, universities quasi-autonomous and committed to inquiry, the initiative in social change rests in the hands of men of thought as well as men of action.

Colleges and universities, too, increasingly support groups that innovate in the arts. The artist of the medieval past was usually subsidized by a duke, a bishop, a wealthy family; later in history, writers gained a livelihood by means of sales to the small public of educated men. But in modern mass markets, there are few patron-sponsors and livelihood by sales depends on a wide popularity. Those whose painting or writing is not in heavy demand need other work for support, such as book reviewing, working in a bank or a publishing house, or teaching students; and artists and writers have been attracted to employment in higher education in increasing numbers. Intellectual magazines are often located around campuses, edited by professors or men with one foot in the academic door. The *Antioch Review,*

[14] For a view that academic men are today less free, critical, and innovating than they were in the past, see C. Wright Mills, *White Collar* (New York: Oxford University Press, 1951), pp. 129–136.

Sewanee Review, and *Kenyon Review* are examples of the campus-based "little mag." Novelists, musicians, and painters become professors or artists in residence at the colleges. The campus is by no means a perfect location, for the burdens of teaching and the conventions of the academic community can stultify and limit artistry. But for many it is the least of the evils, with the man released from the economic necessity of writing for wide acceptance or painting for the specifications of a client. With the campus as shelter, artistic and literary coteries are subsidized and given time to develop their styles. Colleges and universities have become massive patrons of the arts.

Education Liberalizes Attitudes

A second way in which education shapes society is through its effect on the minds of those it trains. This effect is by no means a simple transmission of a traditional consensus, but is quite differentiated and often at the leading edge of the society. A growing body of evidence indicates that education leads toward tolerant and humanitarian attitudes. Consistently it has been shown that the higher the level of educational attainment, the greater the degree to which "democratic" attitudes are held. Similarly, education is a prime correlate of interest in politics and of cultural awareness or sophistication. College graduates are more tolerant than high-school graduates in their attitudes toward ethnic and racial groups; they are more supportive of democratic norms such as having a multiparty political system; they listen more to serious programs and read more magazines. High-school graduates, in turn, are more tolerant and more involved culturally and politically than are those with only grammar-school education. Level of education is related this way even when the influence of age, occupation, and income is "controlled" or ruled out.

Table 1.1 shows that political tolerance in the United States is closely related to education. The percentage of adults who showed a tolerant attitude toward political nonconformists, in a 1955 nation-wide poll, varied considerably when the respondents were grouped according to the amount of education they had received. Even when persons are grouped according to similar occupations, amount of education makes a great deal of difference. For example, the last row in the table reports for persons in high "white-collar" occupations (business executives, owners, and professionals) according to how much education they have had.

TABLE 1.1—EDUCATION AND POLITICAL TOLERANCE

(Percentage of American adults in 1955 nation-wide poll who showed a tolerant attitude toward political nonconformists, analyzed by level of education and type of occupation of the respondents)*

	EDUCATION OF RESPONDENTS				
OCCUPATION OF RESPONDENTS	Grade School	Some High School	High-School Graduate	Some College	College Graduate
Low blue-collar	13†	32	40	—	—
High blue-collar	21	33	48	64	—
Low white-collar	23	29	47	64	74
High white-collar	26	46	56	65	83

* Each respondent was ranked on degree of tolerance according to his answers to a series of questions on willingness to tolerate nonconformists. (For example, "Should an admitted Communist be put in jail, or not?") The percentages report the share of respondents who fell in the upper two of six categories.

† Read: 13 per cent of respondents with grade-school education and "low" blue-collar occupation (unskilled labor) had a tolerant attitude. Rows and columns do not add to 100 per cent.

Source: Seymour Martin Lipset, *Political Man* (Garden City, N.Y.: Doubleday & Company, Inc., 1960), p. 109; figures computed by Lipset from data collected by Samuel Stouffer for his study, *Communism, Conformity and Civil Liberties* (New York: Doubleday & Co., Inc., 1955).

Only 26 per cent of those with a grade-school education exhibited tolerant attitudes (on questions about civil liberties), compared to 83 per cent tolerant among those who had graduated from college, an imposing difference of 57 per cent. Between these extremes, each higher level of education shows more tolerance. The other rows of the table report a similar relationship, each for a set of occupations.

Table 1.2 suggests this relationship is not solely American. A national survey in Germany in 1953 asked citizens whether they favored the existence of several political parties over a one-party system; that is, a democratic structure over a nondemocratic one. Education was here divided into only two categories—elementary, or high-school and higher—and the differences by education within each oc-

TABLE 1.2—EDUCATION AND SUPPORT OF DEMOCRATIC PARTY SYSTEM

(Percentage of German adults in 1953 UNESCO survey of opinion who favored a system with several political parties instead of one; analyzed by occupation and education of the respondents)

Occupation of Respondents	Per Cent of Respondents Favoring a Multiparty System: Elementary-School Educated	Per Cent of Respondents Favoring a Multiparty System: High-School or Higher Educated
Farm laborers	29	—
Manual workers	43	52
Farmers	43	67
Lower white-collar	50	68
Self-employed business	53	65
Upper white-collar	58	69
Officials (government)	59	78
Professions	56	68

Source: Seymour Martin Lipset, *Political Man* (Garden City, N.Y.: Doubleday & Company, Inc., 1960), p. 110; percentages computed by Lipset from the UNESCO survey.

cupation are not huge, but they consistently show the higher level of education to be related to democratic attitude.

Such differences hold, for example, in knowledge and attitude on issues of foreign policy. A review in 1950 of a number of polls in the United States on foreign-policy issues showed greater contrasts between the college-educated and the grade-school-educated than between upper- and lower-income groups. *Interest* in international affairs correlated more highly with education than with any other factor. The lower-educated were characterized by lack of information, limited intellectual horizons, rudimentary analytical skills, and apathy. There were two or three times as many "don't know's" and "no opinion's" among them as among the college-educated. Table 1.3 illustrates these results.

The results from these opinion surveys show the impact of education on opinions at a general level. Specific information can be added through another approach; namely, studies made of changes in the attitudes of students during the college years. These studies generally show a widening of perspective along with increasing liberality; students tend to change toward the attitudes of academic men. The changes often, but not always, include a weakening of religious belief, indicating that college education is a secularizing influence. While these changes have been reported mainly from studies of small, leading liberal-arts colleges (Bennington, Vassar, for example), they have also recently been found to hold true in large state universities.

For example, a study at the University of California, Berkeley, suggests that students on this large state-university campus become more supportive of civil liberties as they go through the four undergraduate years. On the basis of students' attitudes on fifteen issues, such as refusing a passport to a Socialist, students were tagged as slightly, moderately, or highly libertarian. The proportion highly

TABLE 1.3—EDUCATION AND INFORMATION AND ATTITUDE ON FOREIGN POLICY

(American adults, as reported in nation-wide public opinion polls)

	EDUCATION OF RESPONDENT		
PERCENTAGE OF RESPONDENTS:	Grade School	High-School	College
Who show a reasonably correct understanding of what a tariff is (Aug. '46).	22	50	64
Who belong to groups or organizations which discuss national and international problems (May '47).	7	15	32
Who are dissatisfied with the progress the United Nations has made so far (June '46).	42	53	69
Who gave "No Opinion" or "Don't Know" answers to the question concerning the progress the United Nations has made so far.	32	21	8
Who feel it would be a good idea to have reciprocal trade agreements with foreign countries (June '45).	43	67	81
Who gave "No Opinion" or "Don't Know" answers to the question of reciprocal trade agreements.	49	24	10

Source: Gabriel A. Almond, *The American People and Foreign Policy* (New York: Harcourt, Brace and Company, 1950), p. 129.

libertarian almost doubled from the freshmen to the senior years; as seen in Table 1.4, it went from 21 to 40 per cent. The proportion only slightly libertarian dropped from 32 to 14 per cent.

Another study shows that in *both* Ivy League and state-supported colleges, students become more supportive of civil rights as they go through the undergraduate years. (See Table 1.5.) The Ivy schools have a student body that is initially more supportive of civil rights and shows greater

TABLE 1.4—YEAR IN COLLEGE AND ATTITUDE ON CIVIL LIBERTIES
(894 Students at the University of California, Berkeley, 1957)

STUDENT'S ATTITUDE ON CIVIL LIBERTIES*	STUDENT'S YEAR IN COLLEGE			
	Freshman	Sophomore	Junior	Senior
Highly libertarian	21	29	34	40
Moderately libertarian	47	44	50	46
Slightly libertarian	32	27	16	14
	100	100	100	100

* Classified into one of three categories on the basis of the student's answers to fifteen questions about civil liberties.
Source: Hanan C. Selvin and Warren O. Hagstrom, "Determinants of Support for Civil Liberties," *The British Journal of Sociology,* Vol. XI (March, 1960), pp. 51–73.

change over the four years. But the move in student attitude is in the same direction in both cases.

Thus the further the young progress through the educational mill, the greater is the liberalization of attitudes.

TABLE 1.5—YEAR IN COLLEGE AND ATTITUDE ON CIVIL RIGHTS
(Percentage of students in each college class who were classified as supportive of civil rights;* based on 3,796 students in 4 Ivy League and 5 state-supported colleges, 1952)

TYPE OF COLLEGE	STUDENT'S YEAR IN COLLEGE			
	Freshman	Sophomore	Junior	Senior
Ivy League college	45	57	58	68
State-supported college	31	40	41	44

* Each person received a composite score on the basis of his answers to four questions; for example, "It's unwise to give people with dangerous social and economic viewpoints a chance to be elected." (Agree or disagree.) The students were classified in five categories, from strongly pro-civil rights to strongly anti-civil rights, and those falling into the "upper" two categories were taken as supportive of civil rights.
Source: Norman Miller, "Academic Climate and Student Values," paper presented at the Fifty-Fourth Annual Meeting of the American Sociological Association, September, 1959.

The change in attitude results partly from greater knowledge, or the content of instruction, and in part from being socialized to new perspectives through contact with faculties and other students and through anticipation of one's future career. In any case, education is here an active cultural agent, working to change the balance of different attitudes and values in the population, and thus affecting the fortunes of different political and economic interests. At a minimum, education in modern democratic society consolidates and extends some of the liberal attitudes of the immediate past, providing a base for further liberality.

Education's effects on habits and attitudes in the United States take place within a society that has little emphasized the life of the mind. The reading habits of Americans, for example, are always startling when compared to other advanced societies; and they seem at first glance to indict American education. In 1957, 17 per cent of a cross section of adults in the United States were able to answer yes to the question: "Do you happen to be reading a book at the present time?"[15] (This was a decrease from 21 per cent in 1949). A similar poll in 1957 showed 55 per cent of adults in England reading a book, 34 per cent in West Germany, 33 per cent in Australia, and 31 per cent in Canada. The reading being reported covered "any kind of simple identification of black marks on white paper"—a paperback mystery story or a copy of the memoirs of a madam as well as a handsomely bound classic.

This makes the American educational system look completely ineffectual, since over two-thirds of the adult population has attended high school or college; whereas in England, "where three times as great a proportion of the

[15] Lester Asheim, "A Survey of Recent Research," in Jacob M. Price (ed.), *Reading for Life* (Ann Arbor: University of Michigan Press, 1959), pp. 3–26. The data immediately following are also from Asheim's account.

adult population report book reading, only a negligible percentage has attended school beyond the age of fifteen." Yet it is clear that the source of little book reading lies largely in the general society, for the studies also show that education is the major correlate of reading in this country. On the above questions about current book reading, 6 per cent among the grade-school-educated were doing so, 19 per cent among those with a high-school education, and 43 per cent in the case of the college-educated. Or, when American adults were asked whether they had read a book *in the past year,* those who had *not* done so were 26 per cent of the college-educated, 57 per cent of those with a high-school education, and 82 per cent of those with only a grade-school education.

Such comparisons clearly indicate the considerable effect of education on reading habits, even though the differentials stem in part from a weeding out of the poorer readers at the higher levels of education. The common man and the common reader are not the same person; the common man in the United States is essentially a nonreader, at least of books. Education apparently shapes very largely the chances of a person being exposed to the wide, wide world that is found on the printed page between hard or soft covers.

Education Differentiates Culture

A third, largely unplanned, way in which education actively intervenes in modern society is through further differentiating the already complex general culture. A common schooling for most children may be provided up to a point in the educational system. But diversity sets in when preparation for occupation and career takes over, which is now generally upon entry into higher education. At one time, when higher education was for gentlemen, it was "designed to create among them a common core of central knowledge that would make of them a community of the educated."[16] Higher education was then culturally integrative.

In modern technological society, however, the education of the cultivated man is increasingly submerged by the education of the specialist, for colleges and especially universities are not only research agencies but also "play a central role in the economy and the system of stratification as agencies for selection, training and occupation placement of individuals."[17] This occupational and social differentiation has parallel cultural effects: the engineer and the librarian not only take different training in college and go to different jobs, but they also come to think and speak along somewhat different lines. Training for diverse disciplines impels the widening cultural split between men of science and men of the humanities;[18] *education here makes mutual understanding and communication more difficult rather than less.* Ways of seeing are also ways of not seeing; the more that men devote themselves to specialized modes of thought, the less they are able to don other perspectives and to see the world as differently trained specialists see it.

The occupational structure of a technological society not only requires postsecondary training of different types, but also requires training at different levels of complexity within any one major field. These levels of training inculcate different subcultures; the electronic technician trained in a two-year program, the electrical engineer trained up to

16 Richard Hofstadter and C. DeWitt Hardy, *The Development and Scope of Higher Education in the United States* (New York: Columbia University Press, 1952), pp. 11–12.

17 Halsey, "The Changing Functions of Universities," pp. 118–127. The role of education in occupational placement and the allocation of social status will be discussed in Chapter 2.

18 This cultural divide has been described in C. P. Snow, *The Two Cultures and the Scientific Revolution* (Cambridge, England: Cambridge University Press, 1959).

the Bachelor's degree, and the physicist trained through years of graduate work and the Ph.D. degree are somewhat set apart in style, complexity, and content of their thought. The specialization trend, which is irreversible, means that individuals are allocated to a widening spectrum of adult subcultures that are hooked to occupational subworlds. In this general process, the educational system initiates changes as well as reacts to changes forced upon it. Much impetus for further specialization comes from within the academy, for here if anywhere the specialized expert is at home and the process of fields giving rise to subfields continues endlessly.

Education also contributes to cultural diversity in this country through variation in the character of colleges. The more than 2,000 colleges in the United States take diverse forms; there are church-related colleges, especially Protestant and Catholic; secular liberal-arts colleges; public and private universities; state colleges, teachers colleges, junior colleges; and technological schools. These colleges and universities have not been planned or coordinated for a common task, but rather have their genesis and support in diverse interests of private groups, municipalities, and states. In serving these interests the colleges have become quite diversely oriented—from deeply religious to purely secular, from *avant-garde* to backwater. The most important general difference today among American colleges is probably between the colleges, largely private, that are devoted almost entirely to liberal education and the colleges and universities, mainly public, that are committed to servicing a wide range of interests in the local community or the state, principally through occupational training. In any case, the various kinds of colleges represent a cultural diversity in themselves; they educate and train differently, and their "products" are not of a piece.

CONDITIONS DETERMINING PRIMARY CULTURAL ROLE

We have seen that schools and colleges can be both conserving and innovating, passive instruments of other institutions and active forces for change in their own right. In varying degree, in different types of schools, these opposite relationships of education to society will exist side by side. Educational agencies work both ways—and we could leave it at that. However, the useful question is: What are the conditions that tip the outcome one way or the other, making the educational enterprise primarily a passive instrument of the society or a center of initiative and change? We have already discussed several conditions; among these, the extent to which research is institutionalized in the educational establishment, which makes it a source of invention, and the strength of the expectation that the schools should provide a common schooling, which presses toward a passive role of transmission. One condition not highlighted that deserves attention is the operational autonomy of schools and colleges. Antonomous agencies can be critical and innovative; dependent ones usually cannot.

Here we anticipate the topics of control and decentralization that appear later. We will occasionally anticipate a discussion, or partially repeat statements already made, since phenomena that are empirically related but arbitrarily separated in writing must be put back together. Institutional autonomy is sharply affected by the extent to which the structure of control admits the influence of outsiders. The American public schools have relatively little independence since they are an extreme case of control by local citizens. The schools are organized in thousands of school districts, each with its own controlling board of laymen, generally elected. This heavily decentralized system differs sharply from the administration of education in most other countries, where, as in France, the schools fall within a department of the national government. The local-control system, early established in the United States, renders the school heavily dependent on the wishes of the various political factions, churches, business groups, trade unions, and the like that comprise the power structure of the local town or city. This dependent position, paradoxically, may cause the schools at times to change much more rapidly than if they were in a quasi-independent structure, such as a federal department; shifts in public sentiment can cause a dependent school quickly to change its mind but may not be readily reflected in an entrenched, independent system. But whatever the extent of the change, it is largely community-directed, produced by the push and pull of local contending groups, with educational personnel having relatively little control over the direction and extent of change. Local control produces an accommodating institution.

Colleges in the United States are generally in a more independent position. Public colleges and universities answer to state-level boards of control rather than to the local community; at these higher levels, control cannot be so closely exercised. In addition, private colleges and universities answer to no public authorities at all. These schools can be highly independent of public opinion and pressure, especially when supported by a loyal, sympathetic board of trustees. The best private colleges in the country, for example, are often in the forefront of academic resistance to political investigation, and to such outside-inspired practices as loyalty oaths for students. Courage is here underpinned by autonomy, by large degrees of freedom for speaking out. Thus, within the American educational system there are great differences in vulnerability to external influence, and this differential vulnerability makes a difference in the exercising of initiative.

The autonomy of education varies most between totalitarian and democratic societies. The totalitarian society sees education as an instrument of the state, as an apparatus for indoctrination and planned change. In such a society, while the school need not answer to the local community, it is closely controlled by government officials and political functionaries. Education is then an *amalgamated* institution, fused with the government and having little independent power; teachers have relatively little freedom to instruct according to their own beliefs and educators little control over the destiny of their own institution. This is a relative, not an absolute, matter, however, for a large institution always has a momentum of its own; and such unplanned consequences as shifts in attitudes and expectations because of education still take place.

Other factors to which we shall turn in later chapters affect the independence and initiative of educational organizations. For example, the size of the school usually makes a difference, with the large organization more independent than the small. The large school has more resources at its command; the size of its staff and the complexity of its operations screen much of its work from the scrutiny of outsiders. Thus the increasing size of schools and colleges in the United States generally means greater institutional autonomy.

In brief, formal education is always a cultural agent, doing the bidding of the general society and specific social forces in it. But it is also an innovating institution, affecting the general society and indirectly causing other institutions to do its bidding. There is no final answer to the question of whether the school and college are primarily passive agents of the culture or sources of social and cultural transformation. It all depends on the setting, the conditions under which the school or college must work, and the nature of its organization. In democratic societies, education is now a less dependent institution than in the past. The over-all effects of the technological revolution make education a more active force, especially through its participation in research and the training of technologists.

Chapter 2

Education, Occupation, and Status

COMPLEX SOCIETIES have the common problem of training and motivating men for diverse kinds of work and social functions. Much of this necessary training and motivating falls into the hands of education as it becomes a separate institution. The educational system must also select and sort, somehow choosing who is to be trained and later distributed to the various occupations. In so doing, education defines the "life chances" of individuals and groups, their opportunity to reap reward, achieve status, and live preferred styles of life. These primary social roles of (a) training and sorting men and (b) defining their life chances rival in importance the basic cultural roles of education discussed in the first chapter. In analyzing these roles, we shall look especially to the changes that take place as societies advance into the modern age of technology and high mass consumption. With this, we shall again pursue a two-way flow of influence between education and society, searching first for the impact of occupational and social structures on education, and then viewing education as determinant of social arrangements external to it. We also shall have more to say about education as a center of initiative and change, a discussion begun in Chapter 1, and we shall emphasize the role now assumed by education as a means of social mobility.

MANPOWER AND EDUCATION

The occupational structure of a country is determined by the relative strength of what may be distinguished as primary, secondary, and tertiary industry.[1] Primary industry refers to agriculture, lumbering, and fishing. Work is relatively unskilled and, in the case of small-scale farming, closely united with the home. Secondary industry is mining, building, and especially manufacturing, the turning of resources into products through technical processes. Much work is skilled and semiskilled, some is white-collar in the form of office forces in the factory, and work is separated from the home. Tertiary or service industry includes the distribution of products and various forms of service and economic facilitation; for example, transportation, finance, insurance, wholesale and retail trade, government, professional work, domestic labor. This is largely a world of white-collar men, the salesmen and the clerks, the middlemen of economic transactions.

With advancing industrialization, the emphasis in the economy first shifts from primary to secondary industry, and then later to service industry. The United States is in the advanced stage where the service industries increasingly overshadow the others. This picture appears in Chart 2.1, which shows that the workers producing services now outnumber those in primary and secondary industry. The proportion of the American labor force classified as agricultural workers declined from 37 per cent in 1900 to 12 per cent in 1950; over the same half-century, unskilled laborers also declined, from 12 per cent to 7 per cent. Skilled and semi-

[1] Colin Clark, *Conditions of Economic Progress* (London: 1940).

CHART 2.1

EMPLOYMENT IN AGRICULTURE, MANUFACTURING, AND SERVICE INDUSTRIES, UNITED STATES, 1820–1950

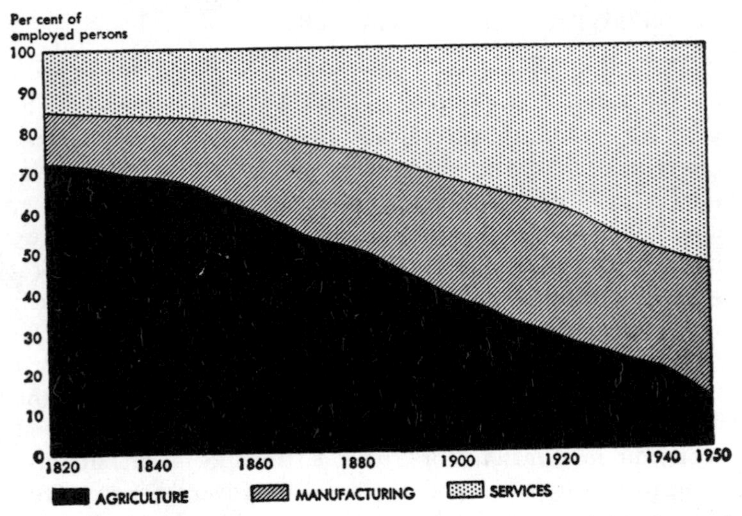

Source: Eshref Shevky and Marilyn Williams, *The Social Areas of Los Angeles* (Berkeley and Los Angeles: University of California Press, 1949), p. 4. Data for 1950 added.

skilled workers increased from 23 to 35 per cent; clerks and sales workers from 7 to 19 per cent; and professionals and semiprofessionals from 4 to 9 per cent in the same years. The growth of professional-technical jobs decade by decade since 1870 and projected until 1975 is shown in Chart 2.2. Note the steepness of the increase between 1950 and 1958. Managers, officials, and proprietors, as a group, increased from 6 per cent in 1900 to 9 per cent in 1950, despite the decline of small-business proprietors. The professional man and the salaried manager—the latter also partially professionalized—are now at the top of the occupational structure in status, influence, and rewards, and these two groups are

CHART 2.2

GROWTH OF PROFESSIONAL-TECHNICAL JOBS

(Millions of workers)

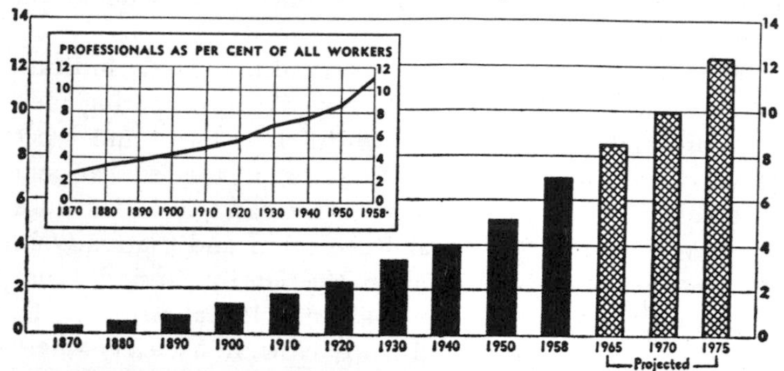

Source: The New York Times, January 3, 1960.

rapidly increasing in absolute numbers and relative importance.

On top of this basic shift from agriculture and manufacturing to service industry, we are witnessing the rise of a small but highly influential fourth sector in the economy, one composed of *producers of ideas and technological innovation.* Research has become institutionalized not alone in the university (see Chapter 1), but also in industry and government. Everywhere there are research bureaus, institutes, and laboratories; in industry, for example, only a few of the largest firms maintained research laboratories as late as the 1920's. Today, industrial laboratories have proliferated so widely that nearly all large firms and many moderate-sized ones maintain them, employing thousands of research scientists and technicians.[2] These workers are not actually in service occupations, but rather represent a new kind of production. Bell Telephone Laboratories, for ex-

[2] Talcott Parsons, "Professional Training and the Role of the Professions in American Society," in *Scientific Manpower, 1958,* National Science Foundation, pp. 80–87.

ample, is one of the most advanced research facilities in the world. From it flows a steady stream of new ideas that reshape technology, industry, and ultimately the other institutions of society. Such a facility is entirely dependent on highly trained brains.

These fundamental trends in occupations clearly indicate why education plays an ever larger role in preparing men for work and allocating them to different levels and types of labor. As mentioned in Chapter 1, the educational threshold of employment has been increasingly raised since the advent of the Industrial Revolution and especially in the last half-century. Labor on the family farm did not demand literacy, but skilled jobs and clerical work in the factory required literacy and more. Now, in a society where automation is taking over the tasks of routine labor, a large proportion of jobs increasingly falls into the upper ranges of skill and expertise, in the range from professional to technician. Large-scale enterprise—big business, big government, big labor, big education—demands managers, professionals, and technicians, and these posts demand training beyond the high school for the most part. Education is becoming so fused with occupations that it may be seen as part of the economic foundations of society. In the technological society—the currently most advanced stage of industrialism—highly trained men replace raw materials and the factory machine as the crucial economic resource; and these men are trained through the educational institution—through schools and colleges and the educational systems that are springing up in industry and elsewhere.

The apex of the pyramid of technically trained men is found in the fourth sector of the economy identified above. This sector has an astonishing appetite for Ph.D.'s, outside as well as within the university:[3]

[3] Bernard Berelson, *Graduate Education in the United States* (New York: McGraw-Hill Book Co., Inc., 1960), p. 56.

The organization in this country that employs most Ph.D.'s today is not Harvard or Yale or Illinois or Michigan. It is Du Pont. Furthermore, General Electric has more than twice as many Ph.D.'s on its staff as Princeton, Shell has more than MIT, Union Carbide or Eastman or IBM has about as many as Northwestern or Cal Tech. As a matter of fact, industrial firms like these probably employ more Ph.D's today than all the liberal arts colleges in the country.

. . . The Federal government has more than any of these, about as many as the top 10 universities put together.

And what of the future? The American manpower structure faces extensive changes during the 1960's.[4] The educational requirements for most jobs will continue to rise and the biggest increases in number of jobs will occur in occupations requiring the most education and training. The trend toward an increase in the number of white-collar jobs requiring college education will become even more marked. By 1970, it is predicted, about 45 per cent of all jobs in the country will be white-collar. The professional workers will be by far the fastest growing occupational group. In 1957, there were 6.5 million Americans in the professional fields; by 1970, there are expected to be 10.5 million—an increase of slightly more than 60 per cent. Thus the occupational pressure for more education will not let up. In 1958, about 366,000 Bachelor's degrees were granted; by 1970, the annual total is expected to be about 718,000. College degrees will be sought by millions of students not because college is so much fun but largely because the connection between educational attainment and occupational attainment grows ever tighter.

The thrusting of education into the economic order is

[4] The discussion that follows is based on Newell Brown, "The Manpower Outlook for the 1960's: Its Implications for Higher Education," *Higher Education,* Vol. 16 (December, 1959), pp. 3–6; and *The New York Times,* January 3, 1960.

changing the face and function of higher education. In the technological society, the primary social function of elementary and secondary education may remain, as in the past, a broad socialization of the young. But in higher education a change in function takes place, from the making of cultivated men to the training of employees, as colleges and universities become the pre-employment training arm of industry and government—and of education itself. One result is that growth in the college population takes place largely in fields of study that are applied or directly vocational, of which the most important numerically are engineering, business administration, and education. The number of graduates in these fields has recently grown almost twice as fast as the whole population of college graduates; in the four years between 1954-55 and 1957-58, the number of degrees earned in these fields increased by 49 per cent compared with an increase of 27 per cent in all Bachelor's and first professional degrees.[5] These fields are now the Big Three among *all* college majors. Business and education majors each account for about one out of six college students, or together one out of three; and two out of three students are now in vocational (professional) programs as opposed to liberal arts programs.[6]

Similar changes are going on throughout the world in industrial societies, with differences in degree determined by the stage of industrialization, its rapidity, and the nation's cultural heritage. Let us consider at some length the case of Russia since 1917. The Soviets have developed a system of education adjusted directly, through central control, to the demand for technological manpower at a high rate of economic growth. Theirs is a system uniquely geared to the training of technicians, engineers, and scien-

[5] Computed by Martin A. Trow from data in *A Fact Book on Higher Education* (Washington, D.C.: American Council on Education, n.d.).

[6] Frank C. Pierson, *The Education of American Businessmen* (New York: McGraw-Hill Book Co., Inc., 1959), pp. 6–8.

tists. The Soviet situation is closely and briefly reviewed in the following article by Nicholas DeWitt, an expert on Russian education. DeWitt makes clear that the specialist is idealized in Soviet society, even more than in our own, and the schools are cast largely in his image.

EDUCATION AND SPECIALIZED TRAINING IN THE U.S.S.R.[7]

In the last few years, since so many people in American educational circles have gained an opportunity to travel to Russia, the new phrase, "Soviet commitment to education," has become popular. But much of the fancy talk about the communist commitment to education comes dangerously close to missing the really important point: what we must ask ourselves is the basic question—*commitment to what kind of education?* The answer is disarmingly simple: first, last, and always, the Soviet commitment to education is a commitment to scientific education, to technological education, to an education which will enable Soviet citizens to perform specialized functional tasks to the best of their ability in their expanding industrial society.

The Russians orient their educational efforts so as to maximize the returns from it for the advancement of their political, military, and economic objectives. The communists do not believe in education for education's sake. They do not believe in education for the individual's sake. The Russians want no part of liberal or general humanistic education. They want no generalists—only specialists. Their main objective is to offer *functional education* so as to train, to mold, to develop the skills, the professions, and the specialists required by their long-run development programs —specialists who are capable of performing the tasks of running the industrial and bureaucratic machinery of the communist state. And in order to accomplish this, the Russians *were, are,* and *will be* training an army of scientists and technologists.

Although professing the aims of general and well-rounded education, the Soviet educational system in reality is uniquely

[7] Nicholas DeWitt, "Soviet Science Education and the School Reform," *School and Society,* Vol. 88 (Summer, 1960), pp. 297–300. The table numbering is DeWitt's.

geared to the training of specialized manpower. By means of mass persuasion, of coercion if necessary, and of bold incentives, the Soviet state makes every effort to channel the best and largest share of available talent into professional occupations and into engineering and scientific professions in particular. This is clearly evident when we compare the professional manpower situation and current training trends in the Soviet Union and the U.S. The total stock of professional higher education graduates [employed in the civilian economy of the U.S.S.R.] at the end of 1959 was 3,300,000. Projected additions of higher education graduates in the next five years amount to 335,000 annually. The total number of Soviet higher education graduates is less than one-half the number of college graduates in the U.S. The Soviet Union's annual number of graduates will be probably 10% less than ours. Turning now to comparisons by field, the following picture emerges:

TABLE 1—U.S.S.R. and U.S. Professional Graduates

	Stock of Soviet professional graduates at the end of 1959	Projected annual additions of graduates in the next 5 years	U.S.S.R.—U.S. comparisons
General education, cultural, and socio-economic fields	1,686,000	146,000	Soviet stock only 1/3 as large as ours. Annual additions half as large.
Agricultural fields	248,000	35,000	Soviet stock about 1/3 higher than ours. Annual additions 1/3 higher.
Health and medical fields	383,000	28,000	Soviet stock about 1/4 larger than ours. Annual additions four times as large.
Engineering fields	974,000	125,000	Soviet stock 1/3 larger than ours. Annual additions three times larger.

The score card looks unfavorable, no matter how many reservations one makes about the validity of such numerical comparisons. It is all the more disheartening because, during the last 10 years, there has not been a single study in the U.S. or in Western Europe which could challenge the proposition that, in qualitative terms, Soviet science and engineering education is not inferior to that in the West. Soviet faults are many and complaints about shortcomings are monotonous; but the basic proposition of qualitative comparability (and, at times, superiority of Soviet science and technical education) remains in force.

Although many American educators may dispute the theory, Soviet leaders believe that engineers and scientists can perform managerial, administrative, economic, and business co-ordination jobs *better* than any generalist or any non-technically trained specialist. This is the simple consideration behind the fact that Soviet engineers manage Soviet industry, Soviet engineers supervise planning and distribution, and a significant part of the Soviet government is even run by engineers and scientists. Perhaps one should not question the wisdom of the presence of American liberal arts graduates and generalists as golden nuggets in the American business world. The fact remains, however, that there are no such nuggets in the Soviet setting, and, what is more, the Soviet regime wants none of them.

Soviet success in training large numbers of specialists on the professional level depends, to a large degree, upon the secondary school training. Today Soviet education is in a state of flux. During the 1950's, two central problems emerged. The first relates to the educational policy of the Soviet regime, and the second to current demographic trends in the Soviet Union. It was not until recently that the goal of universal secondary education has even begun to be approached. As late as 1952, less than 10% of 17-year-olds were able to complete the entire 10-year program of Soviet primary and secondary schooling. Either because of personal circumstances or the stringent academic requirements, some 90% of youngsters fell by the wayside. But by 1956, there were close to 1,500,000 secondary school graduates. In relation to the corresponding age cohort, the rate of completion of the 10-year school increased from less than 10 to 35%. Admission quotas in higher education, however, did not expand appreciably in the intervening period, and, consequently, the *majority* of 10-year-school graduates found themselves outside the walls of institutions of higher learning. Meanwhile, although there have been some revisions in the primary and secondary school curriculum (the introduction of manual training and workshop activities are to be particularly noted), the program of skilled training and vocational preparation has *not* made much headway. As a result, in the course of the last few years, the problem has reared up with full force as to what should be the next step to prepare secondary school graduates for practical occupations.

The second problem is that World War II not only made for tremendous physical devastation within the Soviet Union, but also played havoc with the Soviet population. In 1959, the Soviet population was 208,000,000, while 20 years earlier, just before the outbreak of the war, it was already 192,000,000. Had it not been for the war, the Soviet population would be 30–40,000,000 more than it actually is today. Also, the birthrate declined drastically during the war, and it is only natural to expect that the heavy losses in population were reflected in the school enrollment. While, in the fall of 1948, in the elementary grades (1–4) of Soviet schools there were some 24,000,000 youngsters, by 1953 their number had been cut in half, to only 12,000,000. This staggering decline occurred in the course of five years. Recovery since 1953 has been very slow, and in 1958 there were still only 18,000,000 pupils in the elementary grades. The obvious implication is that the prime age groups for new additions to the labor force, as well as for those who are to serve in the armed forces or to continue their training in Soviet institutions of higher learning, are now considerably reduced. This deficit will continue to be felt throughout the 1960's, particularly during the early years of the decade.

These two social forces were the most influential in triggering off "Khrushchev's Educational Reform." No doubt, political factors also had a role, but the economic considerations predominated. For a year or so, Western observers were quite puzzled by what the future of Soviet education would hold. Now we have enough evidence to state conclusively that the reform will not diminish but, in effect, will *intensify* the scientific and technical orientation of Soviet schooling. As far as general education and as far as the social sciences and the humanities are concerned, the ax will fall. The new educational reform envisages a reorganization of the Soviet complete secondary school from 10 to 11 years. The first eight years will be compulsory. After completion of the eight-year school, most youths at age 15 or 16 will be integrated into productive activity in the labor force directly, and their schooling will be continued on a *part-time* basis only. The three upper grades, 9–11, will be called "general polytechnical school with production training," and these grades will be more selective than were grades 8–10 in 1956. The scientific and technical content will be intensified in these three upper grades, as well as through the general school structure itself, as revealed by a brief comparison of the present 10-year and the new 11-year curriculum:

TABLE 2—Changes in Soviet Curriculum

	10-Year		11-Year		
	1957 Curriculum		Proposed 1963 Curriculum		Net Gain
	Instr. Hours	%	Instr. Hours	%	in Instr. Hours
General (language, literature, humanities, and social sciences)	4,692	44	4,884	38	192
Scientific (sciences and mathematics)	3,332	31	3,727	29	395
Applied activities and vocational skill subjects	2,763	25	4,217	33	1,454
Total	10,787	100	12,828	100	2,041

The bulk of the additional 2,041 hours of instruction will be allocated to vocational subjects (1,454) and workshop and industrial practice. The sciences will gain 395 instruction hours and the addition to the humanities will be only 192 classroom hours. But what this redistribution overlooks is that the "polytechnical subjects" will be science- and technology-oriented. Over one-third of polytechnical instruction will be technology-applied science, and two-thirds will be industrial arts and skill subjects. In other words, although the content will be of an applied nature, it will be closely tied in with regular science and mathematics instruction.

In addition to the curricular changes, one must emphasize the very favorable situation in the supply of teachers. Of the total 1,800,000 teachers on all levels of the Soviet school system, about half are teachers in secondary schools. Among these 900,000 secondary school teachers, 340,000 are science or mathematics teachers. The current trend in teacher training is that of the 110,000 teachers trained annually, about 25,000 are science or mathematics teachers.

Another factor which should give us pause is the question of money. All education, and particularly science and technological education, require money—and much of it. The Soviet state controls all types of education, and most educational expenditures are borne by the state, which spends annually seven per cent of the Soviet gross national product. In proportionate terms, this is *twice* as much as we spend on education; in absolute terms, we are about even. This actually means that a country which is less than half as rich as we are spends as much on education as we do. We, who can afford most, are saving most on an effort which matters critically for the long-run welfare of the nation. Most education in the Soviet Union is tuition-free. A successful student through a system of stipends and scholarships gets paid for going to school. And it is largely by lessening the economic burden of education upon the individual and his family that the Soviet state is able to apply such stringent selection and to channel by means of incentive the national talent into fields of specialization it deems most desired.

Soviet science and education *do* serve the state's military, political, and power objectives. But in pursuing these objectives, they often fulfill their self-purposiveness and thus get full benefit and full credit. We often fail to grasp this in trying to understand the Soviet effort. Today the Soviet Union is in a new phase in its economic evolution: more hands doing physical labor have to be replaced as rapidly as possible by machines and higher quality of skills. The army of Soviet scientists, engineers, and technologists which the Soviet Union has trained in recent years and will continue to train is to be deployed to achieve this task. In order to succeed in this, what the Soviet Union apparently needs most of all today is higher quality in the laboring and technical skills. And Soviet education, as in the past, is being called upon to perform a specific, functional task in developing these skills. This is the essence of Khrushchev's educational reform which has been largely overlooked by many in the West. The age-old issue of education—what kind and what for—is again being resolved *not* in favor of the individual, but in favor of the Soviet state. There is a lesson in this, too. I hope we never will have to resort to such devices, but, in order to avoid them, we will have to begin to do much more for the betterment of our own education before it is too late. For education can be no better than society is willing to make it.

Here, then, is an educational system closely geared to the technical requirements of a technological society. The linking of education to the economy is little restrained by traditional conceptions or by commitment to liberal education. The U.S.S.R. is thus a more extreme case than is the United States in this regard.

England, too, has been moving in this direction but much more slowly than the United States and the U.S.S.R. Cultural tradition restrains the change, since Oxford and Cambridge, national centers of an aristocratic tradition of liberal education, have long dominated English higher education.[8] But provincial universities arose in the nineteenth and early twentieth centuries to train students from their own regions in undergraduate professional schools for the newer technological and professional occupations, such as chemistry and electrical engineering; and English higher

[8] This discussion on England is largely adapted from A. H. Halsey, "The Changing Functions of Universities in Advanced Industrial Societies," *Harvard Educational Review*, Vol. 30 (Spring, 1960), pp. 118–127.

education has been expanding since World War II, especially in science and technological fields. With this, a third tier of colleges has emerged in the form of Colleges of Advanced Technology and Teacher Training Colleges, offering courses of three years duration. The older tradition acts as a brake but does not prevent the gradual movement of the English educational system into the foundations of the economy.

EDUCATION AND LIFE CHANCES

The discussion above makes it abundantly clear that the chance to get ahead in the modern world depends in considerable part on education. This is a new link in an old chain. It has always been true that opportunities in life are shaped by social background, especially the social station of one's family. This was most likely when status was largely *ascribed,* assigned to persons according to the family, tribe, and class into which they were born. The extreme case of ascribed status is membership from birth to death in a particular caste. Where status in part is *achieved,* as in modern industrial nations, the determination of one's life chances by socio-economic background is not so complete. But social origins are still influential, primarily through affecting how far the young go in their schooling, which in turn so strongly affects their later occupational opportunity. Socio-economic level, or socio-educational level as we shall call it, affects interest and aspiration and the capacity to use the schools for an education.

Social Background and Education

Everyone knows that students come to school with widely varying interests and aspirations, but the social categories to which these differences are generally linked are less well known. The most important of these background differences, leaving race and ethnicity aside (see Chapter 3), is the socio-educational level of the family—a combination of father's (and mother's) occupation, income, and education.

The constraint on education that may be exercised by the social setting within which the young are reared is reflected, in the extreme, in the estimated 150,000 children of migratory agricultural workers, now the greatest single source of illiteracy in the United States. Consider the following conditions and their effect on schooling:[9]

Whether the child is a Negro, moving from Florida to New York on a truck with the other members of his crew; a Spanish-American, picking cotton in Texas or Arizona, sugar beets in Colorado, berries in Michigan; an Indian child moving out from the reservation with other members of his tribe to pull carrots or pick lettuce; or an Anglo, like the Kentucky mountain white children who were described by a woman who had worked with them as "chawing tobaccy and using strong language at the age of two," they are children who grow up in a very different context from other American children. Though they move so often, they move from one migratory camp to another, and a migrant camp in one state looks very much like one in another, though the states be as remote as Florida and New York. Their travels are what little they can see of a road uncoiling, glimpsed from the cramped middle of a crowded truck. . . . There often is no single spot conceived of as "home," or if there is, it is simply a shack in a camp where the group stays longer than at other places. There are almost no possessions; little can be taken with a family that moves in a truck.

These children do not easily find their way into the schools, nor remain long once they get there. Their geographical mobility cuts into school attendance; family income is very low—migrant workers averaged $961 in 1958—and the family needs the child as an additional field hand or as

[9] Esther P. Edwards, "The Children of Migratory Agricultural Workers in the Public Elementary Schools of the United States: Needs and Proposals in the Area of Curriculum," *Harvard Educational Review,* Vol. 30 (Winter, 1960), pp. 12–52.

babysitter so that the mother can go out and work. The parents, themselves illiterate or nearly so, can do little to add to their children's education. Most migrant families possess no books and there is no background for learning in the home. The children generally feel out of step and rejected when they do enter school. In addition, from New Jersey to California, the farmers who employ the migratory workers are not anxious to see the young go off to school, for then they are lost to the work and education will ruin them as stoop-laborers. "When a migrant goes to school beyond the seventh grade, you've ruined a good bean picker."[10] The communities where the migrants are employed also encourage them to move on when the harvest is in. The net result is that state laws compelling school attendance up to a certain age, commonly 15 or 16, are widely blinked in the case of the migrants. Most of their children quit school by the fourth grade and few complete high school, let alone enter college. Their background and the encompassing institutional structure restrain their education to the degree that it is difficult to break out of the vicious cycle of unskilled labor to little education to unskilled labor. Illiteracy or near illiteracy in the young condemns them to repeat the life of their parents.

The case of the migrant child illustrates the low end of a general relationship between socio-educational background and education. Broadly, children from the lower class do not have as much interest in education nor opportunity to obtain it as those from upper strata; because of lowered motivation and financial pressure, some drop out of school as soon as they can. However, compulsory attendance laws, and increased interest, now hold almost all students in the high school up through age 15. Ninety-seven per cent of the 14- and 15-year-olds were enrolled in

[10] *Time,* August 8, 1960, p. 66.

school in 1958; and, the same year, 81 per cent of the 16- and 17-year-olds were also in school, an increase of 10 per cent in eight years (1950–1958).[11] Clearly the trend toward completion of high school is running deep and promises soon to bracket all classes. The important locus of the relation between the socio-economic status of the family and the education of the son and daughter now lies at entry to college. Let us look in detail at some recent findings.

TABLE 2.1—GOING TO COLLEGE (1)

(Percentage of high-school seniors planning to attend college, according to scholastic ability and socio-educational status of the family)*

Scholastic Ability	Family Socio-Educational Status (High) 5	4	3	2	(Low) 1	All Students of Given Ability Level
(High) 4	83	66	53	44	43	61
3	70	53	37	29	29	44
2	65	41	31	20	21	33
(Low) 1	53	30	22	16	18	24
All students of given family status	72	47	35	26	24	40

* Based on a study of over 35,000 American high-school seniors who constituted the entire senior class of 500 public secondary schools. The schools were a fairly representative sample of the 20,000-odd senior public high schools in the country, 1955.

Source: Natalie Rogoff, "College, Careers, and Social Contexts," paper presented at the Fifty-Fourth Annual Meeting of the American Sociological Association, September, 1959.

The plans of high-school seniors for going to college reflect the connection between social position and education. Table 2.1 is based on a 1955 nation-wide survey of over 35,000 seniors in 500 public high schools. Each student

11 *A Fact Book on Higher Education* (Washington, D.C.; American Council on Education, n.d.), p. 65.

was rated on *scholastic ability* (as indicated by a special 20-item test) and *"socio-educational" status of family,* an index based on father's occupation, father's education, and whether older brothers and sisters had gone to college. The students were classified into four categories of ability and five status groupings that ranged from well-educated professional and managerial families to poorly educated, unskilled manual and farm families. The share of students in each of the five status categories who planned to attend college varied from 72 per cent at the top to 24 per cent at the bottom, or a difference of 48 per cent; the share of *all* students expecting to go to college was 40 per cent. (See the last row of the table.) The variation in plans for college over the four levels of ability was from 61 per cent among the top ability to 24 per cent among those of lowest ability, a range of 37 per cent. (See the last column of the table.) Note that social status produced greater variation than did ability, 48 compared to 37 per cent, although this may be partly an artifact of having grouped ability only in four categories while status was split into five levels.

The figures "inside" this table—inside the row and column that report the totals—tell several things: they relate ability to college plans, with family background held constant; they relate family background to college plans, with ability constant; and they also show how ability and background are jointly related to college plans. For the effect of ability with family background constant, we simply read down the columns. In families of top status, for example, 83 per cent of the high-ability students and 53 per cent of the lowest in ability plan college; this is a drop of 30 per cent because of less ability. In the families of bottom status, just 43 per cent of the high-ability students plan college and 18 per cent of the low-ability students so indicate, or a difference of 25 per cent.

Then, for the effect of family background on college

plans, for students of similar ability, we read across the rows. Top-ability students range from 83 per cent to 43 per cent according to family status, a difference of 40 per cent because of socio-educational background, or something correlated with it. Here is the loss of talent from education, because of social and economic differences, that is so often remarked. At the second level of ability, the loss is as great, from 70 per cent among top-status families to 29 per cent among the lowest, or a 41 per cent difference. These two ability categories cover the upper half of high-school students.

The joint relationship of plans for college to social background and ability can be studied by comparing any of the figures with another. For example, the extremes are provided by top-status background and top-ability (83 per cent) and bottom-status and bottom-ability (18 per cent), roughly 8 out of 10 compared with 2 out of 10. The dotted line drawn through the table separates figures greater than 50 per cent from those less than a majority; it shows the heavy role played by the socio-educational status of the family. A majority of sons and daughters in families of top status expect to go to college even when they are of lowest ability; whereas for the children of the bottom status, at no level of ability including the highest do a majority plan college.

Much information is summarized in a table of this kind; the results are representative of the best recent work on how social position connects to the education of the young. Similar studies have shown similar gradations. For example, Table 2.2 reports standard intelligence scores instead of Rogoff's ability measure, father's occupation instead of a socio-educational index, and is based on male students in the Boston metropolitan area instead of a coeducational national sample. But the over-all pattern is similar; in fact, a dotted line drawn to separate figures larger and smaller

TABLE 2.2—GOING TO COLLEGE (2)

(Percentage of boys who expect to go to college, by IQ and father's occupation)*

IQ Quintile		Father's Occupation (High) 5	4	3	2	(Low) 1	All Boys of Given IQ Level
(High)	5	89	76	55	40	29	52
	4	82	53	29	22	14	30
	3	79	47	22	19	10	24
	2	72	36	20	15	6	17
(Low)	1	56	28	12	4	9	11
All boys of given occupational level		80	52	26	19	12	27

* Based on a sample of 3,348 sophomores and juniors in the public high schools of eight towns that are part of the Boston metropolitan area, 1950.

Source: Joseph A. Kahl, "Educational and Occupational Aspirations of 'Common Man' Boys," *Harvard Educational Review,* Vol. 23 (Summer, 1953), p. 188.

than 50 per cent has an identical route. The reader might like to compare this table with the Rogoff table for similarities and differences. What are some possible effects on college-going of the Boston locale itself, where society is relatively stratified compared to the country at large and publicly supported higher education is relatively weak? Does social background count for more than does intelligence? More, apparently, than in the country at large?

How do we account for these "class" differences in college-going expectations? One group of reasons lies in objective differentials; higher education costs money and lower-status families do not have much of it. Easily the most important reason given by parents for not expecting their children to go to college is: "Can't raise the money."[12]

[12] Elmo Roper, "College Ambitions and Parental Planning," *The Public Opinion Quarterly,* 25:2 (Summer, 1961), pp. 159–166.

This reason can be an easy excuse, of course, but it undoubtedly reflects cold reality for most families below the average economic level. Other reasons lie in beliefs; often a lower-class person, compared to those higher in status, "doesn't want as much success, knows he couldn't get it even if he wanted to, and doesn't want what might help him get success."[13] In brief, formal education is differently valued and pursued. A nation-wide survey in 1947 asked the question: "About how much schooling do you think most young men need these days to get along well in the world?" Responses varied by economic level and education of the respondents:

Economic level (Interviewer's rating:	Per cent recommending college education
Wealthy	68
Middle class	52
Lower class	39
Highest education achieved:	
Attended college	72
Attended high school	55
Attended grammar school	36

A more direct question, one on parents' *desire* for their own children to go on to college, was put in a 1945 national survey: "After the war, if you had a son (daughter) graduating from high school would you prefer that he (she) go on to college, or would you rather have him (her) do something else, or wouldn't you care one way or the other?" (See tabular matter at the top of page 66.) Whenever such questions are asked, similar gradations by socioeconomic strata are found in the orientation of parents

[13] Herbert H. Hyman, "The Value Systems of Different Classes: A Social Psychological Contribution to the Analysis of Stratification," in Reinhard Bendix and S. M. Lipset (eds.), *Class, Status, and Power* (Glencoe, Illinois: The Free Press, 1953), p. 427. The material immediately following is adapted from Hyman.

Class level	Per cent preferring college
Prosperous	91
Upper middle	91
Lower middle	83
Poor	68

to higher education; it is also known that children of the different classes show values parallel to their parents.[14] Thus class-related definitions of what is valuable and possible connect objective social status and amount of education desired.

On the other hand, too much can be made of these background differences, and the growing urge throughout the population to obtain more education thereby underplayed. The last set of figures above showed that 68 per cent, or over two out of three, of the adults in the lowest class *preferred* that their son or daughter go to college. The absolute number is as important as the comparison; it indicates that even in the lowest category most parents want their children to be educated. Too, this national response was 15 years ago, and the sentiment and opportunity for higher education has increased rapidly since then. In 1959, when a national survey asked 5,000 heads of households whether they actually *expected* (not *preferred*) their own children to go to college, the *percentage of children* expected to go was 44 per cent in the lowest of four economic categories.[15] No social or economic class is immune from academic aspirations.

The democratizing of education in respect to income restriction is now moving rapidly in this country, chiefly through public junior colleges, state colleges, and state universities. The percentage of the 18 through 21 year olds who were enrolled in college was less than 2 per cent in 1870, only 4 per cent in 1900, 12 per cent in 1930, 30 per

14 Hyman, "The Value Systems of Different Classes," pp. 431–432.
15 Roper, "College Ambitions and Parental Planning," p. 160.

cent in 1950.[16] The American labor force had, on the average, gone as far as the freshman year of high school in 1940; half-way through the sophomore year in 1948; and about all the way through high school by 1957.[17]

This schooling trend is moving with amazing speed. *One generation has seen an advance of four years in the median number of years of schooling completed.* The average young adult in urban areas today has completed high school; his rural counterpart has gone almost as far. In contrast, their fathers and mothers had not advanced much beyond the eighth grade.[18] Clearly this schooling trend will increasingly affect the college-going tendencies of the lower classes, as diversified systems of higher education develop to provide colleges that are near home and have low tuition as well as colleges that are costly and out of town.

College-going in one such diversified system shows where the lower-income students will appear in great numbers. Table 2.3 reports that 43.1 per cent of the graduates of California high schools in 1955 went to college in California. However, less than 5 per cent went to private colleges and universities and less than 5 per cent went directly to the state university (more later transferred to the university). All the rest went to state colleges and junior colleges, which for most students are home-town institutions or colleges to which they can commute from home. How did students from different socio-economic backgrounds distribute among the types of colleges? Table 2.4 compares four institutions

[16] *Historical Statistics of the United States, Colonial Times to 1957* (Bureau of the Census, 1960), pp. 210–211.

[17] "Average" here means the median number of school years completed for the labor force, 18 to 64 years old. The shift in the median reflects the retiring of less-well-educated older persons as well as the entry into the labor force of the better-educated young. *Statistical Abstract of the United States, 1960* (Bureau of the Census, 1960).

[18] Sloan Wayland and Edmund de S. Brunner, *The Educational Characteristics of the American People* (Bureau of Applied Social Research, Columbia University, 1958), pp. 1–3.

TABLE 2.3—PUBLIC HIGH-SCHOOL GRADUATES CONTINUING THEIR EDUCATION IN CALIFORNIA*

Type of College	Proportion of High-School Graduates Who Enter
Private college	4.7
State university	4.4
State college	9.4
Junior college	24.6
All California Colleges	43.1

* Based on data from 41 selected California counties, 1955; the 41,423 graduates included were more than half of the total number in the state.

Source: A Study of the Need for Additional Centers of Public Higher Education in California (Sacramento: California State Department of Education, 1957), pp. 130–131.

TABLE 2.4—COMPARISON OF BACKGROUNDS

(Comparison of four colleges, students classified by socio-economic background, in per cent)*

College	Upper White-Collar	Lower White-Collar	Upper Blue-Collar	Lower Blue-Collar	Total
Stanford University	87	7	6	0	100
University of California	69	14	11	6	100
San Jose State College	38	17	29	16	100
San Jose Junior College	23	15	45	17	100
[Total work force of city of San Jose]	26	17	38	19	100

* Based on freshman students from city of San Jose, 1955; socio-economic background determined by father's occupation.

Source: Burton R. Clark, *The Open Door College: A Case Study* (New York: McGraw-Hill Book Co., Inc., 1960), p. 54.

in the San Jose–San Francisco sector as to the socio-economic status of students who came to them from the city of San Jose. For Stanford University, a selective, high-cost private university located only 15 miles from this city, nearly nine out of ten San Jose students (87 per cent) came from families of professional men, business owners, and business officials ("upper white-collar"), with about one in sixteen (6 per cent) from families of blue-collar workers.

At the other extreme, the junior college had a spread of students whose status was distributed similar to the city's total work force, with nearly two out of three (45 and 17, or 62 per cent) from blue-collar families. The difference in the proportion of students from the families of highest social standing between the *state university* (Berkeley campus, approximately 50 miles from San Jose) and the *state college* in the home town (69 compared to 38, or 31 per cent), is greater than the difference between the *private* university and the leading public institution (87 compared to 69, or 18 per cent). The dotted line in the table, drawn at the point of greatest difference in each column, shows that the break-point lies between the state university and the state college. With conveniently located public colleges, most students remain at home; the principle socio-economic cleavage is then likely to occur between the colleges of local draw and the colleges with state and national recruitment. In brief, free, local colleges increase educational opportunity; at the same time they contribute to a socio-economic differential between those who go away from home to the more expensive and generally more selective colleges and those who attend schools at home which are less expensive and usually less selective academically. This cleavage among colleges promises to be as important in the future as the better-understood difference between those who go to college and those who do not attend any kind of college at all.

Education and Occupational Attainment

We have now reviewed briefly the first half of the chain stretching from social station of parents *to* education *to* future social position. Let us now look at the last half, the extent to which education shapes the possibilities of occupational and social attainment. Again we are talking about what is true of a large number of persons, not necessarily the destiny of any particular individual.

First, education strongly relates to occupational achievement. Table 2.5 shows the extent to which the higher

TABLE 2.5—OCCUPATION AND EDUCATION

PEOPLE WHO WORK IN THESE OCCUPATIONS	HAVE THIS KIND OF EDUCATION (In per cent)		
	Less Than High-School Graduation	High-School Graduation	Some College Education
Professional and technical workers	6	19	75
Proprietors and managers	38	33	29
Clerical or sales workers	25	53	22
Skilled workers	59	33	8
Semi-skilled workers	70	26	4
Service workers	69	25	6
Unskilled workers	80	17	3
Farmers and farm workers	76	19	5

Source: Manpower: Challenge of the 1960s (U.S. Department of Labor, 1960), p. 17.

occupations are composed of the fairly well-educated. Professional and technical workers are in a world by themselves in this regard, for three-fourths of them have had some college whereas no more than a fourth to a third of any other *major* occupational group has had that much education.

These categories are useful for the broad picture but each is so inclusive as to obscure some important groups. The category of "proprietors and managers" includes the small shop owner as well as the corporation executive. The small businessman need not have advanced education but the corporation man generally does. The change that has taken place in the education of top business leaders is shown in Table 2.6. The businessmen referred to hold top execu-

TABLE 2.6—EDUCATION OF BUSINESS LEADERS OF 1928 AND 1952 (IN PER CENT)

Highest Stage of Schooling Completed	1928 Business Leaders	1952 Business Leaders
Less than high school	27	4
High school	28	20
Some college	13	19
College graduation	32	57
Total	100	100

Source: W. Lloyd Warner and James C. Abegglen, *Occupational Mobility in American Business and Industry, 1928–1952* (Minneapolis: University of Minnesota Press, 1955), p. 108.

tive positions in the largest firms in each type of business and industry in America. As can be seen, the business leaders of 1952 were much better educated than the leaders of 1928. In 1952, only 4 per cent had less than a high-school education, but 27 per cent did in 1928, or roughly seven times as many. About one-third were college graduates in the earlier group, compared with 57 per cent in 1952. The situation is changing rapidly; today's young men who will be the business leaders of tomorrow will be even more highly educated.

If education relates strongly to occupational attainment, so does it connect to future income. The average annual income in 1958 of American men, age 45–54—the prime of life—differed widely according to the amount of education they had received:[19]

some elementary schooling	$3,008
completed elementary school	$4,337
some high school	$4,864
completed high school	$6,295
some college	$8,682
completed college	$12,269

[19] Herman P. Miller, "Annual and Lifetime Income in Relation to Education: 1939–1959," *The American Economic Review,* 50:5 (December, 1960), pp. 962–986.

Thus a college graduate is likely to earn almost twice as much each year as a high-school graduate and almost three times as much as someone whose education ended with eight years of elementary school. The differences in *life-time* income are almost equally great: as of 1958, total income from age 18 to death was estimated as $182,000 for those who had completed only grammar school; $258,000 for high-school graduates; and $435,000 for those with four or more years of college. The man with a college degree would thus receive approximately $175,000 more income during his life than a man whose education stopped with high-school graduation. The differences in annual and lifetime income among men with these different levels of education is increasing, not decreasing; the largest increase between 1949 and 1958 was made by college-educated men.

We can also guess that the kind of school attended makes some difference in later rewards, with wealthier high-prestige schools leading to greater financial success. Such is the case, for if we divide male graduates into groups by type of school attended we get the differences in median incomes shown in Table 2.7. The different financial rewards still are there even when we take into account the family backgrounds of the students. Poor boys who go to rich schools do much better financially than poor boys who go to the more obscure colleges.

These figures make clear what level and type of education mean for occupational and status attainment on the average. The educational ladder leads to the higher occupations, the upper social statuses, the prestigeful styles of life, and membership in the subsociety of the "educated." It is true in growing degree that without education one has lowered horizons—occupationally, socially, culturally; with education, many doors are open, perhaps even some doors in the mind.

TABLE 2.7—TYPES OF COLLEGES AND FINANCIAL SUCCESS*

Type of College	Annual Income of Graduates, 1947
The Big Three (Harvard, Yale, Princeton)	$7,365
Other Ivy League (Columbia, Cornell, Dartmouth, Pennsylvania)	$6,142
Seventeen Technical Schools (California, Carnegie, Case, Detroit, Drexel, Georgia, Illinois, Massachusetts, and Stevens Institutes of Technology; Rensselaer, Rose, Virginia, and Worcester Polytechnic Institutes; Clarkson College of Technology, Cooper Union, Polytechnic Institute of Brooklyn, Tri-State College)	$5,382
Twenty Famous Eastern Colleges (Amherst, Bates, Bowdoin, Brown, Clark, Colby, Franklin and Marshall, Hamilton, Haverford, Hobart, Lafayette, Lehigh, Middlebury, Rutgers, Swarthmore, Trinity, Tufts, Union, Wesleyan of Connecticut, Williams)	$5,287
The Big Ten (Chicago, Illinois, Indiana, Iowa, Michigan, Minnesota, Northwestern, Ohio State, Purdue, Wisconsin)	$5,176
All Other Midwest Colleges	$4,322
All Other Eastern Colleges	$4,235

* Based on questionnaire replies from over 9,000 college graduates, 1947.

Source: Ernest Havemann and Patricia Salter West, *They Went to College* (New York: Harcourt, Brace and Co., 1952), pp. 178–179.

The educational system moves individuals from one social station to another; it may also move whole groups. The "lower class," for example, may have considerable turnover, if many of the sons and daughters of one cultural group move up a notch or two, replaced by unskilled immigrants of another background who provide the floor of the occupational structure in the next generation. The United States has seen numerous Yankees, Irish, Italians, and others start at the bottom and move right on up the occupational ladder. Education has played an important role in providing the necessary acculturation and training. Then, too, the lower class can be denuded, in a sense, as the number of unskilled jobs decreases and more persons take on the skills, earn the money, and gain the trappings that lead to and symbolize middle-class status. In short, whole strata as well as individuals can be in motion. Such shifts are especially likely to happen in the modern technological society, where improved technique and the trend toward service industry lead to a general upgrading of jobs, in level of skill and thus also in education required. Other reasons aside, the technological society must encourage mass education in order to meet its occupational needs; then education functions to move the lower strata upwards.

When education operates to any considerable degree in this way, it can lead to a pervasive sense of opportunity; with this, it functions to keep the lower classes "in society" as well as "of it." Lower classes become resentful and alienated, in societies where achievement is a value, when low status appears permanent and son follows father in menial labor unto the sixth generation. Resentment is lowered and alienation abated where achievement of the "better life" is thought possible, if not always probable. If the chance to achieve is considered somewhat available, then nonachieving is a *personal* failure rather than the fault of the society. The chance to participate in the general society, through such means as education, also reduces the inclination to extremist politics. "It is in the advanced industrial countries, principally the United States, Britain, and Northwestern Europe, where national income *has* been rising, where mass expectations of an equitable share in that increase are relatively fulfilled, and where social mobility affects ever greater numbers, that extremist politics have least hold."[20] The stability of the democratic process in general is closely related to national levels of economic development, including degrees of educational attainment.[21] In brief, the open society of modern times is likely to remain open and democratic only if, among other conditions, its lower classes have some reasonable degree of access to the educational avenue and other roads leading to social rewards.

We need at this point to resolve a conflict that has gradually built up in this chapter's discussion: What determines life chances to the *greatest* extent—social position or education, ascription or achievement? On the one hand, children from the higher social strata are likely to receive more and better education than their lower-class counterparts. The higher-level education then, in turn, provides access to the better positions. In short, education is a mechanism whereby social-class positions are stabilized across the generations,[22] and is thereby a barrier to the social mobility of those who start from lower rungs. This is one general tendency. Another and contradictory tendency is for a considerable number of the young to be mobile upward from the lower strata by virtue of the availability of schooling, their persistence and success once in school, and then their entry into some higher-status occupation to which their education has admitted them. Here education is a

[20] Daniel Bell, "The Theory of Mass Society," *Commentary*, Vol. 22 (July, 1956), p. 80.

[21] Seymour Martin Lipset, *Political Man* (Garden City, N.Y.: Doubleday & Company, Inc., 1960), p. 129.

[22] See Bernard Barber, *Social Stratification* (New York: Harcourt, Brace and Co., 1957), p. 395.

mechanism whereby social positions are changed rather than stabilized. What is the balance? Until the twentieth century, education's role in providing for mobility was everywhere largely secondary to its role in assigning *similar* social positions across generations. Father's status counted more than the classroom; and mobile individuals were often mobile without education. But the role of the school and college in social mobility grows stronger as (a) education becomes more available to all and (b) men are judged by the universal criteria of scholastic achievement and technical competence—when the question asked is, what do you know, rather than who do you know or what did your father do. In the United States in the middle of the twentieth century, increasing numbers in lower social strata now have the high-school habit; the time is approaching when they, like the middle and upper class, will have the college habit to a considerable degree. Especially in an expanding economy, where there is more room at the top, these habits can lead to the very highest positions; a higher proportion of the American business elite now comes from the lower social ranks than a quarter of a century ago. The gigantic business organizations are particularly open: "The larger the firm the smaller the proportion of men with fathers in the same firm. . . . The stronghold of inherited position today in America is in the smaller enterprises; the larger enterprises are more open to competition for men rising from lower occupational levels."[23] What matters now for social mobility is that one travel the educational road; and access to this highway, despite the handicaps of dirt-road entrances for some, is increasingly open. The lower-class boy majoring in engineering at the state university is a case in point.

[23] W. Lloyd Warner and James C. Abegglen, *Occupational Mobility in American Business and Industry, 1928–1952* (Minneapolis: University of Minnesota Press, 1955), p. 32.

For society, the extending and especially the equalizing of opportunity is a necessary part of a fuller use of talent for trained manpower. When for various economic, ethnic, and motivational reasons, high-ability children leave education early and in large numbers, considerable talent goes undeveloped. A technological society has an insatiable appetite for competence, especially in engineering and allied fields; a bureaucratic society needs trained experts for the myriad specialized positions of the large organization; and on top of this, societies competing internationally also look upon trained men as essential to national vigor. These triple pressures of technology, bureaucracy, and world tension promote the effort in the United States to open wider the doors of educational agencies, train more persons, uncover hidden talent, and draw to higher levels those of obvious ability who otherwise would leave early.

The extending of *larger* amounts of education to *larger* numbers and *larger* proportions of the population in modern society has all kinds of consequences, deeply affecting the nature of education in the lower and the higher grades. We shall touch upon some of these consequences in later chapters, following our interest in the effects of modern social trends on education. One problem raised by the extension of educational opportunity[24] to ever larger numbers is that the upper grades of the school must then face many students who are ill-equipped; when formerly selective schools become unselective, as happened in the American high school, the schools naturally handle more young people of low to average ability. Increased quantity, without quality control, puts pressure on standards, and the deriva-

[24] *Extending* opportunity should be distinguished from *equalizing* opportunity, which will be discussed in Chapter 3. To extend means to offer to a larger number; to equalize means to offer on grounds of ability without regard to such "irrelevant" criteria as race, creed, or ancestry. Extension often implies equalization but need not, as when more education is given to more white children but not to Negroes.

tive problem thus becomes one of maintenance of quality. American secondary education has been plagued with this problem since shortly after the turn of the century, with the schools adapting their programs to a wide range of abilities and the critics of the schools pressing for greater rigor.

Greater schooling for greater numbers also has brought with it, and evidently implies, a greater practicality in what the schools teach and what they do for students. The existence of children of diverse ability and destiny in the schools calls forth the comprehensive school, or the multischool comprehensive structure, within which some students receive a broad, general education but others take primarily a technical or commercial training. In short, increased quantity means greater vocationalism. This tendency hit the American high school around the beginning of the century, changing its character from the strictly academic. It has played a growing role in higher education ever since higher education began seriously to slip out of the liberal-arts-college mold in the last quarter of the nineteenth century. As indicated earlier, the growth in enrollment in higher education in America in recent decades has been in the applied fields, especially business, engineering, and education. Part of the impetus for this growth has come from students of lower social origins entering college intent on a "realistic" training for higher occupations without academic or collegiate frills.

Democratization in the sense of throwing open the doors of educational agencies without regard to *ability* also causes the sorting processes of education to take somewhat different form than was the case, and is the case, when schools are selective. Sorting must take place at some point in the educational structure. If, at that level, it does not take place *at* the door, the time of entry, it must occur *inside* the doors, in the classroom and counseling office. The problem of sorting within the school and classroom is faced acutely at the level in the educational structure where the staff must say to the student, in effect: "From here on, it is ability and not automatic promotion. If you want to be an engineer, you must be able to pass in mathematics and physics. If you can't, then you can no longer kid yourself." This situation is found in the high school, but it is now most critical in the first year of public colleges and universities that unselectively take all high-school graduates. Those who have little or no promise for college are let in to have a try; most of these unpromising recruits are quickly selected out in the first year.

This selecting-out-after-entry means that sorting must become a major internal consideration, affecting the work of the teacher, the counselor, and the administrator. Special procedures arise, for example, for sidetracking or getting rid of the failures, with the procedures leading the student into a counseling orbit. The procedures in some cases lead to quick dismissal, as in state universities where students numbering in the thousands are dropped in the freshman year, or to a change in major to an easy field. In other colleges, the procedures lead to an alternative track, as in junior colleges where students are eased from four-year to two-year programs, to become an "engineering aide" instead of an engineer.[25] Democracy encourages aspiration, and generous admission allows the student whose hopes outrun his capabilities to carry his hopes into the school or now principally the college. But there his desires run into the standards necessary for the integrity of programs and the training of competent workers. The college offers the opportunity to try, but the student's own ability and his accumulative record of performance finally insist that he be

[25] Burton R. Clark, "The 'Cooling-out' Function in Higher Education," *The American Journal of Sociology,* Vol. 65 (May, 1960), pp. 569–576.

sorted out. It is everywhere a problem of democratic institutions that encouragement to achieve runs up against the realities of fewer successes at ascending levels of training and work. With this, situations of opportunity are also inherently situations of denial and failure. Some succeed and some do not.

Thus as ascription has given way to achievement in this country in the very recent past, sorting for adult role has moved considerably from class origin to the classroom. In some democratic countries—England, for example—the sorting through achievement has taken place through national examination and careful selection at a certain level. But in the American educational system, sorting through achievement has become a drawn-out, subtle process. Selection takes place in less formal and less obvious ways. Compared to sorting at the door, selection within the school or college often leads to a somewhat masked and cushioned rearranging of the fate of individuals.

THE TRANSFERENCE OF STATUS

Part of the ever closer connection between education and the occupational structure is the interesting phenomenon of the status of one rubbing off on the other. Let us first consider the transference of prestige that takes place from occupations to schools and colleges. The decisive feature in the assignment of status to levels and types of schools and colleges, broadly, is their relationship to occupations. The university prepares students in its professional and graduate schools for occupations of high social status, such as the established professions, science, business management. The four- or five-year college relates *directly* to occupations of somewhat lower status for the most part, in which neither advanced graduate nor prolonged professional-school training is needed, such as teaching, engineering, lower management positions in business and government. The two-year junior college prepares semiprofessionals and technicians.

The high school now provides relatively little occupational training other than elementary clerical work and, where vocational schools still exist, some training for the building trades and the machine shop. The differential status of the occupations inevitably attaches to the preparatory agencies. Despite the efforts of educators to erase invidious status distinctions among schools, it is unrealistic to expect equality of status for schools when they are differentially geared into the basic outside hierarchy of social status. This is fundamental to the general tendency to rank the university over the state college, the state college in turn over the two-year college, and any level of college over the high school.

This principle of status transference has been observed in the relationship of education to occupations in Britain, even within the limits of secondary education alone.[26] English secondary education contains three types of public schools primarily (public in the American definition of public and private): the Grammar school, the Technical school, and the Secondary Modern school. In keeping with democratic principles, many citizens and government officials would like a parity of prestige for these schools. Yet this is impossible given the encompassing social structure. The several schools relate to occupations of differential status and hence vary considerably in prestige. The Grammar schools, which are selective, lead to the university and the top-status occupations; the Technical school is also somewhat selective, and its graduates typically go into "the new middle class of technologists and industrial managers"; the Secondary Modern school is unselective and leads to all the work of lesser status, from bookkeeper to dressmaker to laborer. A central consideration in this tripartite struc-

26 Olive Banks, *Parity and Prestige in English Secondary Education* (London: Routledge & Kegan Paul, Ltd., 1955), Chapter 16.

ture is how to raise the status of the Secondary Modern school, which handles the majority of students, in the face of the selective schools which have better students on the average and lead typically to the better-paying fields.

In the United States a similar status differential has been attached to the several major programs or curricula *within* the comprehensive high school, with the vocational and the commercial tagged by most teachers, students, and parents as inferior to the academic or college-preparatory major which leads to more education and higher things. Here again efforts to assign a parity of status have largely failed because of the linkage of levels and kinds of education to the general occupational-status hierarchy. Yet Americans have been more "successful" than the English in this matter; the comprehensive school blurs the distinction between curricula more than does a structure composed of three kinds of schools.

An especially interesting feature of the education-occupation connection is the way that status rubs off the other way around, from schools to fields of work. This transference is especially noticeable in the case of occupations that are becoming, or are attempting to become, professions. To be defined as a high-status field, an occupation must usually have high-status educational preparation; a profession must have professional schools in the universities. Entry into the field through training in a university professional program is now one of the several basic hallmarks of a profession, along with licensing or certification of practitioners and a professional association organized for control and protection. Thus it is not solely for reasons of increasing complexity of knowledge and training that some fields come knocking at the door of the university, seeking advanced programs.

The push is on in many fields in the United States today to become known as a profession. Law and medicine long ago arrived; now struggling up the slope and trailing in various degrees come agriculture, business administration, dentistry, education, engineering, forestry, librarianship, nursing, optometry, pharmacy, public health, social welfare, and so on. Fields are being so rapidly upgraded in skill requirements that a very large number of them can claim some degree of "professionalization." The desire for professional status encourages attempts to speed up the already rapid evolution, so that in many cases those in the field attempt a bootstrap operation. An essential part of this professionalization is to get universities to institute professional schools for the field, from which subsequently the field will receive status as well as trained recruits.

We should emphasize in closing this chapter how much the making of the individual's destiny has changed since the days of old. In simple societies, young people are allocated to adult positions and statuses by custom and heritage of the family, clan, and community. Many statuses are ascribed according to birth; for example, the son of a chief is destined to be the ruler after his father. Often only one or two major occupations are available, and the young know quite early whether they will be fisherman or hunter or farmer.

In the complex society, with its elaborate division of labor, one's occupational future is more open and much more likely to be won by dint of individual achievement. The processes of allocating young people to adult positions become complicated and heavily intwined with formal education and training. The more advanced the technology and the state of organization, the more occupational (and social) achievement depend on the possession of special knowledge and skills. The work of the business manager becomes more complicated and specialized, for example, requiring training and perspectives not to be gained by working one's way up from a factory hand. The "self-made man" of the middle twentieth century typically makes himself through four years of college and very probably through additional work in a graduate or professional school. Mobility through education is a core element of the twentieth-century society.

Chapter 3

Education and Minorities

EVERY SOCIETY containing subpopulations diverse in heritage or race needs to define orderly relations among these groups. The differences among the groups, real or apparent, must be reconciled, patterns of control and accommodation found that allow the society to preserve itself and its members to proceed with their work, play, and child rearing. The patterns that constitute an ethnic or racial order may take such disparate forms as: full assimilation of minorities into the society, with gradual loss of separate identity; the integration of minorities to the extent of equal opportunity and treatment, coupled with maintenance of separate heritages or group identities; or, the segregation and subordination of minorities. The patterns vary from forced assimilation to complete preservation of group differences, from erasure of prejudicial attitudes and discriminatory acts to fixation on prejudice and discrimination. Whatever its nature, the ethnic or racial order that evolves, or is planned, will be linked closely to other major parts of the society such as the class system, the distribution of occupations, and the arrangement of housing.

Education is central in any of the patterns of minority relations, since it is the primary system for jointly transmitting culture, socializing the young, and allocating men to jobs and statuses. The paths to assimilation, integration, or segregation extend through the school building as well as across the factory floor, up to the voting booth, and down the neighborhood street. The participation of ethnic and racial populations in education is often a source of great stress, when, as in our own society, the issues are deeply emotional, mixed with strong sentiment about group differences and stirred by parental desire to do the best one can for one's children. Peaceful or explosive, the education of minorities usually stands as a primary problem in the social order of heterogeneous societies. As a problem, it can be tantalizingly subtle and complex, disturbing and baffling to persons of different beliefs. Here, in exploring ways in which education reflects and determines the position of minorities, we shall confine ourselves largely to the education of Negroes in the United States. Negroes are by far the largest minority in this country; the issue of school integration, now important, centers about them; and Negro-white relations highlight ways in which the education of minorities connects with occupation, housing, law and politics—and even the operation of the school itself. In the first two sections in this chapter, we concentrate on the Negro in the urban North; in the last three sections, largely on the Negro in the South.

Again, as in the first two chapters, we shall have an eye peeled for the effect of the technological age. The advanced stages of industrial society are bound to affect seriously, for better or for worse, the position of minorities. The American Negro is physically and socially relocated as population is reshuffled from rural to urban areas, and from one region of the country to another, pushed and pulled by technological advances and related economic development. Many existing majority-minority patterns, surviving from earlier periods, are increasingly called into question. The widespread concern about talent, for example, presses against the discriminatory patterns that sidetrack talent because of race. Democratic industrial societies also suffer in competition with Communist regimes when their own patterns of discrimination are held up to the view of Africans, Asians, and Latin Americans. Notably, the technological age deepens the problem of personal competence for minority members above all others. As suggested in the Introduction and later in Chapter 2, cultural and technical competence becomes a critical matter, and its threshold is raised, as more education and more skill become essential for functioning adequately in society.

The lost young man in our time is the one who does not have a salable skill, or even the cultural know-how necessary to hawk products door-to-door, let alone to comprehend the social forces that shape his world and his life. The problem of competence bears most heavily on those who are culturally deprived, those who migrate from the farm and small town to the city, and those who are defined by others as inherently inferior or different. Minority members tend to be all three—deprived, mobile, and negatively defined. The education of minorities sets in high relief the bearing of technological development and rapid change on the education, competence, and achievement of the individual. Defective education has a prolonged influence, particularly for minorities.

EDUCATIONAL REFLECTION OF THE MINORITY ORDER

The education of the members of a minority is affected in many cases by the traditions and values of the group itself. Japanese Americans, for example, have a strong drive for educational achievement, while Mexican-American boys and girls on the average have not pushed or been pushed so hard and so far in education. Jews traditionally have placed high value upon education and intellectual attainment.[1] Learning in the old European Jewish community gave the individual "prestige, respect, authority—and the chance for a better marriage." Jewish immigrants to this country eagerly sought education for their young. In the Italian culture, on the other hand, the traditional attitude was less supportive of education. School, in Italy, was largely an upper-class institution and remote from the everyday experience of the peasant. Learned men were of another class or were men of the church. First-generation Italians in this country therefore were often negative toward education. "Mother believed you would go mad if you read too many books, and Father was of the opinion that too much school makes children lazy and opens the mind for unhealthy dreams." Such differences in values tend to disappear, however, as the various minorities accept the dominant American values, which emphasize individual achievement and draw attention to education as a means of achievement. The norm is to become pro-education.

Moreover, the education of various minorities has been affected to a greater degree by attitudes from outside the group, by the feelings of the dominant population. The beliefs of white Protestant Americans about the schooling of minorities have been contradictory, not working in a single direction. The dominant population has held strongly to democratic doctrine, stressing opportunity and free schooling. This equalitarian commitment has worked to spread education and to pull the young of the minority

[1] The following account of Jewish-Italian cultural differences is drawn from Fred L. Strodtbeck, "Family Interaction, Values and Achievement," in David C. McClelland, *et al* (eds.), *Talent and Society* (Princeton, N.J.: D. Van Nostrand Co., Inc., 1958), pp. 135–194.

groups into the school house, often against the heritage of the minority and over the obstacles of poverty. Under the impulse of the equal-opportunity doctrine, there are today colleges with scholarships in hand searching for bright Negro youth.

Democratic ideas have restrained many school boards from gerrymandering school areas so as to put white children in one high school and Negro children in another. At the same time, white Protestants have held attitudes that Negroes are inferior, Mexicans are lazy, and Jews are out to get everything; and the prejudicial sentiments have worked themselves out in many ways in education, from separate schools for those thought inferior, to toleration of early dropout for those considered lazy Latins, to quota systems and discriminatory admission policies for Jews seeking to enter medical schools. Too, just as education today can "ruin" a good bean picker, so could education in 1900 "ruin" a good Irish mill worker in a textile town in New England.

Attitudes toward minorities are often intertwined with economic interests. Political power also enters, as we shall see in Chapter 4. In brief, a host of sentiments and motives have combined or clashed in the minds of white Protestant board members and school officials as they have made the decisions, school by school, town by town, whether the various minorities were to receive more or less schooling, academic or vocational instruction, the good teachers or the poor ones condemned to the bad schools. At the level of sentiments and motives, the "treatment" of minorities by the majority in the United States has been exceedingly contradictory and complex.

Apart from the traditional beliefs and attitudes of the majority, features of the social structure of a country affect the education of minorities. Occupation and residence are especially important. The occupational status of the family, as indicated in Chapter 2, conditions the education and life chances of sons and daughters. This linkage bears heavily on minorities since more of their members in greater degree suffer the restraining effects of the poorly paid, low-status occupations. Chart 3.1 compares the occupational distribution of Negroes and whites in the United States. Concentrated in unskilled work—farm laborer, ditch-digger, maid—Negroes have been employed in jobs substantially different from those of most white workers. Their jobs represent low social origins for their offspring—a background of poverty, poorly educated parents, and bad housing that restrains education.

CHART 3.1

OCCUPATIONAL DISTRIBUTION OF NEGRO AND WHITE WORKERS IN 1959

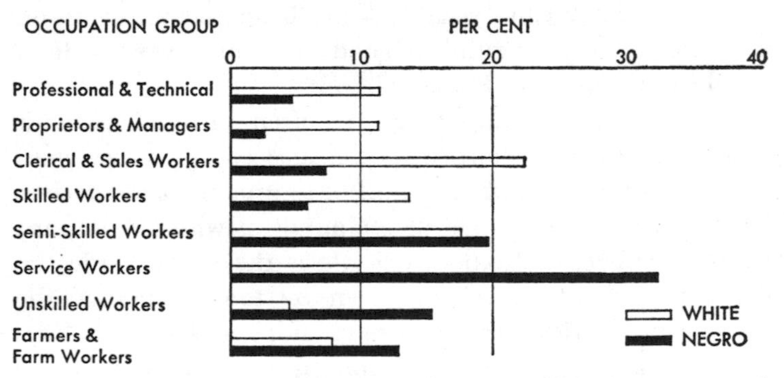

Source: Manpower: Challenge of the 1960s (U.S. Department of Labor, 1960), p. 20.

Together with the special restrictions placed on the Negro in the South after white supremacy was re-established there in the last quarter of the nineteenth century, the Negro's occupational status has been largely responsible for the depressing of the sheer amount of education received by his children. The educational attainment of nonwhites and whites in 1957 compared as follows:[2]

Education Obtained	White	Nonwhite
College	16%	6%
High School	45%	28%
5–8 years	30%	36%
4 years or less	7%	27%

Over one-fourth of the Negroes, twenty-five years old and over, had four years of schooling or less; *nearly two-thirds* had only a grammar-school education.

The residential location of ethnic and racial groups is particularly decisive in determining their integration or segregation in the schools. Schools are dispersed to serve different sectors of a city or town and become linked to the adjacent neighborhood. Ethnic concentrations in neighborhoods means that students will attend segregated or largely segregated schools, since the social composition of the neighborhood determines the social composition of the school. In a large city that has a Black Belt (Chicago) or a Harlem (New York), many schools will be largely all-white or all-Negro, with some mixed schools in the boundary neighborhoods or in areas undergong racial transition.

The carry-over effect of segregation or concentration in housing is strong and stubborn. It can be diminished, at best, only by elaborate attempts to rezone school areas in order to achieve a greater mix, or to reassign and bus students to schools distant from their homes so that there will be no all-white or all-Negro schools. Such efforts encounter many difficulties: new zoning plans designed to produce mixed schools are disrupted by disgruntled parents

[2] Persons twenty-five years old and over. The vast majority of those classified as nonwhites by the census are Negroes. Schooling was unknown for about two per cent of whites and three per cent of nonwhites. Leonard Broom and Philip Selznick, *Sociology* (Evanston, Illinois: Row, Peterson and Co., 1958), p. 486.

who turn to private schools or move to new locations, or the plans are soon outdated by the expansion of the ethnic population past the old boundary lines; the deliberate moving of students different in skin color, social class, and academic achievement into "white" schools by busing them away from their home neighborhood is costly and often resisted by the white parents. As illustration of the almost overwhelming effect of residential concentration, consider the efforts of the New York City school system, where the Board of Education takes the position that racially homogeneous schools are undesirable and attempts to locate new schools and zone old ones to obtain some mixing:[3]

While the Board considers distribution [of students to gain a mixture] in the siting of new schools, the change in population is so rapid, and length of time between planning and opening so great, that very often a school planned for a fringe area, for heterogeneity, opens up finally in a mostly Negro or Puerto Rican area. The Board also considers distribution in setting up zones for old schools; but, as we have indicated, and to put it crudely, there are generally not enough "other" children to go around. The battles that take place between principals and parent groups of various schools over the relatively small numbers of continental white children would be comic—if they were not rather pitiful. And in the end, any victories are likely to be Pyrrhic ones. The assignment of a few blocks containing fifty "other" children to a school that is largely Negro and Puerto Rican does not necessarily mean an increase by fifty in the number of "other" children. Maybe only ten or twenty will show up when school opens, and the battle will have been in vain. There are always alternatives for resisting parents—parochial and private schools (which enroll one-third of the children of school age in New York City); or the move to the suburbs—precipitated, perhaps, by the zoning change.

The Board of Education is unhappily aware of all these problems. If rezoning cannot accomplish much, a certain amount

[3] Nathan Glazer, "Is 'Integration' Possible in the New York Schools?" *Commentary*, 30:3 (September, 1960), p. 189.

of redistributing of the school population can be done by busing. A thousand children from the heavily Negro Bedford-Stuyvesant area of Brooklyn are bused to schools in Queens and Brooklyn, and another 400 are bused from Harlem to Yorkville in Manhattan.

The children bused in 1960 were a small number for a city the size of New York.

The steady and rapid flow of population into cities, and from the cities to their suburbs, is forging larger links in this chaining of the school to residential segregation. Negroes, and in some cities Puerto Ricans,[4] have been migrating in large numbers from their former rural locations into the downtown districts, while whites have been moving from the center of the city to the suburbs—in search of a home, with grass, to call their own and also to escape dark-skin neighbors. These population movements not only shift the ethnic boundaries but tend to put the dark-skin minorities in separate governmental units and school districts in the cores of metropolitan areas, while whites bunch up in the "lily-white" suburbs. In 1960, Washington, D.C., was 55 per cent Negro; Baltimore, 35 per cent; Detroit, 29 per cent; Philadelphia, 27 per cent; Chicago, 24 per cent.[5] Negroes were moving into Chicago at the rate of 2,500 every month in 1957, and New York City's over one million is the largest concentration of Negroes in the country. The striking fact about the social composition of New York City is that "*three-quarters* of the school children of Manhattan are Negro and Puerto Rican; *two-fifths* of the school children of greater New York [Manhattan, Brooklyn, Bronx, Queens] are Negro and Puerto Rican."[6]

4 Nearly all Puerto Ricans in the continental United States are classified as whites by the United States Census, but many are defined by laymen as nonwhites. Puerto Ricans are an important minority in a few American cities, notably New York and Chicago.

5 *United States Census of Population, 1960,* Vol. I, P C 1.

6 Glazer, "Is 'Integration' Possible in the New York Schools?" p. 188.

These concentrations will increase, for the number of Negro and Puerto Rican children in New York City is increasing rapidly. The Negro birth rate is higher than the white birth rate, and the Puerto Rican birth rate is higher still. Light-skin people ("continental whites") continue to move out of the city to the suburbs. Between 1950 and 1957, New York City lost a white population about the size of Washington, D.C. (750,000) and gained a Negro and Puerto Rican population about the size of Pittsburgh, Pennsylvania (650,000).[7] Thus, *within* the largest city in the country, measures taken by school authorities to integrate the schools will continue to be largely checked by residential concentration and population movement.

Meanwhile, out in the suburbs:[8]

> [Levittown] in 1947 . . . had 36 children in two classrooms in six and one-half square miles of potato fields. In 1954 they had 15,000 houses; 45,000 people; 12,500 children in school, and more pre-school children than [children in school]. All of the families were within a few hundred dollars of each other in income, all were beginning families, and not a single family among them would have been classified by the census as "non-white."
>
> . . . There is scarcely a new development created since the war in the metropolitan area of New York which is interracial in character. The developments are "lily-white." Levittown has only recently [about 1958] admitted some six or seven "non-white" families.

In the metropolis, those who live apart are likely to go to school apart.

The Negro's education—deficient in amount and segregated in facilities, North and South—has led nationally to a sizable but unmeasured loss of talent, a feature of educa-

[7] Dan W. Dodson, "Public Education in New York City in the Decade Ahead," *The Journal of Educational Sociology,* Vol. 34 (February, 1961), pp. 274–287.

[8] Dodson, "Public Education in New York City," pp. 275–276.

tion for the culturally impoverished—poor whites, Negroes, Puerto Ricans—that has stirred much concern in recent years. Bright children from culturally deprived families, besides lacking the financial means of going to college, often do not know they are bright and do not aspire to extended education. They may even go unrecognized by school personnel, partly because intelligence tests reflect learning that comes through exposure to books and informed adult conversation, as well as the natural endowment of the child. The sensitivity of the measured IQ to cultural exposure and scholastic motivation has been shown in the dramatic cases where special programs for the culturally deprived have taken students with IQ scores below 100 on entrance to high school and raised them to levels of achievement where they won college scholarships.[9] Without the kinds of exposures that reflect well in test and classroom performance, a bright child from the slum or the tenant farm might appear to grow dumber as he grew older, compared to national norms, and be treated accordingly by the school. Cultural impoverishment in the home and neighborhood can lead, in this way, to low self-evaluation and early school-leaving.

The low estate of many minorities in society also affects the way their children are counseled in the schools as to their occupational possibilities. Counselors, teachers, and other advisors face the problem of whether to direct minority youth toward jobs they can enter easily, or to encourage them to aspire to better positions, prepare accordingly, and take the chance of being shut out by discrimination. The safe road, of course, is to prepare them for the known—to shunt a Mexican-American boy of above average intelligence off to the wood-working shop in the school to prepare for a semiskilled job in furniture repair-

[9] Martin Mayer, *The Schools* (New York: Harper & Brothers, 1961), pp. 124–125.

ing. This decision is most likely if school personnel themselves have prejudicial attitudes or even stereotyped opinions of the talents of minorities.

THE MINORITY CHILD AND TEACHER REACTION

Very important, too, in affecting the education of the child are the ways that teachers react to lower-class characteristics and other related attributes of many minorities. The teaching of culturally deprived youth of the lower class is hard, different from the teaching of middle- and upper-class kids in many cases, and calls out special adaptations. Many of the children come ill-prepared and little motivated for school work. With them, the teachers in the "slum" schools use different techniques from those used in the "better" schools:[10]

> At S—[the slum school], there were a lot of guys who were just waiting till they were sixteen so they could get out of school. At L—, everybody—well, a very large percentage, I'll say—was going on to secondary school, to college. That certainly made a difference in their classroom work. You had to teach differently at the different schools. For instance, at S—, if you had demonstrations in chemistry they had to be pretty flashy, lots of noise and smoke before they'd get interested in it. That wasn't necessary at L—. Or at S— if you were having electricity or something like that you had to get the static electricity machine out and have them all stand around and hold hands so that they'd all get a little jolt.

The administrators and the teachers also come to expect less of the child:

[10] This account and the following quotations are taken from Howard S. Becker, "Social-Class Variations in the Teacher-Pupil Relationship," *The Journal of Educational Sociology*, 25:8 (April, 1952), pp. 451–465.

> So [in the better schools] you have to be on your toes and keep up to where you're supposed to be in the course of study. Now, in a school like the D— [slum school] you're just not expected to complete all that work. It's almost impossible. For instance, in the second grade we're supposed to cover nine spelling words a week. Well, I can do that up here at the K— ["better" school], they can take nine new words a week. But the best class I ever had at the D— was only able to achieve six words a week and they had to work pretty hard to get that. So I never finished the year's work in spelling. I couldn't. And I really wasn't expected to.

The problem becomes worse in each grade, "as the gap between what the children should know and what they actually do know becomes wider and wider." It becomes impossible to follow the normal program of study and teaching is then a struggle to get across a few basic skills:

> The children come into our upper grades with very poor reading ability. That means that all the way through our school everybody is concentrating on reading. It's not like at a school like S— [middle group] where they have science and history and so on. At a school like that they figure that from the first to fourth you learn to read and from fifth to eighth you read to learn. You use your reading to learn other material. Well, these children don't reach that second stage while they're with us. We have to plug along getting them to learn to read. Our teachers are pretty well satisfied if the children can read and do simple number work when they leave here. You'll find that they don't think very much of subjects like science, and so on. They haven't got any time for that. They're just trying to get these basic things over. . . . That's why our school is different from one like the S—.

Similarly, children in the lower-class schools are considered difficult to control. They are more given to unrestrained behavior and physical violence. Many teachers adapt, if they remain long, by using sterner measures than they would in other schools, and by building a reputation "which coerces the children into behaving without attempting any test of strength." For all the teachers, but especially for the newer, inexperienced ones, the greater emphasis on discipline detracts from teaching.

Too, the children from the "worse" neighborhoods also most deeply offend the teachers' moral sensibilities about health and cleanliness, sex and aggression, ambition and work:

> His teeth were all rotten, every one of them. Just filthy and rotten. Man, I mean, I was really shocked, you know. I said, "Don't you have a toothbrush?" He said no, they were only his baby teeth and Ma said he didn't need a toothbrush for that. So I really got upset and looked in all their mouths. Man, I never saw anything like it. They were all like that, practically.

> One thing about these girls is, well, some of them are not very nice girls. One girl in my class I've had two years now. She makes her money on the side as a prostitute. She's had several children. . . . This was a disturbing influence on the rest of the class.

> So we have a pretty tough element there, a bunch of bums, I might as well say it. That kind you can't reach at all. They don't want to be there at all, and so you can't do anything with them.

Such characteristics of many children in the deprived minorities, and the special problems they present, cause teachers anxiety and despair, and commonly lead to the adaptations specified above that retard the education of the child. In addition, there is often wholesale transferring of experienced teachers, by their own request, from the "slum" schools to the "better" ones. Since few move in the other direction, new inexperienced teachers are assigned to the "worst" schools. There a few make the necessary adjustment; more begin the effort to get out. As remarked by a Chicago teacher:[11]

[11] Howard S. Becker, "The Career of the Chicago Public Schoolteacher," *The American Journal of Sociology*, 57:5 (March, 1952), p. 473.

When you first get assigned you almost naturally get assigned to one of those poorer schools, because those naturally are among the first to have openings because people are always transferring out of them to other schools. Then you go and request to be transferred to other schools nearer your home or in some nicer neighborhood. Naturally the vacancies don't come as quickly in those schools because people want to stay there once they get there. I think that every teacher strives to get into a nicer neighborhood.

In short, *the* adjustment of most teachers faced by the unattractive and difficult lower-class, minority student is to manipulate the transfer system, if they can, in such a way as to escape to a better school.

The large and continuing growth of Negro and other dark-skin minority populations in northern cities makes teacher reaction a critical aspect of the education of minorities. The northern urban situation is one in which prejudice alone is not the major factor. It is a matter of the way in which the characteristics (other than skin color and race) of the minority child affect teachers and the operation of the schools. In an important sense, doing away with prejudice would not do away with the minority problem; for as long as a sizable share of the children from culturally deprived and lower-class backgrounds are dirty, violent, and unmotivated—or appear so in the eyes of their teachers—the teachers are likely to handle them differently, teach them less, and want to escape. The consequence is a lessening of achievement, a lowering of opportunity. The problem for the school is to change the "vicious cycle" of interaction between student characteristics and teacher response—through such means as increasing the motivation to achieve on the part of the pupils and strengthening the commitment of the best teachers to the worse schools.[12]

[12] For examples of school effort along such lines, see the attempts to strengthen "the academic subculture" in Chapter 7.

LAW AND EDUCATION

We turn now to the issue of school desegregation and the bearing of law on the education of the Negro. The legal order of a country occupies a key position in determining minority-majority relations, for it spells out the acts and relationships that will be supported or opposed by the authority of the courts and the power of the police. As a fundamental code of the land, a "constitutional" foundation for patterns of behavior, the law can work to maintain the status quo or to bring about broad changes. Its influence on school segregation has been widely debated in this country ever since the Supreme Court decision of 1954 placed the law on the side of change.

For a half-century before 1954, segregated schooling was a lawful institution.[13] In the famous case of *Plessy v. Ferguson* in 1896, the Supreme Court had, in effect, placed its approval on the idea of separate schools for Negroes and whites, provided the schools for Negroes and the schools for whites were equal in quality. This case actually involved a question of seating accommodations for white and Negro passengers in railroad cars. The Supreme Court decided that the separation of the races in public places did not imply the inferiority of either race; further, that state laws requiring such separation, as in Louisiana, were a lawful exercise by state legislatures of their power. Such legally enforced separation, therefore, was not seen as contrary to the Fourteenth Amendment of the Constitution, passed in 1868, which provided that no state shall "deny to any person within its jurisdiction the equal protection of the laws." The Court expressly commented in the 1896 decision that the establish-

[13] This discussion is based largely on J. Lee Rankin, "The Role of the Supreme Court in Equalizing Opportunity in Education," in Francis J. Brown (ed.), *Approaching Equality of Opportunity in Higher Education* (Washington, D.C.: American Council on Education, 1955), pp. 49–57.

ment of *separate schools* for white and colored children was a valid exercise of the legislative power of the states and did not imply race inferiority. At the time, the question of *when* schools were equal was not before the Court and was not discussed.

This separate-but-equal doctrine stood as law from 1898 to 1954, providing a legal underpinning for segregated schools. During this period, however, Negro schools were rarely the equal of white schools in physical facilities and caliber of teacher; moreover, this lawful doctrine was increasingly criticized and attacked on the grounds that separate schools for a minority group were inherently unequal. In cases in 1939 and 1948,[14] the Supreme Court began to put teeth in the equal-facilities interpretation, requiring the states of Missouri and Oklahoma to provide within their own borders for the law-school education of Negroes. In 1950, in the *Sweatt v. Painter* case, which again involved the right to a legal education, the Department of Justice of the federal government for the first time spoke out before the Court on what it saw to be a serious inconsistency between democratic ideals and the law of the land; the Solicitor General advised the Court to repudiate the separate-but-equal doctrine of 1896 as "an unwarranted deviation from the principle of equality under law." The Court did not choose to re-examine the Plessy case at this time, but it did construe tightly the equal-facilities doctrine. The Court maintained that the legal education offered at a separate law school for Negroes in Texas was not equal to that offered at the University of Texas Law School, this because of a number of tangible and intangible factors—variety of courses, library facilities, reputation of the

[14] The "Gaines case," 1939; *Missouri ex rel. Gaines v. Canada,* 305 U.S. 337. The "Sipuel case," 1948; *Sipuel v. Board of Regents,* 332 U.S. 631 (*per curiam,* 1948).

faculty, influence of the alumni. In a second case decided on the same day in 1950,[15] the Court also decided that a Negro could not be segregated spatially within a formerly all-white graduate school, since such restrictions would impair and inhibit the student's ability to study, to exchange views with other students, and in general to learn his profession.

These decisions left the 1896 doctrine still standing—but barely. Here a lawyer describes how the separate-but-equal doctrine was then decisively struck down:[16]

In May 1954 the Court in two historic unanimous opinions delivered by Chief Justice Warren expressly rejected the fifty-year-old doctrine of "separate but equal" in the field of public education, holding with respect to the states that it did not satisfy the "equal protection" clause of the Fourteenth Amendment, and with respect to the District of Columbia, the due process clause of the Fifth Amendment. Altogether there were five cases before the Court—four from the states (South Carolina, Virginia, Delaware, and Kansas), and one from the District of Columbia. In each instance Negro children had been denied admission to public schools attended by white children under laws requiring or permitting segregation according to race. And in each case, except Delaware, the lower courts had denied relief under the Plessy doctrine; in the Delaware case, the lower court also had adhered to that doctrine but ordered admission to the white schools because it found that they were superior to the Negro schools.

The Chief Justice, after pointing out that the history of the Fourteenth Amendment, with respect to segregated schools, was inconclusive, said that the question had to be resolved not in the light of 1896 conditions but in the light of present-day conditions. Stating that education today "is the very foundation of good citizenship" and "a principal instrument in awakening the child to cultural values, in preparing him for later professional train-

15 The "McLaurin Case," 1950; *McLaurin v. Oklahoma State Regents,* 339 U.S. 637.

16 Rankin, "The Role of the Supreme Court," pp. 55–56.

> ing and in helping him to adjust normally to his environment," the Court held that where the state undertakes to provide an opportunity for education it had to be "made available to all on equal terms." This, it said, was not done when schools were separate even though physically equal. Modern psychological authority amply supported a finding, the Court held, that segregation with the sanction of law had a tendency to retard the educational and mental development of Negro children and to deprive them of some of the benefits they would receive in a racially integrated system. Accordingly, the Court concluded that: ". . . in the field of public education the [Plessy] doctrine of 'separate but equal' has no place. Separate educational facilities are inherently unequal. Therefore, . . . the plaintiffs . . . are by reason of the segregation complained of, deprived of the equal protection of the laws guaranteed by the Fourteenth Amendment."

It was on the basis of these beliefs that the 1954 decision put federal law on the side of change from segregation to integration in the public schools. Education had to be equally available and separate schooling was inherently unequal.

The Court did not set a timetable for school desegregation, however, and the pace of change in southern schools has been slow since 1954. Table 3.1 shows the extent of school desegregation by 1960 in the 17 states, and the District of Columbia, where the schools had been entirely segregated before 1954. Some border states (Oklahoma, Missouri, Kentucky, West Virginia, Maryland) had largely or completely complied with the Court's decision, while some others (Tennessee, Arkansas, North Carolina) changed little. The states of the Deep South, resisting the decision all the way, had not desegregated at all. The table also shows that even when a state has completely or largely desegregated the school districts that contain both white and Negro children, the number of Negroes in schools with whites may be only a small proportion. In Maryland, for

TABLE 3.1—DESEGREGATION BY STATE, 1960

State	Per cent of Biracial School Districts that Are Desegregated	Per cent of Negroes in the Desegregated Districts Actually in School with Whites
Much desegregation:		
Delaware	41	84
District of Columbia	100	82
West Virginia	100	50
Missouri	94	47
Kentucky	72	39
Oklahoma	78	34
Maryland	100	24
Little desegregation:		
Texas	18	4
Florida	2	3
Tennessee	4	2
Arkansas	4	1
Virginia	9	0.4
North Carolina	5	0.1
No desegregation:		
Alabama	0	0
Georgia	0	0
Louisiana	0	0
Mississippi	0	0
South Carolina	0	0
Total for 17 states and District of Columbia	27	29

Source: Based on information contained in *Southern School News,* 7:4 (October, 1960), p. 1.

example, all of its 23 biracial districts are desegregated; yet only 24 per cent of the Negro children in these districts are in school with whites, the rest remaining in all-Negro schools. Table 3.1 lists the states in descending order of the proportion of Negroes in biracial districts who are actually going to school with whites; the table shows 11 states where

4 per cent or less of the Negroes are thus integrated (Texas and below).

As a summation for these 17 states and the District of Columbia, 27 per cent of some 2,800 biracial districts had been desegregated by 1960, and 29 per cent of the Negro youth in these districts (approximately 183,000 out of 622,000) were in integrated schools. For all Negro youth in these states in the fall of 1960, just 5.9 per cent were in schools with whites. There were over 3,800 school districts in these states that contained only whites or only Negroes, and the bulk of the school population is in such districts. These one-race districts, not subject at all to integration, result in part from the geographic location of whites and Negroes. They also are produced by gerrymandering in the setting of district lines. The zones of individual schools *within* districts can also be drawn and redrawn so as to keep the races largely in separate schools. Through such means as gerrymandering and the reassignment of individual pupils from one school to another ("pupil placement" provisions), many school districts, especially in the Deep South, will have only token integration when they reach the stage of compliance with federal law.

The Supreme Court decision of 1954 has raised again the old argument voiced succinctly in the phrase "the law can't change the mores." The course of events in education in the southern and border states since 1954 could be taken as evidence for either side of the argument. In considering the role of law in this issue, it is useful to distinguish between attitudes and actions, prejudice and overt discrimination. An edict of the courts may not directly change attitudes, but it works directly on actions by defining certain behaviors as lawful and others as illegal. The 1954 Court decision does not say that whites cannot have prejudicial thoughts about the Negro race; what it has done is to make certain discriminatory acts toward Negro youth unlawful—actions that previously had the support of the law. The decision thus is a fundamental pressure for change in patterns of action. Indirectly, such a decision also strikes at attitudes. Most citizens think of themselves as law-abiding and the 1954 decision turns law-abiding inclinations against attitudes of prejudice—one attitude against the other. People's thinking about the rightness of their own attitudes is affected by whether the law supports or opposes those attitudes, just as the law makes a difference in the upholding or striking down of particular actions.

Of course, the law cannot be so out of step with public opinion or so unenforceable that it is honored mainly in the breach, as happened in the case of the Prohibition Amendment. The legal edict needs a moral backing, provided by a sizable, influential segment of the population. The Supreme Court decision of 1954 on school desegregation has had strong backing in all sections of the country outside the South; as resistance to the decision has hardened in the South, there has been an increasing inclination in the North and West to intervene, to have such federal officials as the Attorney General actively seek to help the Negro achieve certain rights.

The relationship of the legal institution to the education of minorities is highly complex, and there is no simple answer to the question of whether the law can change the mores. In the technological society, however, the law is constantly extended to cover more relationships; recent decades have seen labor-management relations, for example, increasingly spelled out in legal arrangements. As a behavioral code backed by police power, and as a primary system for settling conflicts, the law clearly can play a potent part in accelerating or retarding social change. Norms that have the force of law are not easily ignored, especially when they are pushed vigorously by interest groups in the pursuit of their own welfare or their conception of social rights.

EDUCATION AS AN ACTIVE AGENT

What is education's active role in shaping the minority order? Education affects society by changing attitudes, as we saw in Chapter 1, and we can first inquire into its effects in changing attitudes toward minorities. Generally, education makes for greater tolerance; larger amounts of education are related to a lowering of prejudice and the relation is apparently causal. Chart 3.2 shows how approval

CHART 3.2

APPROVE SCHOOL INTEGRATION
(According to Education, 1956)*

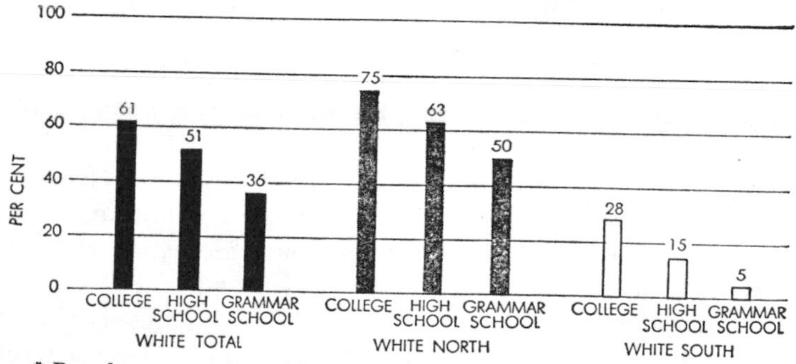

* Based on a nation-wide survey of white adults conducted by the National Opinion Research Center in 1956.

Source: Herbert H. Hyman and Paul B. Sheatsley, "Attitudes toward Desegregation," *Scientific American,* Vol. 195 (December, 1956), pp. 35–39.

of school integration changes with level of education, for whites in the South, in the North, and in the nation as a whole. In each case, consistently, the percentage of whites approving school integration increases for higher levels of schooling. The greatest change, proportionately, is in the South, for there the uneducated whites provide a very low base; only 5 per cent of those who had gone no farther than grammar school, in 1956, approved of school integration. The proportion among the college-educated was five to six times larger—still, however, amounting to only 28 per cent. While education is probably an attitude-changer in this case, it is not an overwhelming determinant.

Education has apparently played a considerable role in the long-run trend toward a more appreciative conception of the characteristics of Negroes. Much of the sentiment of whites toward Negroes in the United States has been conditioned by the Negro's early status as slave, and by persisting belief since the time of slavery that Negroes are not as intelligent as whites, inferior by reason of native endowment. Recent years have seen this belief slide from majority to minority opinion in all sections of the country. In a series of national polls between 1942 and 1956, white adults were asked: "In general, do you think Negroes are as intelligent as white people—that is, can they learn things just as well if they are given the same education and training?" In the whole country, those believing Negroes are as intelligent swelled from about 40 per cent in 1942 to over 75 per cent in 1956; in the South alone, the change was from 20 to 60 per cent. (See Chart 3.3.)

This change in belief on Negro intelligence has undoubtedly contributed to the growing approval of school integration, for if Negroes are thought to be as intelligent as whites, they are probably also considered equally educable, and hence a strong argument for segregated schools is knocked out. Approval of school integration increased during the 1942–1956 period from 30 to 48 per cent for whites in the country at large, 40 to 61 per cent for whites in the North, and 2 to 14 per cent for whites in the South. The trend toward approval of school integration has noticeably lagged, however, behind change in belief about Negro intelligence, especially in the South. For the South, in 1956,

CHART 3.3
BELIEVE NEGROES ARE AS INTELLIGENT
(as Whites, 1942–1956)

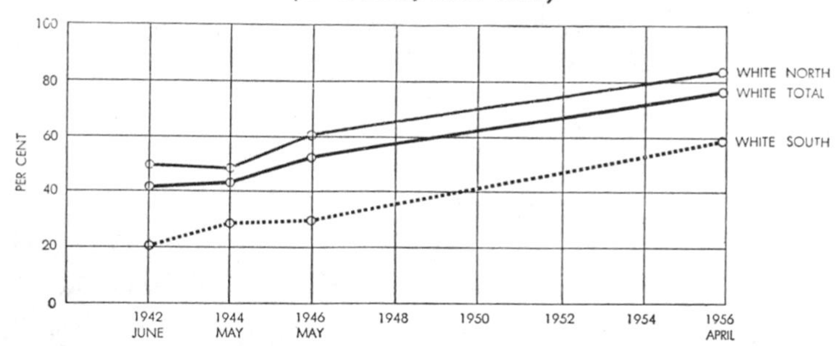

Source: Herbert H. Hyman and Paul B. Sheatsley, "Attitudes toward Desegregation," *Scientific American,* Vol. 195 (December, 1956), pp. 35–39.

60 per cent believed in the equal intelligence of Negroes but only 14 per cent, one out of seven, approved of school integration. Many other beliefs and sentiments intrude here, such as fear that Negro children are dirty and rough, and that close contact among the young could lead to friendship, love, and marriage.

The strife attending desegregation of schools in the South since 1954 has demonstrated the intense emotionalism that attaches to racial issues in this country, about which we spoke earlier in the chapter. Pollsters in this country have also taken note of the depth of feeling, North and South, on racial segregation:[17]

[People] consistently showed a livelier interest in this topic than in almost any other public question on which [they] are polled. As one respondent said when the interviewer, after a series of questions about Russia, the Suez Canal crisis, the hydrogen bomb and similar problems, came to school segregation: "Now you're asking the right questions." In the overwhelming majority of

[17] Herbert H. Hyman and Paul B. Sheatsley, "Attitudes toward Desegregation," *Scientific American,* Vol. 195 (December, 1956), p. 37.

cases, the answers, and emphatic comments, fairly burst forth: "We moved last year because some Negroes moved into our block." "I'll go to jail before I let my kids go to school with Negroes." "I don't have to think about *that* question, I'll tell you right now." In contrast to most issues, on which anywhere from 10 to 20 per cent of the public have no opinion or can't make up their minds, on questions about racial segregation the "Don't know" group is never higher than 4 per cent. Almost everyone knows exactly where he stands in the matter.

The effects of education in liberalizing attitudes toward the country's largest racial minority must thus work in a climate of opinion unfavorable to change, where views are rigid and intense. Opinions are most amenable to change when they are unformed or lightly held; the investment of emotion turns an opinion into a sentiment, a feeling-state little amenable to change through rational argument. Parents may or may not communicate a lightly held opinion to their children; but by direct instruction or otherwise they are sure to communicate beliefs they feel deeply. Any formal instruction in the classroom to the contrary probably has only modest effect.

But many social changes are made without the backing of majority opinion, especially regional or sectional opinion, and educational systems have effects other than what is accomplished through larger doses of knowledge. Like other facilities, school systems can be demonstration projects, showing that an instituted change actually works and without the consequences most feared. The American army found during World War II that whites in racially integrated units became more favorable toward working and associating with Negroes than whites in nonintegrated platoons, companies, and battalions. In short, attitudes changed because of experience in relationships that were initially resisted.

Somewhat similar outcomes can be predicted in education

where integration is introduced over popular opposition. But there are important differences between the military and the school contexts, and the degree of change depends more on the larger social setting. The authority structure of the military can enforce a change—"It's an order!"—until such time as it is accepted in spirit. Men in the military are also considerably isolated from normal ties of family, neighborhood, and club, and thus the influence of other groups is walled off. The schools, in contrast, have less authority to push through a change undesired by students, parents, and public officials. The student also remains under the influence of home, neighborhood, and friends. Integration "from the top," against majority sentiment, is therefore more difficult in education than in the military. Traditional sentiment supported by the primary social groupings of the youth does not readily yield.

Despite the entrenched position of segregationist opinion, changes made toward integration under the pressure of law and the efforts of Negroes may simply have to be accepted as fact, or as inevitable, by those who continue hostile:[18]

> In the Southern areas that have integrated their schools during the last two years [1954–1956], two thirds of the white public continue to mutter that Negro children really should go to "separate schools." But the fact of integration has been accepted, . . . Segregationists are themselves inclined to agree that theirs is a lost cause. When Gallup Poll interviewers recently [1956] asked Southerners, "Do you think the day will ever come in the South when whites and Negroes will be going to the same schools, eating in the same restaurants, and generally sharing the same public accommodations?", only one in three answered, "No, the day will never come."

The percentage of Southerners conceding that desegregation is inevitable has continued to rise, reaching 76 per cent in

[18] Hyman and Sheatsley, "Attitudes toward Desegregation," p. 39.

1960.[19] The changing patterns of race relations in the schools affect people's feeling of what actually is going to happen compared to their feeling of what ought to be.

Turning from attitudes, education affects the minority order through the occupational and social mobility gained by some minority members when they receive more education. Earlier (page 91) we pointed to the sizable difference in the amount of education obtained by whites and Negroes. Negroes have made the greater gains over the century since the Civil War, however, having started out closer to zero. Eighty per cent of the nonwhites were illiterate in 1870, compared to 11 per cent among whites. In 1900, the rate was 45 per cent illiteracy for nonwhites and 6 per cent for whites; in 1950, about 10 per cent for nonwhites and 2 per cent for whites.[20] The reduction in illiteracy for both populations is, of course, a direct result of greater numbers getting into the schoolhouse. For whites and nonwhites, 1860 to 1957, the proportion of the 5 to 19 year olds who were in school is shown in Table 3.2; the difference between the two populations on this school enrollment rate dropped from about 58 per cent at the time of the Civil War to about 3 per cent in 1957. Such crude indices reflect the gain in schooling produced by nearly all Negroes receiving an elementary education and some a secondary schooling. Too, for Negroes as for whites, and in greater degree, young adults are better educated than their elders. The figures on amount of education that are reported on page 91 are based on all adults 25 or older, and thus are greatly weighted by the educational histories of the generations who went to school between 1900 and 1940. In the population over 65, nonwhites have only half the amount of schooling of whites; in the age

[19] *Time,* April 7, 1961.

[20] U.S. Bureau of the Census, *Historical Statistics of the United States, Colonial Times to 1957* (Washington, D.C.: 1960), p. 214.

TABLE 3.2—SCHOOL ENROLLMENT RATE, 1860–1957

(Rate per 100 population, 5 to 19 years old)

Year	Whites	Nonwhites	Difference Between Rates for Whites and Nonwhites
1860*	59.6	1.9	57.7
1890	57.9	32.9	25.0
1920†	65.7	53.5	12.2
1950	79.3	74.8	4.5
1957	88.2	85.3	2.9

* Enrollment of students of *all* ages compared to base of those 5–19 years old.

† Population 5 to *20* years old.

Source: U.S. Bureau of the Census, *Historical Statistics of the United States, Colonial Times to 1957* (Washington, D.C.: 1960), p. 213.

group 25 to 29, the nonwhites have nine-tenths of the schooling of whites.[21] While Negroes are still relatively deprived in sheer quantity of education, the trend is toward closing the gap. More Negroes will be equipped with more of the educational means of better social and occupational placement.

Recent times have also seen southern states improving the quality of the segregated—the supposedly separate-and-equal—Negro schools. This upgrading has been encouraged by the hope that it would help forestall integration.[22] In 1896, the former Confederate states were spending twice as much for the education of whites as for Negroes. This difference *widened* to three and one half to one by 1930. After the depression, the trend was reversed, and, by 1956, the per-pupil expenditure for the instruction of Negro students compared to each dollar spent for the white

21 Murray Gendell and Hans L. Zetterberg (eds.), *A Sociological Almanac for the United States* (New York: The Bedminster Press, 1961), p. 21.

22 Information taken from *Southern Schools: Progress and Problems* (Nashville, Tenn.: Southern Education Reporting Service, 1959), pp. 3–4.

students as follows: Georgia, Alabama, and North Carolina, 95 cents; Florida, 94 cents; Texas, 93 cents; Louisiana, 79 cents; South Carolina, 77 cents; Arkansas, 75 cents; Mississippi, 63 cents. The low Mississippi figure was an increase of over 100 per cent in the years 1952–1956.

With Negroes moving into the cities, gaining in educational attainment, and facing less discrimination in some fields, larger proportions of the Negro work force are appearing in the higher-status, better-paying occupations. The occupational composition of the Negro population has undergone a radical change since 1950, according to the population experts.[23] During a short period of eight years, 1950–1958, "the number of nonwhite male farmers (largely sharecroppers in the South) was estimated to have declined by 55 per cent, and the number of farm laborers by 21 per cent . . . The Negro woman, even more than the Negro man, was emancipated from low-income farm jobs during this period." In all, there was a "wholesale desertion of agriculture."

In the urban occupations, the number of nonwhite workers increased at all levels: 49 per cent increase among those in professional and technical work; 69 per cent among clerks; 24 per cent in sales workers; 20 per cent among craftsmen; 12 per cent among operatives; 20 per cent in service workers; and 12 per cent in laborers. "The Negro stenographer, switchboard operator, business machine operator, and receptionist have become commonplace in many cities. Jobs as laboratory technicians in hospitals and in industrial plants, as bus drivers, and as policemen are now freely available to nonwhite persons, at least in larger cities." To understand the magnitude of the change, it must

[23] The following information and quotations are taken from Donald J. Bogue, *The Population of the United States* (New York: The Free Press of Glencoe, 1959), pp. 502–507.

be remembered that only since 1940 has the Negro been admitted to the factory and to the office.

At the same time, the effects of history and discrimination still blunt the effects of education and job opportunity. Large numbers of Negroes have simply moved from unskilled labor on the farm to unskilled labor in the city, swelling the ranks of janitors and porters. It is the children of the migrants who stand to make greater strides, as they remain in school longer and acquire a better education than their parents.

THE SHIFT TO MILITANCY

In our concern with education as a source of change in the position of a minority, we should not overlook the broad influence of trends outside the classroom—industrialization, urbanization, bureaucratization—that change where people live, how they work, and the ways they are bound to one another. To take the South: the social location of the Negro changes as the city replaces the farm, the large mill pushes out the small-town forge, and the national chain takes over from the family store. The close, informal control of whites over Negroes in the small town is replaced by the looser web and greater anonymity of the city, where race relations are mediated more by the police, the courts, and the politicians who jockey between interest groups and voting blocs. The nature of work changes radically for both whites and Negroes as they enter the large plant and move into urban service industry. The growing industrialization of the southern states brings plant superintendents, corporate technicians, and managerial policies from other sections of the country.

Long distinctively different in its rural character, its lack of industry, its leisurely pace, the South now becomes ever more like the industrial states of the North and the West as its industrialization gains on these other sections. The southern white is moving into a new social frame, as the land of cotton becomes a neighborhood of split-level and ranch-style housing. On top of the relocation of population in the South, the large migration of Negroes out of southern states has been almost entirely to urban centers in the North. Thus, increasingly, the American Negro is an urban man within an urban society.

The technological revolution accelerates and extends these social relocations, as it reverberates throughout the economy and society. It speeds up the obsolescence of traditional social orders as well as of plant and equipment. In place of the spent need for unskilled agricultural workers in the South, there is not only a need for the city service worker, skilled and unskilled, but also a growing need to see ability without seeing skin color. The norms of science are notably impartial on such attributes; more important, so are the rational perspectives of the growing technological establishment—the "think factories." The modern far-flung corporation is also prone to adopt impartial criteria of skill for hiring and firing and promoting, compared to its antecedents.

The premises of the expert society broadly undercut the premises of the nonexpert community, especially one centered on paternal dominance of a minority. Perspectives may be almost wholly different. The young executive in steel, with his Master's degree from the Harvard Business School, hardly speaks the same language as the cotton-growing oligarch and the other remaining survivors of the rural society. Further down the technological trail appears the electronics expert, headed for space in a transistor tube and clearly on another wave length. Still further, the guided-missile encampment appears, run by the same rules in Florida as in Nevada or Tahiti—and a world apart from the plantation.

The shrinking of the world through rapid communication transforms domestic problems into foreign affairs. Negro-white relations in the United States have long been largely a domestic matter, occasionally remarked abroad but mainly out of sight and out of mind for other countries. Now these relations are a part of international relations, an issue in diplomacy, United Nations debate, and casual discussion with foreigners. The television camera and the correspondent's cablegram place racial incidents under immediate world scrutiny. Thus the nature of the modern world insures that a struggle over school desegregation in Little Rock becomes part of the national face. This nationalizing and internationalizing of town disputes feeds back upon a society in many ways, at many levels, affecting the attitudes of citizens and the policies of officials. It draws attention and leads to more and stronger calls that something be done, and done sooner rather than later. In particular, the bad name that discrimination gives the country in the eyes of the nations of Latin America, Africa, and Asia, presses the federal government to take a stronger hand in seeking equal rights and treatment for Negroes. Through legislation, executive order, and court decision, national policy promises to play an expanding role in changing the position and participation of minority groups in education.

Notable in Negro-white relations is the shift toward militancy. The tenor of these relations, long in slow evolution, began to change sharply after 1954, as southern whites stiffened their resistance to school desegregation. This resistance, centered in the well-organized, influential White Citizens Councils, was followed a few years later by a leap in militancy on the part of young Negroes, grown impatient with the pace of court cases and searching for other methods of gaining rights they considered overdue. This mutual toughening of attitudes makes over Negro-white relations into a contest of political and economic power—a series of skirmishes fought with the economic boycott, the home eviction, the sit-down, the jail sentence, the physical beating, the law suit. Older, informal ties between members of the two races, especially paternalistic relations, have broken as attitudes have hardened and clashed, and as many moderates have been silenced or forced into an unequivocal commitment to one side or the other. In this situation, gains are not given but are won, and tactics rather than changes in opinion become the primary levers of change. Schools are slowly desegregated largely as the result of law suits, the power of the federal courts, and the anticipation by city fathers that bloodshed and civic decline will follow if they fail to find formulae that preserve order and keep the schools open. The schools are kept segregated in many communities through the tactical maneuvering of segregationists in and out of the law courts.

As many minorities have done before them, American Negroes are moving out of the backwaters and idle ponds of the central institutions and into the main stream of group contention. Along with the militancy of young Negroes, there is a changing distribution of political power in many cities and states as Negroes learn to use the vote and other means of political persuasion. Minorities exert their *own* influence on school matters through such means as: the election of friends to the city council and school board; the behind-the-scene meeting at which bargains are made and concessions won; the vigorous public statement of inadequacies in school facilities; the defeat of school bonds by votes of resentment, when officials have ignored minority sentiments and interests; the threat of a parents' strike that would embarrass the school administration. The rising political power of Negroes in many northern cities makes them a strong special-interest bloc; as the voting right is extended to more Negroes in the South, first in such large cities as Atlanta and Houston, their influence on school policy will also rise there. The growing strength and militancy of American Negroes together with the movement of federal authority into relationships handled formerly, if at all, by the state and local government, will help to determine the quantity and quality of their education.

The web of institutional factors affecting the education of a minority is thus intricate: traditional sentiments, occupations, residence patterns, teachers' careers. The sources of change are various, from changes in the law and in public opinion to political action and violence. All these institutional forces will weigh heavily in the scales as education becomes increasingly a main road to personal achievement and group attainment. For the American Negro minority, the heart of the matter now and in the immediate future varies, however, between the South and the North. In the South, it lies in the impact of law and political action on the speed of school integration. In the North, the critical issues are the effects of residential concentration in the metropolis on school integration and the impact of the characteristics of lower-class Negro youth on the capability of the schools. The metropolitan context should loom ever larger as time goes by, becoming characteristic of cities in the South as well as in the North.

We can predict that the schools will integrate throughout the country, even though in token form in many cases. We cannot predict on the basis of present trends that residential concentration will soon greatly lessen, nor that the bulk of Negro youth in the metropolitan ghetto will soon become middle-class, highly motivated, and culturally sophisticated—in short, the kind of students that teachers prefer. The problem of education of the Negro minority, as of white lower-class children in lesser degree, promises to turn increasingly into one of the ability of the school to motivate and teach large concentrations of students whose background is not middle-class, whose drive to achieve through education is *relatively* weak or unformed, and whose cultural characteristics repel teachers, causing them to flee the scene, or to adjust in such a way as to offer at best, half a loaf—at worst a few crumbs of education.

Chapter 4

The Problem of Control

WE HAVE argued thus far that the educational system transmits culture, socializes the young, allocates men to occupations and statuses, and shapes the racial-ethnic order. These primary roles, defining education as a key institution, generate the problem in every advanced society of how schools and colleges are to be controlled. The policy question is: Who *ought* to control this institution that is moving toward the center of the stage? The research question is: Who in fact *is* in control of this institution or its major components? It does not help much to speak elliptically of "society" determining what the schools do; society is plural, composed of many factions, and actual control in democratic societies is always a somewhat open question, decided largely by political interplay and institutional trends. We should not expect all groups comprising an elaborate social structure to agree readily on educational issues. They speak about education with many voices, impelled by divergent points of view, and the public argument over school policy is continuous and often raucous.

In this chapter we first identify some forces external to the schools that seek to shape school policy. We then consider the problem of centralized versus decentralized control, and lastly take up the major conceptions of authority that contend with one another in the governing of schools and colleges. Thus we shall be asking who controls education, what is the shape of the control, and what principles legitimize control? Here again we wish to point up effects on education of modern social trends. How does advancing technology, expanding population, and large-scale organization affect community control? Is the educational institution becoming more centralized under the impact of advanced industrialism? Does growing size give more power to administrators or teachers—or both? On such large matters we can make only broad and tentative judgments. There are a few facts available to inform our judgment but for the most part we shall instead have to use reasoned speculation to estimate the shape of the facts.

COMMUNITY FORCES

Whoever controls education is in a position to mold if not control the minds of the next generation. In totalitarian societies, the issue of educational control is decided by centralized state power, behind which lies the power of the ruling party. Education in the Third Reich was controlled by the Nazis through the state apparatus. Education in the U.S.S.R. is explicitly controlled and directed by the Communist Party through the machinery of the central government. No other groups—unions, business associations, churches, other political parties—seriously contend with the state and the ruling party. In short, centralization is combined with a one-party system, and the issue of educational control is fairly well settled. If struggles do take place, they are within the political-educational system itself, and most likely take the form of educational expert versus the noneducational official. Most conflict is therefore thrown into the shadowland of bureaucratic maneuver, since effective power lies almost entirely within the network of bureaucracies.

The Public School

Democratic societies, in comparison, depend upon a certain amount of free play of group interests, permitting diverse groups to organize and campaign for their own point of view. This characteristic of democratic societies holds whether the educational system is centralized, a national system such as found in France, or decentralized, a mélange of discrete state and local systems as in the United States. The degree of centralization does not change the fact of a plurality of interests; what it changes is the level at which factional contention has its greatest play and the kinds of groups who must be heard. In democracies with unified educational systems, interest groups contend at the level of national politics; for example, attempting to influence the policies of the national ministry of education, or the platform of national parties as they struggle for office. In democracies with decentralized educational systems, the battle of interest groups goes on at middle and lower levels of government—the province, the state, the city or town—where, to influence school policy, groups must seek to influence the local board of control or the state legislature. Such is the situation in the United States. The historic and extreme decentralization of education in this country has made control a problem of state and local government, and until recently these have been the locales of nearly all the conflict of interest.

Elementary and secondary education in the United States have been very much a *local* matter. Much authority to run the schools has been scattered, placed in the hands of separate districts that numbered over 100,000 in 1945, about 40,000 in 1960, and that will probably still number 10,000 in 1970 after great progress in consolidation.[1] This decentralization has placed the formation of educational policy down at the level of town politics. Such state-level authorities as the state legislature and the state department of education play a role, but in most states this has historically been secondary to local influence. The state authorities generally declare minimum educational standards for the school program, disburse state funds to the local districts, set minimum requirements for the certification of teachers, and sometimes buy and prescribe textbooks for certain grades. But it is the local officials who hire and fire the school personnel, from the superintendent to the "custodial engineer"; they build the buildings; they determine the curriculum for the most part. In short, most key areas of policy formation are in the hands of the local authorities.

School politics in American communities are ostensibly nonpartisan, separate from city hall and the county courthouse, from Republicans and Democrats. Thus the election of board members commonly proceeds without party labels or party slates of candidates. But what is not explicit is often implicit, and the conservative-liberal opposition in a town that may explicitly take the form of Republicans versus Democrats for the city council will find a similar, only unannounced, alignment for the school board. The taxpayers association offers its support (conservative) for certain candidates; the local chapter of the Americans for Democratic Action backs the liberal opponents. Conservative and liberal groups seek candidates for the school board whose opinions are congenial to their own; the candidate may be already within the ranks or at least a frequent lunch partner. Election to the school board is often a first step in the political career of a local man; after

[1] Edgar L. Morphet and John G. Ross, *Local Responsibility for Education in Small School Districts* (Berkeley: Bureau of Public Administration, University of California, 1961), p. 5.

board membership has brought some public attention, the man sheds his nonpartisan clothes and runs redressed as a Republican or Democrat for the city council or the office of mayor.

One important division of interest swirling around American public schools in the last quarter of a century has been the proponents of the "three R's"—reading, writing, and arithmetic—versus the believers in progressive education. The most vigorous proponents of the three R's have been traditionalists outraged by changes in the curriculum that tore it from its rigorous academic pattern and annoyed generally by the many social changes that have been tearing apart the fabric of the old. The parents most interested in the progressive school have generally been of liberal persuasion, sympathetic to experimentation and interested in changes that promised to free their children from the traditional lockstep. School personnel during this period have, in most cases, been largely in the progressive camp. Controversy between advocates of the three R's and proponents of progressive education has commonly taken the form of an attack by the "outs" on the "ins"; an attack on current school policy—at board of education meetings and elsewhere—by small, vocal conservative groups from the churches, women's clubs, and business associations.

The battle of traditionalists versus progressives takes many specific forms, and each camp is quite diverse within. One extreme case in the early 1950's centered on classroom discussion of world government. Certain conservative groups took the position that the schools should not teach anything about the United Nations, especially about UNESCO (the United Nations Educational, Scientific, and Cultural Organization). In Los Angeles, a militant campaign against the schools on this issue was sustained by some church groups and patriotic organizations, who were against imparting information to school children that would in any possible way promote world government. The controversy caused several articulate spokesmen for the anti-UNESCO forces to be elected to the school board, and hastened the departure of the then superintendent of schools. It reverberated throughout the system for some time, leading to adjustments in the curriculum and to apprehension on the part of teachers over the kind of protection they would receive in discussing controversial issues. The neighboring city of Pasadena also experienced an attack by extreme traditionalists on liberal school policies, in even more traumatic form.

Such attacks subsided considerably in the late 1950's. After sputnik the foreground of the traditionalist attack on doctrines and practices of progressive education in the schools has been occupied increasingly by well-educated professionals, notably college professors, who would not be seen dead with the far-right groups. The weapons used by these traditionalists are the critical book, the study report, and the mimeograph machine, rather than the packed audience and the violent denunciation at board meetings. The sense of national concern about the schools, which has become part of the temper of the times, has swung the attention of many educated men of both conservative and liberal persuasion to the schools and motivated them to try to save the schools from what appear to be their progressive faults. Thus driver education became more controversial than world government. The professor-critic is concerned about the interruption of learning by athletic and social activities, rather than about communism in the schools.

University professors, little active over the last half-century in shaping school policy, are becoming again an active force, one similar to community groups in being external to the public schools but unlike them in being within education and there occupying some of the commanding heights. This traditionalist force is manned in part by liberal intellectuals, and has a general esteem among the educated who over the last three or four decades have provided a public base for the innovations of progressive education. New national concerns are producing new national moods and reshaping the adherence of groups to doctrines. The neighborhoods of the well-educated business and professional families are especially in flux; their demands add resonance to the professors' criticism of the schools, though they attempt at the same time to hold to many of the patterns of progressive education.

Above all, the educated and near-educated want their sons and daughters to get into college—in many cases, a very good college—and this family desire is a base on which the traditionalist demand for rigor in a circumscribed curriculum gains support from persons and groups long known to be "pro-education" or "friends of the schools." This swing among opinion leaders in upper-middle-class neighborhoods is one to which many school authorities must pay heed; for others it is the climate for which they have long waited. Any self-respecting school system is now experimenting with "unique new science projects"; the announcement for the next PTA program now commonly reads: "Can your first grader explain what force is? Does your sixth grader know what influence orbit size has on centrifugal force? Come to the PTA meeting Wednesday evening at 7:30 p.m. to hear how elementary-school children are studying these questions and enjoying it." In community after community, changed ideas and stronger interests in the schools among the educated middle class have fostered the current attempt to revamp the curriculum and radically upgrade the competence of teachers in the "hard" subjects.

In many communities where there is a large Catholic population, a basic cleavage exists between Protestant and Catholic interests. Controversy along the lines of this cleavage has been strongest in the cities and towns of New England. There the "Yankees" long occupied the heights of the economy—being the factory owners, the merchants, the bankers—and they also were the political leaders. These "Brahmins" gradually lost political power, and some of their economic control, as the Catholic immigrant families—Irish, Italian, Polish, French Canadians—became acculturated and educated in the second and third generation and learned to use their vote.

By the 1920's, Catholic majorities in the cities began to take political power—Irishmen became mayors—and also began to control school boards. Soon the key to local public office was to be a Kelly or a Kennedy rather than a Lodge, a Cabot, or a Lowell as previously. This change-over was a bitter one, with religion, class, ethnicity, and industrial conflict all fused—the Catholic, lower- and lower-middle-class Irish factory worker against the Protestant, upper- and upper-middle-class Yankee mill owner, merchant, and clerk. In the climb of Catholic groups to power in this setting, control over the public schools has been described as playing an important part; a prospective board member's religion and nationality mattered greatly. The school superintendency has sometimes been second only to the position of mayor in symbolizing the former minority's new place in the sun. In some New England towns, this has been shown twice over: first, in the ascendance of the Irish to power, replacing the Yankees; and secondly in the later ascendance of Italians, and in a few cities of French Canadians and Portuguese, to replace the Irish or lingering Yankees. For the rising group it has often seemed crucial that the school superintendent as well as the city officials be one of their own, even if he served quite impartially after his appointment. Thus, the Catholic majority has subdivided in many cases into factions based on ethnicity, with a Kelly having to give way to a DeAngelo or a Jean-Baptiste Ladéroute.

The aspiring politicos of an ethnic population coming into power are more likely to use school-board membership for direct political purposes than are the entrenched factions with long security who are more attached to lofty ideals of civic duty. Table 4.1 shows, for example, that more Catholic

TABLE 4.1—MOTIVATION OF SCHOOL-BOARD MEMBERS

(Differences between Catholics and non-Catholics in motivation for seeking election to Massachusetts school boards, as judged by school superintendents)

	Catholic	Non-Catholic
Motivated by civic duty	49	73
Motivated to represent some group	38	23
Motivated to gain political experience	36	11

Source: Neal Gross, Ward S. Mason, and Alexander W. McEachern, *Explorations in Role Analysis: Studies of the School Superintendency Role* (New York: John Wiley & Sons, Inc., 1958), p. 199.

than non-Catholic members of Massachusetts school boards seem motivated to serve in order to further their own political career or represent a group, as over against "civic duty." The difference reflected in this table between Catholic and non-Catholic may be connected with the existence of Catholic parochial schools in these same localities, a subject later discussed, and with this some lowering of commitment to the public schools. But it seems largely a part of a passing historical situation in which "civic duty" has been the ideology of an established elite, while representing a group and gaining political experience are the motives of rising factions.

The clash of interests in the local community over educational policy, interestingly, often takes a form in which organized blocs play only a minor role. The Old-Timer versus the Newcomer is a common schism of this kind, one that has developed in small communities from Maine to California as population movement has taken millions of city folk into the suburbs. These two types are easy to describe. The Old-Timer's family has *been* the community since way back when, and he works in the town or runs a farm; he owns property, often the farmland on which the new suburbs are spreading, or has the little home with land where he hopes to live out a peaceful retirement; his children are grown and out of the schools; he is not too well educated, perhaps completed high school; he likes Main Street quiet and the tax rate low; he sees most of his local taxes going for new sewers and new schools for the Newcomers and he does not like it.

The Newcomer has been on the scene ten years or less; he may be renting but he too is likely to own a house—generally one of the new ones in the tracts out from town; he is a young professional or corporation man and commutes to the nearby city; he is raising a family and his first concern at home—other than the blasted crab grass—is good schools. He sees education as a Good Thing, since he went to college and as a result now has a good job and feels culturally sophisticated. He finds Main Street quaint and the town dead, but still a good place to raise one's children away from the dangers of the city's streets. He wants better schools and playgrounds; he is willing to pay higher taxes and does not see why the Old-Timer is so penny pinching and reluctant to accept change.

These two sectors of the community find expression in some organizations—the Property Owners Association, the PTA, and Dad's Club—but often fight their main battles as numerical aggregates in which most members are publicly silent. The silent members turn out on election day and vote for or against the school bond issue and then return home to glow or grumble about the results. The schools can be much influenced by these periodic expressions of sentiment. A system that repeatedly passes its bond issues and wins tax-limit increases gains the financial resources for new buildings, more teachers, and varied courses; it also develops a feeling that the town supports the system and its policies. But a series of defeats at the polls, often due to a silent "taxpayers revolt" or a hard-to-explain general distrust of current policy and personnel, pulls the financial rug out from under the "extra" features of a modern system and encourages a mood of staying with the fundamentals.

The cultural and political climate of a community inevitably gets through to the local school system, whether the climate is expressed openly by interest-group spokesmen or is something to be sensed by prolonged, informal contact. Climates may vary from one region of the country to another. Many California towns and cities, expanding rapidly in population and wealth, have a vigorously optimistic climate of opinion on community matters. This climate supports the growth of "progressive" school systems. Experimentation is in the air in many of these communities, with new buildings and new teachers—indeed whole new systems springing up over night—offering the chance to introduce new arrangements in the curriculum and in the treatment of students. Unhampered by tradition, progressive education has been extensively developed in the newly settled areas and suburbs.

A notable contrast to the boom psychology of California is found in the many industrial towns and cities of New England that have continued to experience economic depression and decline even in good times for the nation at large. Here the local citizenry has faced for 20, 30, or 40 years the vicious cycle of industry lost, property values down, taxes up. This state of affairs, unless changed by vigorous effort, promotes a town psychology ranging from "stiff upper lip" to sheer despair. The young and the adventurous leave, throwing the city more than ever into the hands of an aging leadership. The general mood of pessimism, underpinned by the hard fact of scarce money, sharply constrains school development. Educators are typically forced to a traditional, conservative style whether they like it or not.

Lastly, while change and conflict in the local community are characteristic of a society that over-all is changing rapidly, there are also many relatively stable communities. Often a small conservative group of city fathers quietly exercises control over town government and school affairs. Power in the hands of a few is coupled with apathy on the part of the vast majority, and the apathy is reinforced by lack of interest and lack of influence. In towns with an oligarchy of city fathers, successful school superintendents are those who learn to consult informally with the few who count, securing their nod before making an important move. Such towns are located from coast to coast but are more heavily concentrated in the long-settled states of the eastern seaboard. Many such towns have been broken out of this pattern by industrial and population movement, such as the flight to the suburbs, which brings new blood willing and able to challenge the old leadership.

The Private School

Pressuring the public schools is not the only way by which various segments of the population seek an educational system congenial to their own point of view. An alternative is to establish a private school that reflects one's own interest. Private schools take two main forms—religious and secular.

The religious private school. In this country, schools outside the public systems have been primarily established by churches, the better to transmit the faith and shape the values of the next generation. These instruments of church control are premised generally on the twin beliefs that (a) the religious values of the particular church are fundamental to the education of "its" children, and (b) the secular public schools cannot or will not satisfactorily instill these values, hence special schools are necessary. Catholic schools constitute by far the largest system of religious schools; approximately one-half of Catholic youth attend Catholic elementary schools. Among the Protestant denominations, only the Lutheran Church, especially the Missouri Synod, has been able to maintain a sizable school system (approximately 160,000 students). As part of the general secularization of American education, the parochial schools of other churches have largely passed from existence.

Nonpublic school enrollment has been rising both in absolute numbers and as a proportion of the total school population: 1.4 million, or 8 per cent in 1900; 2.7 million, or over 9 per cent in 1930; 3.4 million, or 12 per cent in 1950; and 6.5 million, or 15 per cent in 1960.[2] About 80–85 per cent of the nonpublic enrollment is in the parochial schools of the Roman Catholic Church, and it has been the growth in Catholic enrollment that has accounted for the increase in size of the private sector.

For a lucid review of the historical roots of the parochial school in America, we turn at this point to an excerpt from the work of Peter H. and Alice S. Rossi. The Rossis first make clear how necessary was the invention of the *public* school, together with the separation of church and state, in a society peopled by a host of denominations and sects. The "nonsectarian" public school of the nineteenth century was to be a common meeting ground for the numerous Protestant groups. The Roman Catholic Church had not yet become influential. But after they were established, the public schools moved away from religion, and various

[2] *Health, Education, and Welfare Trends* (Washington: U.S. Department of Health, Education, and Welfare, 1960), p. 56.

churches then attempted their own school systems. The only large church school systems that have persisted, however, have been ones linked to particular ethnic groups as well as to militant doctrine.

THE HISTORICAL ROOTS OF THE PAROCHIAL SCHOOLS IN AMERICA[3]

At the time of the adoption of the Federal Constitution, nine of the American states had established churches, with several denominations represented. Perhaps only the little state of Rhode Island had complete religious liberty as we conceive of it today. When supported as a state enterprise or as an arm of local government, the schools of the time were denominational in character, upholding in instruction the doctrines of a particular church. Today's great secular universities were then primarily denominational seminaries: Harvard was a state-supported Congregational seminary. For some decades after Independence, this condition persisted. While the First Amendment prohibited the Federal Government from establishing a national church, it did not prevent the individual states from following a variety of patterns of special recognition to particular denominations.

The state churches of the 18th century did not last long into the 19th. Immigration and internal schisms within the established denominations brought about a proliferation of sects, so that by 1840 the separation of church and state had taken place in every state within the Union. During the same period, interest was growing in public education. In Massachusetts, for example, where public education had been left to the initiative and discretion of small school districts, the General Court passed a series of administrative reforms, consolidating school districts and providing for a State School Board, whose function it was to disseminate information on educational matters to the local school boards. The distinguished Horace Mann was the first

[3] Excerpt from Peter H. and Alice S. Rossi, "Background and Consequences of Parochial School Education," *Harvard Educational Review,* 27:3 (Summer, 1957), pp. 168–199.

secretary of the State Board. In Massachusetts, as in the other states, the solution to the diversity of denominations was to make the new schools "non-sectarian." The interpretation of this rule in practice was a major preoccupation of Horace Mann throughout his term of office.

Originally "non-sectarian" meant primarily that the doctrinal tenets peculiar to any one Protestant sect could not be taught, but that the elements of Christianity common to all would be both permissible and desirable as elements of the common school curriculum. This was apparently no attempt to keep religion out of the schools, but only to prevent control by one sect. However, the definition of what was common ground was by no means easy to achieve. In time, "non-sectarian" has come to mean that religion has had less and less place in the elementary schools.

As the public schools extended their coverage and became increasingly "non-sectarian," they came under fire from the more orthodox denominations. In some cases, these denominations had been operating their own schools, and the new public schools achieved a popularity which threatened the existence of the denominational schools (for example, the schools operated by Lutherans and Dutch Reformed in Pennsylvania). In other cases, religious leaders felt that a secular education would weaken the faith of their children. Several denominations began to consider the advisability of setting up parochial schools. In the 1840's the Presbyterian Church urged its congregations to set up schools for children between the ages of 5 and 12. The Presbyterian experiment was at best but a feeble attempt and by 1870 this denomination had given up its attempt. The various Lutheran denominations, which since their arrival in this country had maintained denominational schools, renewed their emphasis on the importance of church schools. In 1846, the Evangelical Lutheran Church (Missouri Synod) was established in this country. From its inception, the Missouri Synod emphasized denominational schooling and today operates the largest parochial school system among the Protestant denominations.

It was also during this period that the Roman Catholic Church began to grow in size to the numerical stature of a major denomination. Heavy Irish immigration to the Eastern seaboard cities plus the arrival of many from the German Catholic states swelled the ranks of the Church. To the church leaders of the time, the "non-sectarian" public schools, where the King James version of the Bible was used, were "Protestant" schools. Early in this period the bishops of the Church urged each parish to establish a denominational school. The religious teaching orders established in Europe were asked to set up communities in this country in order to supply the personnel to run the schools. But it was not until the Third Plenary Council of the hierarchy, held in Baltimore in 1884, that the Church made it obligatory for each parish to set up its school and for each Catholic to send his children to the parochial schools. Catholic parochial schools—state supported, if possible, privately financed, if necessary—were seen as the answer to the felt need for the religious education of Catholic youth.

Of the several 19th-century attempts to set up mass denominational school systems in the United States, only the German Lutheran and the Roman Catholic efforts were successful and survive to this day. The Presbyterian schools, which at their peak had enrolled 15,000 pupils, had disappeared by 1900. The efforts of the Swedish Lutherans and the Dutch Reformed Church in Pennsylvania gradually died out or were incorporated bodily into the public school systems of their locale. A few secondary schools have survived, but these are primarily serving an elite clientele. Only the Catholics and the Missouri Synod managed successfully to establish school systems which serve a mass clientele.

It is crucial for understanding the contemporary functioning of parochial schools to consider what were the factors which made for the success of the Roman Catholic and the German Lutheran denominational schools. . . . To begin with, in both cases, more than denominational purity was at stake. In each case very self-conscious ethnic groups were identified with each denomination: the Irish and Germans in the case of the Roman Catholics, and the Germans alone in the case of the Lutheran Church. In each case the church was a major point of identification in the old country, and the strength of identification was augmented by experience in the new land. Both the Irish and the Lutherans had had some experience in maintaining their church under unfavorable conditions, the Orthodox Lutherans against a reformed state church in Germany and the Irish against the established church of Ireland. The Irish particularly had developed the institutions for maintaining their church in a hostile environment and had also evolved customs favoring heavy financial support of church activities. In addition, each group brought with it an experienced religious cadre, and when established in this country quickly set up organizations for the recruitment and training of future cadres.

In the case of the Lutheran schools, their ethnic character was quite obvious. These were German language schools in which at least the religious subjects were taught in that language. German was the liturgical language of the Missouri Synod up to only a few decades ago and the church leaders today are primarily from German ethnic stock. It should be noted that the success of the Lutheran schools was greatest in rural areas and small towns of the Midwest, where many Germans had settled. Even as late as 1947 a majority of Lutheran schools were one- or two-room rural schools. Although the amount of instruction conducted in German has decreased considerably since the anti-German hysteria of World War I, it is highly likely that these schools played an important part in keeping German as the most widely spoken foreign language in American households: in 1940, of the fourteen million Americans who spoke a foreign language as their "mother tongue," over three and a quarter million spoke German, more than twice as many as spoke the next most popular language, Italian.

While the rural isolation of the German Lutherans helped them to maintain a viable denominational school system, the urban Irish Catholic schools derived a similar strength from their position on the bottom of the urban heap. The anti-Catholic movements of the 19th century helped to maintain the strong attachment of the Irish to the Roman Catholic Church. The German Catholics benefited from very much the same geographical isolation as the Lutherans.

Undoubtedly these two denominations were aided in the struggle to maintain their parochial schools by their ideologies of non-compromise with their environments. Both the Roman

Catholic Church and the Missouri Synod were militant and dogmatic bodies whose leaders consistently insisted that their churches alone were truly Christian. The disappearance of some of the other Lutheran bodies, e.g., the once strong Swedish Lutheran Church which had settled in Pennsylvania and Delaware, is a witness to the strength of this factor.

Thus, the successful denominational schools were those which were identified with particular ethnic groups and were run by religious organizations which either already had or quickly developed the institutions for maintaining and recruiting a cadre of teaching personnel. In more recent times, the success of the French Canadian immigrants in establishing and maintaining an extensive foreign-language parochial school system provides another illustration of the importance of this pattern. . . . These historical origins have left their mark on the Roman Catholic schools of today.

Although these are factors which apparently make for initial success in establishing a successful denominational school system, they are not as well suited to the maintenance of such systems over long periods of time, given the processes of assimilation which all ethnic groups in America sooner or later undergo. As the period of initial entry into this country recedes into the past, the attachment of each group to its national origins tends to be dissipated and the continued success of a denominational school system may perhaps be best assured by calling upon other types of motivation. The denominational schools, compared to the public schools, must provide as much or more aid to the aspirations of the emerging middle classes and at the same time lose some of their ethnic stamp. In this connection we may note the increasing emphasis during the past two decades in both the Roman Catholic and Missouri Synod schools on increased educational standards and a corresponding decline of instruction in foreign languages. Even so . . . evidence seems to point to a considerable decline in the popularity of the German Lutheran schools. Apparently the Roman Catholic schools have been more successful in accommodating to the mobility aspirations of at least part of the Catholic masses.

The secular private school. The nonreligious private school in this country is generally a nonprofit agency attempting to offer a special education to selected groups of students. Many secular schools had religious origins; some of the top-rank private schools of today were established as arms of Protestant denominations but gradually evolved away from church influence until their religious ties became nominal. These secular private institutions find clientele in upper-middle-class and upper-class families who are seeking a level or type of education they do not believe is available for their children in the public schools; many of these families are also seeking a school of high social and educational status whose graduates land in the best colleges.

The control of these schools varies greatly. They tend to be influenced by the constituencies from which they draw most of their students—by the manners and mores, whims and wishes, of their typical supporting families and class circles. As private ventures, of course, they avoid the public control that comes through dependence on a local public board and public funds. But their nonpublic footing compels them to find annually the financial resources that will keep them going; namely, a sufficient number of tuition-paying students plus endowment and other funds gathered from alumni and wealthy benefactors. Control by those who provide the financing, or who are devoted alumni, can be as extensive and compelling as the control of a public board over a local school system or the control of a church over a parochial school. The private school's board of control, for one thing, may consist largely of its leading benefactors or those who have a way with financial angels, and school policy may be more influenced by their desires or the wishes of influential clients than by the wishes of the administrative and teaching staff.

Yet, of all the types of formal control over elementary and secondary education, the secular private probably on the average offers the greatest possibilities of independence. Free of both general public and specific church authority, some of these schools have reached positions of great autonomy. They have done so by securing the resources that would make them financially secure and building a reputation that guaranteed ample clientele. They have over a period of time developed controlling boards devoted to the welfare of the private schools and educated to a division of authority in which the board sets policy in broadest terms and the school staff has much autonomy in daily administration.

The Achilles heel of the secular private school is financial weakness, especially in times of inflation, and it is chiefly through this weakness that such schools are vulnerable to external influence and control. When this weakness is overcome, this type of school is generally the least susceptible to the push and pull of various interest groups or to close supervision by any one single external body.

The College

The influence exercised by external groups over colleges generally operates at a different level and in more diverse ways than do external controls over the lower schools. The public schools, for example, are all of a piece in that they are under local boards of education or a similar unit of authority located in the community. But public colleges vary greatly in their control and hence by whom they are influenced. Municipal colleges often serve largely their city and are controlled by a city-connected board of trustees; state colleges may be charged with serving a section of a state and thus take heed of the demands emanating from the groups of that area; state universities, established "to serve the needs of the people of the state," are subject to all the interests that reflect themselves through the state legislature and to the direct demands of interest groups who feel that they are among the host that should be served. However, the most common forms of control in this variety exist at state level. The boards of regents of the state universities are constituted at this level, and so also are the boards responsible for state colleges.

This shifts the arena of action, and also generally the degree of autonomy as mentioned briefly in Chapter 1, from that of the public schools. The public colleges for the most part are not under the gun of interest groups in the city or town where they are located, in the way the public schools are. Their area of responsibility is wider, their board membership is drawn from a larger area, many if not most of their students come from elsewhere, and—most important—their money comes not from the local city treasury or taxing system but from the state. Being not locally dependent, they are not so locally vulnerable. Thus public colleges and universities commonly escape most of the local "supervision" that public schools experience because of their intimate relationship to the neighborhood and town.

The dependency of the higher education units is upon the state government, and the degree of this dependency varies considerably among the states according to their political structures and their traditions of campus-state relations. In some states the university is by tradition closely watched, especially in matters that touch sentiments widely and deeply held in the state. State legislatures in the hard-core southern states today, for example, observe closely the utterances and actions of the university professors on desegregation. In other states, the state university may have a strongly autonomous board of regents whose independence from the rest of state government is traditional or even written into the state constitution.

It also must be remembered that one thing going for nearly all state universities is that their graduates people the state legislature and state government, and loyal sons will often not wish to question alma mater too closely, even when she seems to be falling upon errant ways. Too, the sheer size of the state universities has tended everywhere, increasingly, to mask much of what they do from close public scrutiny, and also to add to their prowess as a fighting force. Most state universities have learned to be effective lobbies in their own behalf at the state capitol—an interest group in themselves, ready to fight bills that appear injurious and to push measures of their own.

Where there are several major state colleges or universities within one state, or even several major systems such as a set of state colleges on the one hand and a set of university branches on the other, then their respective lobbies are often at odds with one another. With this, a growing tendency is for the public colleges of a state to be one of the chief sources of constraint upon the development of one another. The colleges often compete for faculty and students, they nearly always are competitive for programs, prestige, and state funds. Out of this situation of public colleges acting and reacting upon one another, we are seeing the growth of state superboards—coordinating councils and boards placed over all the public colleges of a state to allocate functions, prepare unified budgets, and adjudicate conflicts. The tendency in these ever-larger state systems of higher education is for the system as a whole to grow more powerful and independent, and thus less vulnerable to the demands of the public-interest groups; but in turn the colleges and branches that constitute the system lose some of their autonomy to internal administrative controls. In short, as in other institutions, bureaucratization plays a large role.

Our efforts here to catch up with the fast-moving developments of the present should not be allowed, however, to obscure the historic dependency of the American state universities and colleges on the politics of state government.

The condition of having to extract money every year from state legislators who are elected from every corner of the state and who face the lobbyists of every major and minor interest group in the state has been of great importance in determining the character of these colleges. This condition has promoted a service-mindedness—service to the basic industries of the state, service to many groups who step up and ask for courses or curricula relevant to their own interests, service to the youth of the state who are setting off down the multitudinous lines of specialized training.

It was mentioned in Chapter 2 that occupations in the process of becoming professions seek to have training programs established for them in the centers of higher education. Many other interests similarly approach the public college or university, and the amount of power they wield in the state capitol must be considered. A philosophy of service to the state supports the introducing of occupational curricula that are demanded. "Wouldn't the university like to offer some courses in its extension division for real estate men?" asks the realtors association. "We would like to see the development of a curriculum in retail marketing," remarks the business association. Sometimes the university says yes, sometimes it says no; the greater the political influence of the claimant, the more likely it is to assent. A state university in an agricultural state is never without a large school of agriculture.

After occupational curricula are established, then much of their institutionalization in the college or university rests on the expectations of outside supporters that "their" program will be a permanent matter—plus the power of these supporters to see that it remains so if others have serious ideas about reducing or terminating it. Most colleges and universities periodically reassess their component departments and schools, especially those that seem somewhat marginal, and occasionally attempt to do away with one. But if the professional school, for example, that is being questioned can rally outside supporters of some influence, then the battle that would have to be fought is generally judged not worth it. Few programs of this kind are discontinued. In such ways, the structure of influence and control around state-supported colleges has shaped their character from their origins to the present time. The extent to which the structure of control over public colleges has admitted the influence of state interest groups is an important source of the greater service-mindedness of public colleges over their private-college counterparts.

CENTRALIZED VERSUS DECENTRALIZED CONTROL

The federal level of government in this country has not been, until recently, the center of much interest-group pulling and hauling on education. Pressure goes to where the decisions are made, and historically the decisions have been made in the detached private school or college itself, or in the local and state agencies that govern public education. But everywhere in modern society policy making is gravitating upward, from smaller to larger units of governance, from agencies of local control to agencies of broader jurisdiction, as modern technology and communication shrink the world and the large organization outproduces and outorganizes the small. Issues and problems are increasingly national and international in scope rather than local or state. The corporation and the union have grown into huge enterprises; American trade unions have undergone considerable centralization, as they have found it effective to perform such functions as collective bargaining out of national rather than local headquarters.

Partly because the economy is dominated by national

firms, associations, unions, and the like, public action on domestic issues tends toward higher levels of government. The upward drift in public decision making is also impelled by national needs in international affairs, which press for centralized decisions in national defense, the allocation of resources, and the training of men.

The speed with which decision making flows from local to national levels in the private or the public sector depends considerably upon the amount of opposition offered by old machinery and traditional sentiments. In the economy, there has been relatively little drag exerted on the growth of the large corporation by its smaller antecedents. Large firms have been demonstrably more efficient and profits have gone to those that could make bigger and cheaper mousetraps. So, too, in the case of most unions, where the advantages of a national united front in bargaining with industry or lobbying around government centers have outweighed the desire of local union officials to keep power at their level. In short, authority in the private sector has moved rapidly upward.

Opposition to the nationalizing of control, however, is noticeably stiffer in the case of public authority, for here there is an historic, constitutional division of power between the national government and the states, and secondarily between the state and the local municipalities. These constitutional separations have been supported by a national consensus in sentiment that dates back to the very beginnings of the republic. Values in this realm have tended to be somewhat sacred; and of all the public enterprises, education has been most sacred. Resistance to the upward flow of control has been vigorous in the case of education. There are several reasons: education has been strongly institutionalized as a local and state function, legally, structurally, and in the common understanding; the local public schools are a core element in the identification of adults with their own community, and to alter the control of the schools threatens further the weakening sense of community in many localities; there is a traditional fear that control from higher levels is intrinsically bad, that it replaces democratic control with central dictation. The existing structures, backed by these sentiments, are strong enough to insure that control over education (especially for the lower grades) will remain largely out of Washington, D.C.

A modest upward drift in educational authority is taking place *within* the states, as the school-consolidation movement replaces small districts with larger ones, and as state departments of education and state associations of school personnel grow in size, strength, and number of state-wide rules and requirements.

Yet, in the face of the obstacles to more centralized control, the future clearly will bring more national legislation on public education and enlarged activity in such federal establishments as the United States Office of Education and the National Science Foundation. Many educators and citizens have long been interested in obtaining federal money for the schools, feeling that the local property tax was fast exhausting itself as a financial source and that state treasuries were also showing signs of being unable to finance necessary expansion and improvement. The large increase in the number to be educated, brought on by the high post-1945 birth rate, has called for rapid expansion in school funds—and a greater inclination to look toward Washington. International tension has encouraged a *national* approach to the problems of quantity and quality of American education.

With such forces at work and public interest aroused, we find emerging a comparatively new phenomenon for this country—education in national politics. Leaving aside the matter of school desegregation, interest groups are increasingly submitting, or opposing, various bills on education in the United States Congress. School personnel have their own lobbies; the National Education Association through its Washington headquarters works for "strong" bills on education, for large sums of money for school construction, teachers' salaries, and scholarships. In this they are generally supported by labor unions and liberal organizations, such as the AFL-CIO and Americans for Democratic Action. On the other side, such conservative groups as the United States Chamber of Commerce are chary about federal aid to education and work for weaker legislation. Some groups wish no federal legislation in education at all. Here is a new battleground whose existence is due to education's increasingly important role in our society and to its growth into a big enterprise.

The growing contention over education in national politics is reflected in the attitudes of the two major political parties. Both the Democrats and the Republicans now see education as a national issue, one in which there is political capital and on which positions must be taken. The growth of their interest in recent years is shown in the following summary of the attention given to education in the party platforms at the time of presidential elections:

PARTY PLATFORMS ON EDUCATION, 1944–1956

The Democratic Platform	*The Republican Platform*
1944	
Three lines on education, favoring federal aid to the states.	No mention of education.
1948	
Nine lines on education, favoring federal aid.	Three lines on education, favoring equal opportunity and the promotion of education.

1952

About twenty-five lines on education, favoring (a) equal opportunity, (b) shared responsibility among local, state, and federal governments, (c) aid for school construction, salaries, federal scholarships. The first sizable "education plank" by either party.	Six lines on education, subscribing to the principle that responsibility is local and state.

1956

Twenty-seven lines on education (in addition to a vocational education section), favoring equal opportunity, federal aid for school construction, and the training of teachers.	Twenty-three lines on education, within a "health, education, and welfare" plank, pointing to a prior White House conference on education and reaffirming need for federal aid in school construction.

Then, in 1960, both parties broke loose on education with long planks containing many subjects and promises. Some typical passages were:

Democrats:

We shall act at once to help in building the classrooms and employing the teachers that are essential if the right to a good education is to have genuine meaning for all the youth of America in the decade ahead.

The new Democratic Administration will end eight years of official neglect of our educational system.

Only the Federal Government is not doing its part.

We believe that America can meet its educational obligations only with generous Federal financial support, within the traditional framework of local control. The assistance will take the form of Federal grants to states for educational purposes they deem most pressing, including classroom construction and teachers' salaries. It will include aid for the construction of academic facilities as well as dormitories at colleges and universities.

Republicans:

Primary responsibility for education must remain with the local community and state. The federal government should assist selectively in strengthening education without interfering with the full local control of schools. One objective of such federal assistance should be to help equalize educational opportunities.

[We pledge] federal support to the primary and secondary schools by a program of federal aid for school construction—pacing it to the real needs of individual school districts in states and territories, and requiring state approval and participation.

The federal government can also play a part in stimulating higher education. Constructive action would include: the federal program to assist in construction of college housing; extension of the federal student loan program and graduate fellowship program.

We believe moreover that any large plan of federal aid to education, such as direct contributions to or grants for teachers' salaries can only lead ultimately to federal domination and control of our schools to which we are unalterably opposed.

With the very sharp expansion of interest of the two parties in 1960 also went a new-found interest in science and technology. Republican platforms had said nothing about these matters until 1960, except for a few words about an Atoms for Peace proposal in 1956. The Democratic platforms have had items about atomic energy since 1948, with a major plank on this subject in 1956, but had not expanded into a broader consideration of science and technology. In 1960, both parties had major planks, one on "Science" and the other on "Science and Technology," with the Democrats underscoring "the special role of our Federal Government in support of basic and applied research," and the Republicans maintaining that "Government must continue to take a responsible role in science to assure that worthwhile endeavors of national significance are not retarded by practical limitations of private and local support."

Federal aid to education is controversial precisely because it is thought to bear heavily on control. The common understanding is that he who gives the money calls the tune, thus that federal financing means federal control and the undercutting of local and state authority. Those experienced in finance and organization can usually testify that this belief has some basis in fact. Earlier we indicated that public colleges were generally subject more to state than to local community pressures, and this is in part because of funds coming from state rather than local government. Yet it is clear that the degree of control exercised through the allotment of money can vary within wide limits, from virtually no impact to dominance. Federal funds can be allotted and directly supervised by an arm of the national government, that is, a ministry or department of education. Or they can be disbursed to an existing decentralized and varied structure of state offices, separate schools, and independent colleges in ways that change relatively little the distribution of authority.

The federal government has been in the business of subsidizing the colleges of agriculture of state universities since 1887. Have these colleges come under governmental control or supervision because of the federal grants? Apparently the grants have not been the means of federal political control. The pressures on these agricultural colleges have continued to come from the state and local areas in which they are located; and the federal money has strengthened the colleges so that they are better able to resist these state and local political pressures as well as others.[4] Agricultural education and research remains decentralized and has been

[4] Charles M. Hardin, *Freedom in Agricultural Education* (Chicago: The University of Chicago Press, 1955).

made into a more independent force, while continually dependent on the federal funds. The ways in which funds are allotted are thus more important in determining control than is the amount of the financial support or the sheer fact that money is given at all. The national government will play a greater role in American education in the future—dispensing scholarships, supporting research, paying for new buildings, and even contributing to teachers' salaries. Yet, it is also likely that compared with other countries the educational structure will remain decentralized.

One of the basic problems of this decentralized structure in an age of rapid technological and social change is its consequences for institutional adaptation. Decentralized systems possess certain flexibilities that systems under central control do not have. The "lower" units can innovate or experiment or change as they see fit, and new patterns can thus arise. But highly decentralized systems are also difficult to influence quickly and decisively with new ideas and often have the inflexibility of institutional drift. When each autonomous subsystem decides for itself what is best, the composite institutional trend "just happens." Thousands of school boards separately make policies on the basis of what is best for the local town or area—and what the decisions add up to is the national product.

In earlier eras, it mattered relatively little, perhaps, whether the national outcome was appropriate to the national need. Now it matters greatly. We have shown earlier that education is adaptive to changing occupational requirements and social conditions. Yet it is an open question whether a decentralized institution operating under local impulse can adapt rapidly and appropriately to the needs of a society in which other institutions are more centralized and changing at a very high rate, primarily under the impulse of a technological revolution.

PRINCIPLES OF AUTHORITY[5]

Authority takes many forms in academic organizations—control by external power (such as a parent church), lay trustee, autocratic chief, bureaucratic official, academic colleague. Even students occasionally have some influence. Related to these forms of control are certain *principles* of authority, general beliefs about who should exercise power and how. Three principles are especially important because they are now most actively in contention: the first is the principle of public trust; the second, the principle of bureaucracy; the third, the principle of colleagueship.

Public Trust

The principle of authority most widely accepted by Americans for the administering of schools and colleges is one of public control vested in a board of laymen. The lay board is empowered legally to direct the organization and is held responsible for its welfare; it is to have final authority over the work of the employed staff. This principle relates to a wider belief, long a part of the American tradition, that schools and colleges should be directed ultimately by community interests rather than by professional personnel or government departments. In tax-supported schools and colleges, board members are considered representatives of the whole community or the population of the state. In private schools and colleges, the members of the board are often considered representatives of a sponsoring constituency; for example, "the Quaker community."

In both the public and the private sectors, the board member's position is a "public trust." The board is seen as an instrument of external control and of control by persons who are part-time and amateur rather than full-time and

[5] This discussion is drawn largely from Burton R. Clark, "Faculty Authority," *AAUP Bulletin*, 47:4 (Winter, 1961), pp. 293–302.

expert. Additionally, in the case of the public schools, authority in the hands of a *local* lay board is a way of insuring that the schools will not be completely controlled by state departments of education, even though the local district is legally and formally a part of a larger system. The lay board ideally is also "above" politics; but as we noted previously, school governance in practice strays measurably from the ideal of impartial citizen control.

Bureaucratic Authority

The legal provision that authority rests ultimately with the lay board does not insure that laymen will determine policy. Schools and colleges are organized in an hierarchy of personnel and staffed with full-time, paid officials; operating authority is either delegated to senior officers by the lay board or is assumed by the officers in the course of affairs. The board members, part-time and amateur, are removed from actual operation, while the officials—full-time, expert, informed—are on the spot, making the daily decisions. Even though the board is supposed to make policy and the hired staff to execute it, much policy determination falls into the hands of the trained officialdom. The organization assumes, to some degree, the form of a bureaucracy, with a hierarchy of officers assigned to positions that have fixed jurisdictions and duties.

Because of the strength of the lay-board idea in this country, authority in the hands of trained officials has not been so fully accepted for education as in many other realms. But as educational systems grow larger and more complex, and as educational administration becomes more dependent on expert knowledge and hence on the trained professional, bureaucratic authority increases naturally and contends more vigorously with trustee authority. The larger of the academic systems simply cannot be run without layers of administrators, an elaborate network of staff units, and the advice of experts. The interests and values of administrators also push in the direction of staff control. As experts in educational matters, the administrators feel better qualified to make policy than the inexperienced layman. They know they are better informed about what is going on in the schools, they are trained in this realm, and they often feel they can see the long-run welfare of the schools better than local pressure groups and their representatives on and off the board.

While disagreeing over whether laymen or administrators should direct policy, the principles of public trust and bureaucratic authority agree that authority is hierarchical. The "higher" authorities—the school board or the superintendent, the trustees or the college president—are expected to command the work of lower administrators, who in turn direct the teachers and control the students. There is wide public acceptance of control through hierarchy, for the idea is strongly rooted in practical experience and hence in common sense. Many board members take the business firm as a model of how to organize the school or college. This borrowed conception stresses clear lines of authority and sharply demarcated jurisdictions for which officials are held responsible.

Colleague Authority

The above two principles of authority do not have the field to themselves, for some men feel that much if not all authority in academic enterprises should be in the hands of the faculty. The notion of self-governing communities within which teachers, sometimes together with students, control policy and practice is an old one in the history of *higher* education. The first universities, established in Europe in the twelfth through the fourteenth centuries, were composed of teacher guilds and student guilds. Some of the universities even grew out of detached bands of teachers and students who, if displeased with the way they were treated by the landlords and good burghers in one town, could pick up and move on to another place. These groups of scholars and students continued to govern themselves even when encumbered with a sizable physical plant, and in Europe today and in many other countries influenced by the European tradition there is a heritage of faculty control.

This principle was absent in the early years of American higher education. The colonial colleges were established and closely watched by religious denominations, with the teacher hired to further the orthodoxy as defined by the board of control. These colleges were cases of control by outside interest as expressed through close supervision by board members selected from the parent group. The president had some authority, the faculty was inordinately small and weak in most cases. As American education became more secular, these early church-controlled colleges moved away from this close control and came to be directed primarily by their own trustees and the appointed president.

With some major regressions (the early nineteenth century saw a resurgence of denominational interest and control), the American liberal-arts college moved toward autonomy. After 1875 the university helped to make the principle of colleague control a strong contender. With the university came a broadening of function in education; to the task of conserving and transmitting knowledge was added the mission of creating knowledge, an inherently more critical function that required more elbow room for academic men. Research and scholarly writing are kinds of academic work that only peers can evaluate and assess, in contrast (somewhat) to the transmitting of certified, existing knowledge. With the introduction of the university also came the European ideal of a community of scholars. The functional requirements *and* the ideals of the university thus both worked toward greater autonomy for academic systems and for faculty influence. At the same time, the scientific ethos and the university sentiments spread into the small colleges.

Faculty control over instruction and curriculum is now widely accepted, uniformly so in the best colleges. Faculties have also promoted the concept of tenure, or guaranteed employment after a trial period; and tenure provisions are rapidly becoming a standard part of the "law" of higher education. Many faculties have much to say about who will be hired and fired, in some places virtually full control, and set the standards for admitting and retaining students. The ethos of colleague control continues to spread, invading the halls of teachers colleges, for example, where it used to be almost totally absent. Surveys conducted by the American Association of University Professors compared faculty self-government in 173 colleges for the two years 1939 and 1953, and found that faculty influence had increased. The greatest change was in state teachers colleges, which as a group were "conspicuously autocratic" in 1939 (as put in the AAUP report) and were still comparatively low in 1953.[6]

The AAUP surveys also compared faculty influence in 1920 with 1939 and 1953, for 36 colleges, and increases in influence were noted over the longer period. Table 4.2 reports the 1920–1939–1953 comparisons. However, American higher education contains colleges today in which the faculty is completely under the control of the administration and the board of trustees. In some cases, the right to flunk students has not yet been won by the faculty.

Over-all, the long-run trend in American higher education has been for authority to move from external to internal sources, with faculties increasingly contending with the administration about who has authority over what. The faculties march under the banner of self-government and

6 "The Place and Function of Faculties in College and University Government," *AAUP Bulletin*, 41:1 (Spring, 1955), pp. 62–81.

TABLE 4.2—INCREASE IN FACULTY INFLUENCE, 1920–1953
(36 Institutions)

ACTIVITY OR PROCEDURE IN WHICH FACULTY INFLUENCE HAD CHANGED	NUMBER OF COLLEGES REPORTING INCREASE OR DECREASE IN FACULTY INFLUENCE			
	1920–1939		1939–1953	
	Increase	Decrease	Increase	Decrease
Exchange of opinion with trustees	3	0	11	4
Choice of new president	8	0	14	2
Appointments, promotions, and dismissals	4	2	7	0
Selection of deans	2	1	18	1
Budgetary procedures	11	2	14	2
Faculty control of committees	0	0	6	0
Selecting departmental executives	1	0	6	0
Total number of changes reported	29	5	76	9

Source: "The Place and Function of Faculties in College and University Government," *AAUP Bulletin,* 39:2 (Summer, 1953), p. 311.

academic freedom, emphasizing equality of relations among colleagues and de-emphasizing administrative hierarchy. The administrations move forward under the banners of increased efficiency, unified effort, public relations—and the reducing of chaos to mere confusion.

"Academic freedom" is a critical part of the general struggle between professors who wish to say and do as they please and outside groups who want only certain opinions expressed to the young and some topics not discussed at all. This struggle takes the form in many cases of a contest between the faculty and the administration. In 1960, a faculty member at a midwestern state university made statements supporting an unconventional approach to sexual relations among unmarried students. He was promptly fired by the administration. If colleague authority had been dominant on this campus over the authority of the administration and the board, the professor probably would not even have been censured for his statement, since faculty sentiment is usually permissive on expression of opinion. In commenting on this case, a professor at another university stated vigorously the point of view that a university is not a university unless teachers and students are free from control by others:[7]

> [This discharge of a faculty member] indicates that there is still on the part of some University Administrators and Governing Boards indifference to, or incomprehension of the necessity for safeguarding to a maximum degree, the rights of students and teachers to express publicly their considered beliefs regarding scientific, social and moral matters. A University is a body of teachers and students actively engaged in learning and teaching what they suppose is the truth concerning man and nature. Any action that interferes with or suppresses such activity is incompatible with the idea of a University. . . . A University subject to unfavorable publicity or without a maximum budget is perhaps unfortunate; a University without free speech is a contradiction in terms.

To this, administrators might reply that a university with a budget curtailed by a hostile state legislature is not much of a university either. Administrators are generally more sensitive to public reaction and more concerned about the over-all security and equilibrium of the university than are the faculty. The pressures they face in their external relations strain their commitment to academic freedom. The discussion of controversial issues versus public relations is a sore point between the faculty and the controlling board on many campuses, with the administration sometimes in one camp, sometimes in the other, but more sensitive than the faculty to board and outside opinion.

[7] University of California *University Bulletin,* Vol. 9 (January 23, 1961), p. 101.

While the notion of a self-governing academic community waxes strong in American higher education, it is only weakly voiced in the public schools. This divergence stems from fundamental differences in work, status, history, and organization. As discussed earlier, the public schools relate closely to the local community in financial support and clientele, while colleges usually do not depend on such nearby sources of support; hence the teaching and administrative staffs of the public schools are more exposed to public scrutiny. Too, all children are compelled to attend elementary and secondary schools with little or no choice by their parents as to which school they will attend. When families must entrust their tender young, whom they are not yet ready to relinquish to society, they are likely to inquire closely about the values and practices of the teachers. College on the other hand is later and voluntary, the child has matured somewhat, and a particular college can be chosen from among many. The college is not just around the corner, physically and psychologically, as is the elementary school; it is a more distant, unknown enterprise. Hence the concern of parents about the character of any one college is different; they can send their youngster elsewhere if the values of a college seriously violate their own sentiments. Parents are less interested in controlling colleges than the public schools.

Freedom to pursue new ideas wherever they may lead has *not* been seen in this country as crucial to the effective performance of the public-school teacher, at least not as much as for the college professor; and the teaching staffs of the lower grades have neither been given nor have actively sought the modest degree of freedom of expression found in most college faculties. The skill and knowledge of the teacher has also not been so specialized and thus has been more easily understood by laymen. Citizens who are unlikely to criticize the ability of a physicist will freely comment on the work of the public-school teacher, in part because they are closer to it and better informed, but also because they feel competent to comprehend a less esoteric skill.

In sum, the interests and values of laymen in the United States have led to more lay control over the public schools than over the colleges, and teachers in the lower grades have been less inclined to assert their own authority and less in a position to do so. College staffs are more strongly impelled by their own interests to control policy and practice. The college teacher has generally been defined as an expert in his discipline and granted greater independence.

What does the future promise for these major forms of control in American education? Trustee authority will undoubtedly continue to be recognized legally and formally as the dominant type of authority; schools and colleges will continue to have lay boards as their highest formal element. But in actual operation we may expect bureaucratic administrations on the one hand and self-constituted groups of teacher colleagues on the other hand to assert themselves increasingly and contend more actively for decisive influence in school matters. We know that the influence of the expert administrator will increase because the administration will grow in size and will become ever more specialized and expert. Everything we know about bureaucratization and managerial technique points in this direction for the decades immediately ahead. At the same time, the influence of the teaching staff will continue to increase, because the faculty grows in size and also gains influence through its growing expertness. This is most apparent in the case of physical scientists and mathematicians in the universities, but even first-grade teachers are now privy to theories and techniques —Gesell on the "fives" or the "nines," for example—known generally only within the ranks.

Everywhere in modern society, professional men gain in authority by virtue of expert knowledge. Many groups of teachers today are pushing their own professionalization, pulling themselves up by the bootstraps through strengthening their associations, establishing standards of training, recruitment, and retention, and promulgating codes of conduct. This drive for professionalization promises to have some success, with the result of greater protection for the teacher from control by laymen and administrators. In higher education, as we have observed, conflict in authority is already taking the form principally of the administration and the governing board on the one side and professors on the other, with the professors holding to the principle of a self-governing body of academic colleagues. In the public schools, this form of conflict will grow as teachers press for authority along with their own professionalization, and, occasionally, unionization.

In short, there is now in the organization of education an inherent strain toward greater conflict between the administration and the faculty. This conflict is similar in many respects to the growing conflict in other major institutions between The Organization and The Profession. The expert located within an organization is subject to the authority, the influence, the appeal to loyalty, of both his organization and his professional group. The technological society both creates more and better experts *and* puts them to work within complex organizations, where technical authority must come to grips with administrative authority.

In the age of the expert, it is not easy for managers to decide what structure of authority is most conducive to long-run effectiveness. Central coordination that appears efficient this year may be detrimental in the long run if it discourages staff initiative, lessening the will to create and innovate. Rational administration in this regard is a special problem in schools and colleges. Rationality in most settings has been served well by bureaucratic structure—in the United Auto Workers Union as well as in the Ford Motor Company, the prison as well as the hospital. But rationality in academic settings often seems best served by flat structures with relatively little hierarchy, a minimum of rules, and much freedom for the typical practitioner. Why this is so, is not entirely clear; but of all classes of workers, the academic man perhaps most needs a large amount of freedom for effective performance. Not only does his teaching necessitate daily communication of ideas, often subtle and unclear in nature and sometimes controversial, but scholarly writing and research require free-swinging imagination and a willingness to venture into the unknown as well as to critically re-examine and reconstruct the known.

Professors and teachers are widely committed to the notion that their work—teaching and research—is best performed under a condition of maximum independence, with the layman and the administrator providing the resources and then remaining at arm's length. In part because of the work itself and in part because of this belief, able professors and teachers gravitate from systems where they feel unduly pushed around to colleges and schools where greater freedom exists. Maximizing faculty recruitment and productivity seems to call for administrations oriented to establishing the conditions that leave the teacher relatively free. The loose, meandering, overlapping structure of authority we often find in colleges may be there because it is in the service of rationality rather than of madness.

Chapter 5

Organization of the School and College

AFTER CONSIDERING control and authority, we turn now to other organizational features of schools and colleges. He who says action in the modern world says organization, for organizations are *the* tools for the accomplishment of major tasks. If we wish to comprehend why schools and colleges perform the way they do, we do well to look for the impulses of their own character, as well as to environmental forces that exert push and pull.

Organizations have certain features that contribute to their character. Each recruits outsiders to come in and staff its positions and offices, and who is recruited makes a difference; each has a scheme for dividing work and delegating authority; in each, friendships are made and a network of informal relations arises spontaneously to condition work; and, in each, habits form and routines set in—a development that is at once necessary but potentially dangerous in leading to rigidity, a hardening of the organizational arteries. Various features and processes constitute a composite character that determines the organization's capabilities. Organization character embodies competence in certain efforts, together with inability to assume other roles, just as the personality of the individual offers both promise and limits for personal functioning.

Out of the large number of features of schools and colleges that could be discussed, we shall touch only a few. In each case we point to the apparent impact of major social trends. How is the organization of the school and college affected by the current technological stage of modern society, with its explosion of knowledge, its high rate of change, its high birth rate and mass population?

We turn first to the recruitment process, the securing of the necessary work force. Very little is known, but recruitment is so important that the topic begs for attention. Second, we inquire into the formal structure of educational agencies, how they group people and arrange work, and how these arrangements are evolving. Here more is known and speculation can be somewhat firmer. We know for instance that the schools of the future are bound to hire more staff experts, to have more diversified teaching forces, and to give a larger place to counseling. Third, we discuss how schools and colleges tend to become institutions, in the sociological sense. Fourth, we consider the ideologies and images of schools and colleges, the beliefs to which they are attached and the impressions that the public holds of them. Here we enter into matters that have received almost no attention, yet are of growing importance in the interaction of schools and colleges with their environment. Educational agencies in varying degrees compete for students, financial resources, personnel, and moral support; and the sustenance they each receive is conditioned by their organizational reputation.

RECRUITMENT

The persons recruited to staff an organization are often a prime determinant of its character, because they bring not only certain skills but also their values, their affiliations, their personalities. Perspectives developed in the outside world are thus carried inside, and it matters greatly which particular values are acquired in this manner, deliberately or unintentionally.

An established organization with narrow goals and routine tasks may neither care much about nor be affected by the values of its newer members. Only their technical competence may matter. But to new organizations, especially to those whose goals are broad and hence somewhat unfixed, the orientations of newcomers are quite influential. The values held by recruits are most important when the organization is established to defend and develop certain values; and to some degree all schools and colleges fall in this category. Educational agencies that seek close conformity to a set of norms and values recruit very carefully, securing new members who already have the "proper" outlook. As remarked in Chapter 4, early American colleges, established by various church groups, recruited with an eye to a man's religiosity: "In the making of appointments an effort was commonly made to be sure at the beginning that the incoming president, professor, or tutor was one who accepted the requisite theological doctrines."[1] Doctrinal acceptability was an explicit criterion, generally dominant over scholarship and teaching competence.

Conformity to creed became less important as a secular trend diminished church control and increased the use of professional criteria of competence. But recruitment on the grounds of a man's values is still practiced, although less rigidly for the most part than in the past. Church-related schools and colleges still "care" to some degree about the

[1] Richard Hofstadter and Walter P. Metzger, *The Development of Academic Freedom in the United States* (New York: Columbia University Press, 1955), p. 155.

faculty recruit's religiosity; a college committed to the education of Lutheran youth and tied financially and traditionally to a Lutheran church federation requires at least a modest level of Lutheran commitment in its personnel and hence recruits partly on this basis. The pursuit of academic excellence in such a college must be reconciled with the church framework; students, faculty, and administrators are not recruited solely on the ground of academic performance or competence but on a combination of their values and their ability.

Recruitment with an eye to a man's values also comes about in more implicit, subtle ways; for example, through selecting those who will be "congenial." This may even occur in a leading college when a faculty of liberal (or conservative) political persuasion chooses recruits to match their own political preferences. Such selection is often largely unconscious, a result of the college having a public image that attracts liberals and repels conservatives (or vice versa), and the tendency of like to select like. In such ways, the recruitment pattern, backstopped by the pattern of who stays and who leaves from among the junior faculty, may largely decide the tone of the college.

The public junior college is an interesting instance of the influence of recruitment. Located educationally between high school and four-year colleges and universities, part of both the public-school system and higher education in most states where it exists, the junior college may select its teachers from many sources: directly from graduate schools, as do most colleges; or from the ranks of those already teaching in the public schools, or in teachers colleges, or in liberal-arts colleges—or from among those who have never taught but are instead in business or industry. The various sources offer personnel who differ somewhat in orientation. Teachers with high-school experience have been habituated to different norms than those who have taught in the four-year college or whose expectations have most recently been formed by the graduate school. The normal classroom load is 25 hours a week in the one case, 9 to 12, or less, in the other; supervision by administrators is practiced in the public schools but rarely, if ever, in colleges; the school teacher has worked with students of all levels of ability and ambition, while the college teacher has not seen the worst, although he often feels he has. Different experiences, expectations, and tolerances are brought to bear within the junior college according to whether it principally finds its teachers within the public schools or elsewhere. Junior colleges actually recruit most heavily from the ranks of high-school personnel, and this pattern of recruitment influences them toward assuming the character of secondary education.

We know little about the effects of recruitment and selection on the character of elementary and secondary schools. It is generally known that public-school teaching historically in the United States has not been an attractive occupation for the ambitious and the talented, especially among men, and the recruitment pool therefore has not contained a fair share of talent. Even though education attracts some students from the top 10 per cent, the ability of school teachers has been relatively low, on the average, and the education majors on most college campuses are among the least promising students—again "on the average." About 25 per cent of the education majors with a Bachelor's degree score less than 110 on intelligence tests on which the average for the total population is 100, the average for high-school graduates is 110, and the average for college graduates is 121.[2] Comparisons of the *scholastic achievement*

[2] Dael L. Wolfle, *America's Resources of Specialized Talent* (New York: Harper & Brothers, 1954), p. 146 and p. 199.

of high-school seniors and college seniors preparing to teach have shown that:[3]

> . . . substantial numbers of high school seniors were scholastically better qualified than large numbers of college seniors preparing to teach, often in the very subject which the prospective teachers had been preparing to teach. It appears that if persons of average or slightly above average intelligence are permitted to become high school teachers, they will inevitably be teaching sizable numbers of students who are scholastically better qualified in the teachers' fields of specialization than the teachers themselves.

Public-school teaching has also been a woman's occupation, for the better part of a century, especially in the elementary schools. Sixty-one per cent of the teachers in 1870 were women; 70 per cent in 1900; 83 per cent in 1930; 75 per cent in 1955. About 12 per cent of the elementary and 45 per cent of the secondary teachers in 1955 were men.[4]

In social origins, teachers used to be drawn largely from the established sectors of the middle class. Teaching was a respected occupation for women from hard-working, thrifty, respectable families, especially farm families, and the "schoolmarm" was a carrier of middle-class values. The social origins of teachers have become diverse, however, and teachers increasingly come from lower-middle-class and lower-class urban families.

It is unclear what such social sources mean for the values carried into the public schools by recruits. Women of average or slightly above average intelligence from lower-middle-class and lower-class families probably, it can be guessed, tend to be plodding and unimaginative. But nothing follows from this for the character of particular schools. The recruitment net of the field as a whole is wide and

[3] Myron Lieberman, *Education as a Profession* (Englewood Cliffs, N.J.: Prentice-Hall, Inc., 1956), p. 231.

[4] Lieberman, *Education as a Profession,* p. 242.

picks up a multiplicity of types from which individual school systems select, according to their means and their inclinations. Elite suburban or urban schools are able and inclined to select highly talented, often scholarly, teachers, much in the model of a select private school. Such public schools could be characterized as private schools run at public expense. Other public schools select, deliberately or accidentally, according to subtype: a conservative system, conservative teachers; a progressive school, progressive teachers. Some small towns that cherish the rustic virtues are on guard against the big city man. Such towns particularly like to use home-town girls who have strayed no farther than the nearest state teachers college; they are safe as well as cheap. If not enough home-towners are available, then their country cousins are the next best thing. One small town in upper New York state, controlled by rural interests on the school board, showed this pattern:[5]

> Preference is shown for native daughters who return to the community from college. Three or four teachers are the wives of farmers, and several more represent village families. The great proportion of teachers, however, must be hired from the "outside," which usually means the importation of 30-35 families into the village; the school chooses these carefully. One of the primary criteria used in selecting teachers is their social origin—whether they were "reared" in a city or the country. The applicant who comes from a farm or a small town is uniformly appointed if a choice between two candidates is available; by and large, the staff is composed of teachers who have a rural background. Through such processes of teacher selection an attempt is made to perpetuate the rural tradition and to minimize innovative tendencies which might run counter to it.

The common pattern of using home-towners or persons raised nearby often stems from low salaries, convenience in

[5] Arthur J. Vidich and Joseph Bensman, *Small Town in Mass Society* (Garden City, New York: Doubleday & Company, Inc. [Anchor Books], 1960), p. 183.

recruiting, or unimaginative effort—and can be found in sizable cities as well as small towns. In 1957 in the public-school system of Pawtucket, Rhode Island, a city of over 80,000, 83 per cent of the educational personnel—teachers, supervisors, administrators—were born within the area or educated in the local elementary schools. Three-fourths of the staff had received their college education within the local area and of the remaining one-fourth the great majority of degrees were acquired within Rhode Island.[6]

Yet the trend in recruitment to the public schools is undoubtedly toward wider geographic, cultural, and social origins. Many school administrators are now recruiting nation-wide by such aggressive means as an annual recruiting safari to bag choice specimens in other states. The elite public schools in the Chicago and New York areas that have a national reputation for quality are now thoroughly national in staff. There are also drifts in teacher mobility from poor-paying and otherwise undesirable systems to the better-paying and otherwise more attractive schools. The states of New England, outside of Connecticut, have experienced some drift of their better teachers toward Connecticut, New York, and New Jersey, where new or growing systems have offered good pay and attractive work conditions. In brief, the trend is toward increasing numbers of school systems moving into wider recruitment and toward a greater national mixing of teachers. But the situation is enormously diverse and uneven, with many smaller systems seeking particular value orientations in their teachers, the better to maintain a desired climate of thought in the schools.

The trend toward state and national mixing, and away from purely local draw, is closely related to the major trends of a technological society. The high rate of change,

[6] *Pawtucket,* A Report by the Center for Field Studies, Graduate School of Education, Harvard University, 1957, pp. 147–149.

the explosion in knowledge, and the other features of the modern era that we have earlier stressed raise the importance of the well-trained teacher—for the college-preparatory suburban school or the tough slum school or the rural school at the crossroads. All, including the rural school, are being dragged into the main stream of educational change and reform, facing alike the problem of preparing the young for a world in which skill is raised to ever higher levels of importance and in which science is becoming increasingly important. One outcome of the modern era is that the schools must find more highly competent people for their staffs just to remain even, to do as good a job of preparation for the current generation, relatively, as for its predecessors. Selection by personal pull, or hiring the home-town girl in order to economize—or even selection to maintain the traditional values of the town or city—is thrown increasingly into question. The criterion that steadily forges ahead is professional or technical competence.

The high school now requires a more diversified staff, than in the past, to cover the widening array of subject matter and to have at hand specialists who can keep abreast of the work done in depth in various fields. Increasingly the high-school teacher must return to the college campus, not alone to pick up credits toward salary increases or have a summer romance, but to retread his or her knowledge, to keep up with the revisions being made. Apparently the summer teacher-training institute is here to stay, one more indication that our underlying social trends will increasingly insist on expert competence in the high school.

ORGANIZATION STRUCTURE

Let us now turn to some structural aspects of schools and colleges, their formal schemes for organizing effort, for getting the work done. A primary process in the formal system is *delegation*. The controlling board delegates authority to a full-time officer; he in turn splits and delegates authority to subordinates, and so on down the line. The larger and more complex the organization, the greater the need for the subassignment of authority. So, too, for work processes. These are delegated and subdivided, and just as the division of labor in society grows ever more complex, so does the division of work within organizations. The large organization is thus a web of work jurisdictions, offices, and assigned responsibilities. There is a splitting of purpose, from the most general at the top to the most specific at the bottom; purpose at the lowest level may amount to two turns of a bolt by a worker on the assembly line, or a daily lesson by the teacher. These elaborate divisions of effort that we call formal organizations, necessary in modern society, also require great effort in putting the pieces together; coordination becomes a central task of officers and internal communication one of their basic problems.

"Formal structure" is the name generally given in social science to the officially contrived web of arrangements; "a system of rules and objectives defining the tasks, powers, and procedures of participants according to some officially approved pattern."[7] This "officially approved pattern" is reflected in part and in skeleton form in tables of organization, such as the one shown in Chart 5.1. This organization chart, involved as it is, is only the roughest approximation to the formal structure of the Los Angeles school system. No complex organization can express more than a segment of its official scheme in a chart or in a set of written specifications. It generally requires considerable experience in an organization to know in detail its formal system of allocation and coordination. Of course, in a simple system, a school with one administrator and a handful of teachers,

[7] Leonard Broom and Philip Selznick, *Sociology* (Evanston, Illinois: Row, Peterson and Co., 1958), p. 208.

CHART 5.1

ORGANIZATIONAL STRUCTURE

(Los Angeles School System, 1952–53)

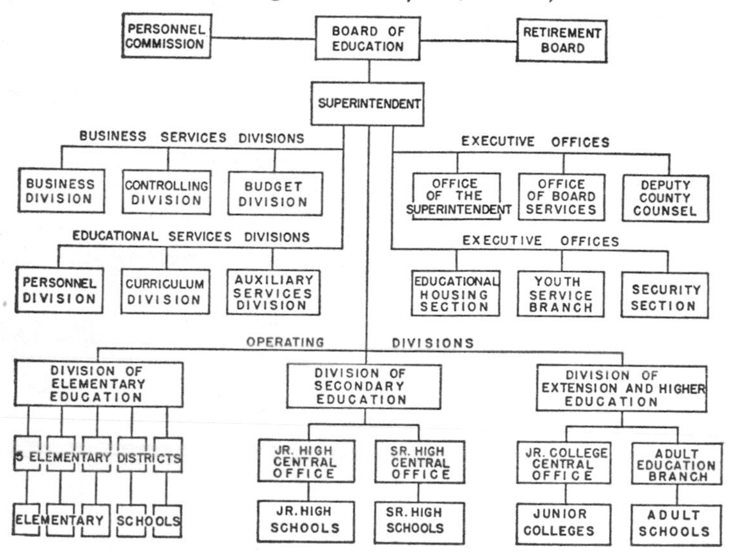

Source: Burton R. Clark, *Adult Education in Transition: A Study of Institutional Insecurity* (Berkeley and Los Angeles: University of California Press, 1956), p. 68.

the formal arrangements do not even need to be written down for them to be apparent to all.

The concept of bureaucracy is sometimes used in social science to mean virtually the same thing as formal structure; often, however, bureaucracy refers to administrative officials alone—and hence within *their* realm, to the division of labor, the delegation of authority, and the channeling of communication and coordination. In either case, "bureaucracy" does not directly connote red tape, petty officials, and inefficiency, as the common usage of the term does. It refers rather to highly formalized social systems, based on law, with fixed offices within—a means of social action efficient for the most part compared to its predecessors or alternatives. The bureaucrat is hired for his competence rather than because of his family name, his ties of friendship, his political connections, or his manners.

The formal structure may be most simply portrayed as a set of work positions, and a common sociological conception of the school sees it as a system of interrelated roles. We can inquire into the formal structure of educational organizations by analyzing their primary roles, and seek the changes in these organizations by determining what is happening to the roles. Roles are relatively concrete units with which to work.

Basic Educational Roles

A role is a social position that has certain patterns of behavior associated with it. Roles are mandates on behavior; regardless of personality, individuals who occupy a role are likely to behave in roughly similar ways because of what is expected of them. The teacher must meet classes, keep order, teach, grade papers, not because of any inclination of personality—that may not be there, especially for grading papers—but because such actions are part of what a person has to do as teacher. Place the same person elsewhere and he behaves differently, often even changing his style of response. Teachers promoted to principal take on a different perspective; beloved professors turned college president seem no longer to be the persons they once were. The new roles present tasks and relationships of a different order, and urge the man to adopt a different mental set. In part, men are the roles they play. In the analysis of any social setting we should understand the influence of roles, comprehending what men are impelled to do or are likely to do because of the mandates built into the system.

In American educational organizations, there have been

four basic roles: board member, administrator, instructor, and student. These roles normally complement one another, the behavior specified for each helping to make interaction orderly and reliable. Each role has expectations about which most people agree; a school-board member should concern himself with general policy but should avoid attempting to supervise classroom practices. But over and above the elementary expectations, there is much room for ambiguity and conflict.

Conflicting requirements. Any role in itself may call for inconsistent kinds of behavior, leading to strain. The role of school teacher asks that the teacher be fair to students, judging them impartially. But the role also asks that teachers shape students; and to "reach" them, one needs to understand their differing capacities and temperaments and be capable of sympathetic, "emotional" relations. Teachers have difficulty in reconciling such impersonal and personal considerations, to be friend and judge at the same time.

The college instructor faces conflicting demands in the form of teaching versus research. Much of his time goes to teaching and counseling, and students press for more time than he gives. In large and small colleges alike, "we do not see enough of the faculty" is a persistent student complaint. Yet most rewards for the faculty man, especially in the universities, are linked to research and scholarly publication. The professor who gives all his time to students may hurt his career—for example, jeopardize his chances for promotion. On the other hand, the instructor who invests heavily in research must to some degree turn his back on students, giving less time to preparing for lectures and reducing the hours in which he is available. Consciously or not, the college teacher adjusts to these two streams of demands; he so often makes research his primary commitment because of the pressures and rewards of the system.

Nearly all administrative positions also contain such

inconsistencies and strains. The school principal must communicate with his teaching staff in order to understand their problems and have rapport with them to foster cooperation and morale. It is useful for the principal to be "close to the teachers," at least be able to take their point of view and represent them to higher authorities. But the principal must also act as an agent of his superiors, the superintendent and board of education, and exercise authority over his subordinates. Like lower-level officials in business, the principal is a man in the middle who must reconcile two sets of interests that play on him from above and below. The principal who falls in with the teachers dims his prospect of rising higher in the administrative ranks; if he acts solely as an arm of the school headquarters, he cannot claim to champion his teaching staff and widens the schism between the teachers and the administration. The principal must search for the compromise that serves both sets of interests, or live with the consequences of satisfying one party but not the other.

Conflicting expectations. Many conflicts in roles take the form of different groups having contrary expectations, as reflected in the case of the principal caught between the teachers and the central administration. Board members and superintendents frequently differ in how they define their respective roles. In theory, the school board sets policy and the superintendent serves as chief executive, translating policy into practice. But there is actually no clear line between policy and administration; policies are made at different levels of organization and often occur as by-products of administrative action. Administrators tend to enter into the determination of policy more than the school board would like. On the other hand, a school board may define its province so widely that it becomes deeply involved in the running of the schools; in one case known to the author, board members themselves checked drinking fountains in the schools to ascertain their working condition. Such a board sees its superintendent as little more than a handy assistant to whom specific tasks are assigned and withdrawn at will. A superintendent normally resists this definition of his role, and rapid turnover in the superintendency often signifies a "meddlesome" board. At the other extreme, the superintendent's headquarters staff in a large school system may virtually control policy making, with the school board merely ratifying staff decisions. Board members usually resent a rubber-stamp role, however, and seek ways of intervening effectively. They may, for example, establish subcommittees on curriculum, personnel, or budget that meet with middle- and lower-level administrators, by-passing the superintendent. New boards bent on reform—elected with a "mandate from the people"—often are inclined, we may note, to define their own role broadly as they hasten to make the changes they desire.

Complexity of tasks. The roles of board member, administrator, teacher, and student have all become increasingly complex in recent decades as educational organizations have become larger and assumed more functions. The elementary-school teacher collects money, meets with the PTA, counsels students, and has numerous other chores besides keeping order and teaching. Committees occupy much time. More than most organizations, the modern school operates by committee; a change in the curriculum calls for a committee of teachers and administrators working together over a considerable length of time. This consulting-before-decision is widely practiced, if for no other reason than to involve those who later will implement the change. Many teachers also engage in quasi-administrative tasks such as planning new programs or special events, supervising practice teachers, and coordinating the work of a department. The complexity of tasks pulls the time and attention of the teacher in many different directions, confronting the teacher with the question: What really is my role?

The increase in number and types of tasks is great at the administrative level. The college presidency is a case in point. The president of a private college, for example, is normally held responsible for the educational leadership of his institution. To exercise such leadership, he need concern himself with the selection and orientation of faculty and the organization of the curriculum. He must give much time and energy to the daily internal affairs of the college, chairing innumerable committee meetings and meeting individually with faculty and students. But college presidents in modern times have had to turn their attention to other matters, especially public relations and fund raising. The president is often the chief solicitor of funds, visiting foundations and wealthy old ladies with "hat in hand." Foundations will openly tell him: Don't send your assistant money raisers, we want to see *you*. He also meets with alumni groups from coast to coast, since the college depends on their loyalty, moral support, and money.

The college president serves, often extensively, as a national spokesman in education, participating in conferences, giving speeches, publishing articles and books—activities that, among other things, add to his reputation and the renown of his college. These external matters now make it difficult for the president to involve himself in the life of the college as called for by his role of educational leader. The strain is acute, causing some ex-presidents to maintain that the role of college president has grown beyond manageable size.

The overburdening of the traditional positions acts as an impulse for the proliferation of new roles, a topic to which we now turn.

Proliferation of roles. The strain exerted by the loading-on of tasks encourages a greater division of labor. New roles arise in schools and colleges to supplement the old, and new specialists find a niche. Specialization of skill and function is proceeding rapidly as in other institutions. Even small liberal-arts colleges of 500 to 800 students have come to the point within the last ten years of adding men who specialize in alumni affairs, fund raising and development, publicity, and admissions, to relieve the president and deans of overwhelming tasks. In large universities and large school systems, the administration has long consisted of layers of officials and clerks, with nonteaching personnel numbering into the hundreds and sometimes thousands. The university administrative superstructure includes bureaus devoted to government relations, housing, job placement, and budget.

"Counselor" is perhaps the most significant role emerging in educational organizations. Teachers have long advised students on their educational program, the job market, and personal problems. But guidance is becoming a large business, a specialized line of work separate from teaching, especially in mass institutions. The growth of a distinct counseling sphere inside schools and colleges stems from the greater complexity of society and education. As occupations grow more numerous and specialized, occupational choice becomes more difficult, necessitating the help of guidebooks and experts. So with course work, experts in reading the catalogue are needed. Students especially need help in aligning career choice with capability —and then selecting an appropriate course of study. Schools and colleges also seek ways of allocating students to educational and occupational tracks without prodigious waste of time and effort; for this they need to measure ability and progress, maintain a cumulative record of promise and performance. Around such personal and organizational needs, professional counseling has already become a primary endeavor in many places, as important as teaching to the progress and destiny of the student.

The best public-school systems commonly start a file on the student in the lower elementary grades. Records accumulate and pass along through channels as the student moves up through the grades, and counselors are increasingly the custodians and interpreters of the records, especially in the upper grades. The student is "known" and judged through the dossier which shadows him, often precedes him. A student entering high school may be studied by means of the achievement history and the scores made on aptitude and achievement tests, and typed as underachiever, overachiever, bright, "hoody," normal, or problem child before he begins his high-school work. Counseling is a distinct operation in the public junior college where some students end their education and set off for jobs while others prepare to transfer to a host of different colleges. The two-year college is a classification and distribution center; in the short time students are there, the college needs to counsel them into a program and career appropriate to their capabilities. Counseling also grows in four-year colleges and universities, especially in the large public enterprises, but in many cases, the faculty effectively resists its growth, and there are liberal-arts colleges that pride themselves on the absence of professional counselors.

Official counseling duties are usually first assigned to teachers as part-time work. Then as the counseling tasks grow in magnitude and complexity, they call forth a variety of full-time professionals. Some of the "pros" counsel on choice of occupation and academic program primarily, others have psychological or psychiatric training and specialize in emotional and personal difficulties. Some schools also have social workers on the staff. There are even liaison counselors who work in a high school and specialize in gathering information from junior-high-school personnel on the students about to enter high school. In short, school counseling itself already contains a number of subspecialities, and has "professional" problems of training requirements and relations with other fields.

Despite opposition by teachers and professors who feel that counseling is already overdone, it will continue to grow as a sphere of work and as an influence on the careers of the young. The technological age requires it. Increasing specialization and longer formal instruction make hit-and-miss and late identification of ability more costly to both the individual and the society. To this has been added the pressures of the Cold War for locating and training talent. We will see greater effort to develop and apply methods for identifying the potentially talented students early in the schools and for later steering their choices and judging their progress. Those interested in how modern society presses on the organization of the school and college can learn much by exploring further the developing place of counseling.

Other possible changes in educational roles are in the air. Which ones will take hold is hard to tell, but it seems likely that a differentiation of teaching positions is on its way in the public schools. Generally speaking, there is now only one official status for teachers in the schools—teachers are "teachers," with pay differentiated by years of service and amount of educational preparation (the Bachelor's degree, the Master's degree). As knowledge becomes more specialized and teaching a more complex task, a dividing of the teaching role enters into consideration. Teachers vary greatly in training and ability, and only some can handle certain demanding tasks. Some school boards and administrators are seeking ways of paying higher salaries to a few teachers without disastrous effects on the morale of the others, in order to attract and retain exceptional persons who otherwise are likely to pursue a career outside of education.

Many administrators and teachers feel that the heavy load of paper work now carried by teachers could be assigned to assistants. Such developments and concerns have generated attempts to rearrange teaching positions; schools have been inquiring into the possibilities of "team teaching" and the use of master teachers and teaching aides. In team teaching, several teachers consolidate their classes part of the time and one teacher lectures or demonstrates to the large group while the others help out around the room or attend to other tasks. In such groupings, one teacher is often designated as master teacher or captain; aides who are not yet trained teachers are used; and mothers are hired on a part-time basis to do the most routine work. With the work differentiated for master teachers, teachers, aides, and part-time assistants, a school can offer salaries at several levels of capability for work of differing complexity. Previous attempts to pay teachers according to their perceived competence, namely "merit pay," have largely come to grief in the face of teacher opposition. Differences in financial reward may be seen as legitimate when teaching is subdivided into several roles ordered in authority and competence.

Informal Relations

The formal structure specifies what the members of a school or college shall do in their assigned positions. It treats persons as if they were roles, ignoring personal considerations and interests other than those technically demanded. But people resist being treated as if they were cogs, and the formal system is never enough, either for personal satisfaction or for organizational achievement. Around the formal relations arise informal ties. In the organization, as in the community, groups emerge based on personal likes and dislikes, on the need to interact with emotional warmth and regard, on the need to face problems and interests other than those technically defined. These informal groups often counter or subvert the formal scheme: workers band together and restrict output; managerial cliques war with one another to the detriment of the whole enterprise; students bring down school standards by ostracizing those who study hard. But informal associations are also necessary and functional. Personal contact helps in getting the job done; a lunch-table discussion, informally arranged or spontaneously developed, may lead quickly to an agreement on policy that otherwise would take weeks to form through official channels. Subordinates work hard and responsibly for superiors with whom they identify closely, and will "produce" for a friend. Informal relations, in short, promote levels of loyalty and work not otherwise obtainable. The formal and the informal depend on one another and act on one another, not the least in schools and colleges.

Informal links are especially important in colleges and universities because of the diffusion of authority (see Chapter 4). The chain of command is ambiguous and members of the faculty are consulted on many matters. When many men are "in" on policy, whether in a department, a division, a college, or a whole university, the situation calls for extensive informal give-and-take. Unless members of the faculty and administration worked out many matters informally, they would spend nearly all their time in meetings, instead of merely a good share of it. Much "politicking" is required, because agreements must be thrashed out among individuals and groups with divergent views and interests, as in a community. Whom to hire, whom to fire, what courses to add, who should take leave of absence, and similar matters are often thrashed out informally, and the resulting decisions then ratified through formal processing of the necessary papers. Where authority is broadly and ambiguously diffused, "the proper channels" may play a relatively small role compared to the informal exchange, the informal agreement, and the informal veto.

Informal relations among teachers in elementary and secondary schools apparently do not play so strong a role in decision making, since these instructors have less authority. But informal relations can serve other functions. Informal alliances among teachers often serve as mutual-protection societies in warding off the authority of the administration. As Becker points out in the adapted reading below, when teachers and a principal disagree, "the teachers may collectively agree on a line of passive resistance, and just do things their way, without any reference to the principal's desires," or they may use their connections outside the school to create sentiment against the principal. Teachers may also band together socially outside the school in order to avoid the surveillance of community groups. Too, as discussed earlier, the authority of teachers in these schools may be increasing; if so, administrators must take the teachers more into account, consulting and winning consent through informal as well as formal means.

In brief, each school and college has a web of informal ties as well as a structure of formal relations, with both types of relations controlling behavior. The formal structure normally directs behavior toward official purposes. The informal system may either support the official machinery, be neutral to it, or subvert it—or do all of these things. Regardless of outcome, informal relations will arise spontaneously, establishing norms that will appear to managers as a check upon their own authority.

The following reading, taken from an article by Howard S. Becker on the Chicago school teacher, offers examples of several matters we have reviewed: conflict in expectations between teachers and administrators; the formal arrangement of authority; the informal means available to teachers and the school principal for obtaining what they wish or for warding off undesired control. Becker portrays dramatically the stress experienced by teachers and principals, and the ways in which they exert control over students and parents—and each other.

TEACHER AND PRINCIPAL [8]

The principal is accepted as the supreme authority in the school:

> After all, he's the principal, he is the boss, what he says should go, you know what I mean . . . He's the principal and he's the authority, and you have to follow his orders. That's all there is to it.

This is true no matter how poorly he fills the position. The office contains the authority, which is legitimated in terms of the same principles of professional education and experience which the teacher uses to legitimate her authority over parents.

But this acceptance of superiority has limits. Teachers have a well-developed conception of just how and toward what ends the principal's authority should be used, and conflict arises when it is used without regard for the teacher's expectations. These expectations are especially clear with regard to the teacher's relationships with parents and pupils, where the principal is expected to act to uphold the teacher's authority regardless of circumstances. Failure to do this produces dissatisfaction and conflict, for such action by the principal is considered one of the most efficient defenses against attack on authority, whether from parents or pupils.

The principal is expected to "back the teacher up"—support her authority—in all cases of parental "interference." This is, for teachers, one of the major criteria of a "good" principal. In

[8] Abridged from Howard S. Becker, "The Teacher in the Authority System of the Public Schools," *Journal of Educational Sociology,* Vol. 27 (November, 1953), pp. 128–141.

this next quotation the teacher reacts to the failure of a principal to provide this:

> That's another thing the teachers have against her. She really can't be counted on to back you up against a child or a parent. She got one of our teachers most irate with her, and I can't say I blame her. The child was being very difficult and it ended up with a conference with the parent, principal, and teacher. And the principal had the nerve to say to the parent that she couldn't understand the difficulty, none of the other teachers who had the child had ever had any trouble. Well, that was nothing but a damn lie, if you'll excuse me. . . . And everybody knew it was a lie. . . . And the principal knew it too, she must have. And yet she had the nerve to stand there and say that in front of the teacher and the parent. She should never have done that at all, even if it was true she shouldn't have said it. (INTERVIEWER: What was the right thing to do?) Well, naturally, what she should have done is to stand behind the teacher all the way. Otherwise, the teacher loses face with the kids and with the parents and that makes it harder for her to keep order or anything from then on.

This necessity for support is independent of the legitimacy of the teacher's action; she can be punished later, but without parents knowing about it. And the principal should use any means necessary to preserve authority, lying himself or supporting the teacher's lies:

> You could always count on him to back you up. If a parent came to school hollering that a teacher had struck her child, Mr. D— would handle it. He'd say, "Why, Mrs. So-and-so, I'm sure you must be mistaken. I can't believe that any of our teachers would do a thing like that. Of course, I'll look into the matter and do what's necessary but I'm sure you've made a mistake. You know how children are." And he'd go on like that until he had talked them out of the whole thing.
>
> Of course the teacher would certainly catch it later. He'd call them down to the office and really give them a tongue

lashing that they wouldn't forget. But he never failed them when it came to parents.

Not all principals live up to this expectation. Their failure to support the teacher is attributed to cowardice, "liberalism," or an unfortunate ability to see both sides of a question. The withholding of support may also, however, be a deliberate gesture of disapproval and punishment. This undermining of the teacher's authority is one of the most extreme and effective sanctions at the principal's command:

> [The teacher had started a class project in which the class, boys and girls, made towels to be given to the parents as Christmas presents.] We were quite well along in our project when in walked this principal one day. And did she give it to me! She wanted to know what the idea was. I told her it was our Christmas project and that I didn't see anything the matter with it. Well, she fussed and fumed. Finally, she said, "All right, you may continue. But I warn you, if there are any complaints by fathers to the Board downtown about one of our teachers making sissies out of their boys you will have to take the full responsibility for it. I'm not going to take any responsibility for this kind of thing." And out she marched.

Teachers expect the same kind of support and defense in their dealings with pupils, again without regard for the justice of any particular student complaint. If the students find the principal a friendly court of appeal, it is much harder for the teacher to maintain control over them.

The amount of threat to authority, in the form of challenges to classroom control, appears to teachers to be directly related to the principal's strictness. Where he fails to act impressively "tough" the school has a restless atmosphere and control over pupils is difficult to attain. The opposite is true where the children know that the principal will support any action of a teacher.

> The children are scared to death of her [the principal]. All she has to do is walk down the hall and let the children

> hear her footsteps and right away the children would perk up and get very attentive. They're really afraid of her. But it's better that way than the other.

Such a principal can materially minimize the discipline problem, and is especially prized in the lower-class school, where this problem is greatest.

The principal provides this solid underpinning for the teachers' authority over pupils by daily acts of "toughness," daily re-affirmations of the intention to keep the children "in line." The following quotation contrasts successful and unsuccessful principal activity in this area:

> For instance, let's take a case where a teacher sends a pupil down to the office. . . . When you send a child down to this new principal, he goes down there and he sits on the bench there. . . . Pretty soon, the clerk needs a messenger and she sees this boy sitting there. Well, she sends him running all over the school. That's no punishment as far as he's concerned. Not at all.
>
> The old principal didn't do things that way. If a child was sent down to the office he knew he was in for a rough time and he didn't like it much. Mr. G— would walk out of his office and look over the children sitting on the bench and I mean he'd look right through them, each one of them. You could just see them shiver when he looked at them. Then he'd walk back in the office and they could see him going over papers, writing. Then, he'd send for them, one at a time. And he'd give them a lecture, a real lecture. Then he'd give them some punishment, like writing an essay on good manners and memorizing it so they could come and recite it to him the next day by heart. Well, that was effective. They didn't like being sent to Mr. G—. When you sent someone there that was the end of it. They didn't relish the idea of going there another time. That's the kind of backing up a teacher likes to feel she can count on.

The principal is expected to support all teachers in this way, even the chronic complainers who do not deserve it:

> If the principal's any good he knows that the complaints of a woman like that don't mean anything but he's got to back her just the same. But he knows that when a teacher is down complaining about students twice a week that there's nothing the matter with the students, there's something the matter with her. And he knows that if a teacher comes down once a semester with a student that the kid has probably committed a real crime, really done something bad. And his punishments will vary accordingly.

The teacher's authority is subject to attack by pupils and may be strengthened or weakened depending on which way the principal throws the weight of his authority. Teachers expect the principal to throw it their way, and provide them with a needed defense.

The need for recognition of their independent professional authority informs teachers' conceptions of the principal's supervisory role. It is legitimate for him to give professional criticism, but only in a way that preserves this professional authority. He should give "constructive" rather than "arbitrary" orders, "ask" rather than "snoop." It is the infringement of authority that is the real distinction in these pairs of terms. For example:

> You see, a principal ought to give you good supervision. He ought to go around and visit his teachers and see how they're doing—come and sit in the room awhile and then if he has any constructive criticism to make, speak to the teacher about it privately later. Not this nagging bitching that some of them go in for, you know what I mean, but real constructive criticism.
>
> But I've seen some of those bastards that would go so far as to really bawl someone out in public. Now that's a terrible thing to do. They don't care who it's in front of, either. It might be a parent, or it might be other teachers, or it might even be the kids. That's terrible, but they actually do it.

Conflict arises when the principal ignores his teachers' need for professional independence and defense against attacks on authority. Both principal and teachers command sanctions which may be used to win such a conflict and establish their definition of the situation: i.e., they have available means for controlling each other's behavior. The principal has, as noted above, the powerful weapon of refusing to support the teacher in crucial situations; but this has the drawback of antagonizing other teachers and, also, is not available to a principal whose trouble with teachers stems from his initial failure to do this.

The principal's administrative functions provide him with his most commonly used sanctions. As administrator he allocates extra work of various kinds, equipment, rooms, and (in the elementary school) pupils to his teachers. In each category, some things are desired by teachers while others are disliked—some rooms are better than others, some equipment newer, etc. By distributing the desired things to a given teacher's disadvantage, the principal can effectively discipline her. A subtle use of such sanctions is seen in this statement:

> Teacher: That woman really used to run the school, too. You had to do just what she said.
>
> Interviewer: What did she do if you "disobeyed"?
>
> Teacher: There were lots of things she could do. She had charge of assigning children to their new rooms when they passed. If she didn't like you she could really make it tough for you. You'd get all the slow children and all the behavior problems, the dregs of the school. After six months of that you'd really know what work meant. She had methods like that.

Such sanctions are ineffective against those few teachers who are either eccentric or determined enough to ignore them. They may also fail in lower-class schools where the teacher does not intend to stay.

The sanctions teachers can apply to a principal who [does not] respect or protect their authority are somewhat less direct. They may just ignore him: "After all the principal gets to be too big a bother, all you have to do is walk in your room and shut the door, and he can't bother you." Another weapon is hardly a weapon at all—making use of the power to request transfer to another school in the system. It achieves its force when many teachers use it, presumably causing higher authorities to question the principal's ability:

> I know of one instance, a principal of that type, practically every teacher in her school asked to leave. Well, you might think that was because of a group that just didn't get along with the new principal. But when three or four sets of teachers go through a school like that, you then know something's wrong.

Finally, the teachers may collectively agree on a line of passive resistance, and just do things their way, without any reference to the principal's desires.

In some cases of extreme conflict, the teachers (some of whom may have been located in the school for a longer period than the principal) may use their connections in the community to create sentiment against the principal. Cooperative action of parents and teachers directed toward the principal's superiors is the teachers' ultimate sanction.

The principal, then, is expected to provide a defense against parental interference and student revolt, by supporting and protecting the teacher whenever her authority is challenged. He is expected, in his supervisory role, to respect the teacher's independence. When he does not do these things a conflict may arise. Both parties to the conflict have at their disposal effective means of controlling the other's behavior, so that the ordinary situation is one of compromise (if there is a dispute at all), with sanctions being used only when the agreed-on boundaries are overstepped.

INSTITUTIONALIZATION

In the study of schools and colleges, we should also note what happens to their machinery over periods of time. A primary process is institutionalization. Schools and colleges, like other organizations, may start out as impersonal tools—organized means of getting something done—but they rarely remain merely that. As we have indicated, informal ties emerge, putting flesh on the formal skeleton. Also, organizations tend to become institutions, in the sociological sense: certain patterns of behavior become firmly established and take on a lasting meaning to participants and supporters. Schools and colleges notably become objects of sentimental attachment; one reason why they resist dying is that they develop a body of people who care enough to fight for the welfare of "their" school. When an organization becomes an end in itself, instead of purely a means of reaching an end, it is then an institution. The Marine Corps is strongly institutionalized—and so is the University of Wisconsin and the Bronx High School of Science.

Organizations become institutionalized in part through the formalizing of procedure. Out of trial and error come practices that are explicitly promoted and codified—in short, are made part of the formal arrangement of work. The practices become routines and the personnel become accustomed to their pace. The routines conserve time and energy, as habits do generally, but they tend also to promote rigidity. If the personnel invest themselves emotionally in their routines, and in this way transform means into ends, then the means becomes fixed, resistant to change when a change in purpose or a change in the environment demands the scrapping of the old and the instituting of something new. Professors may come to love their old lectures, and teachers to feel that certain classroom techniques are a very extension of themselves. Formalization, always necessary to some degree, thus may develop to the point where it impairs the viability of the organization. Because mature organizations so often incorporate a fixed point of view and a particular style of work, leaders in government or business often decide to establish a *new* organization when a new task is on the horizon rather than attempt to change the old. The established units may have their procedures so firmly grooved that they could not develop a fresh approach.

Formalization is a source of the common definition of

bureaucracy as consisting of red tape, buck-passing, and inefficiency. Where procedures are heavily formalized, the client, the customer—or the student—is handled in an invariant manner; assigned to just the right office, given the correct forms, and moved through the appropriate channels, step one, step two, step three. How nice it is from the student's point of view when college registration treats him as a unique individual, considering his case on its own merits, in all its complexity. But the registration that students encounter on large campuses does not offer this face; rather, students are processed in batches through a sequence of steps, shunted from one office to another, with set forms and rules, and with personal identity exchanged for a six-digit number on a registration card.

In general, the institutionalization of schools and colleges is inevitable, necessary, and useful on the one hand, and rigidifying and potentially costly on the other. The problem of leadership presented by institutionalization is to reap its benefits without paying a high price in rigidity and complacency. The problem is not always present: each organization has its own historical time line, with problems changing from one stage of development to the next, and institutionalization becomes a problem only during certain periods.

A new college, especially a self-defined "experimental college," has an air of excitement in its formative years, while all is unformed and fresh and the character of the enterprise is being thrashed out. Then, usually, come years of settling down—a college cannot remain new forever or indefinitely experimental. After a while, the settling down may reach a plateau of equilibrium where nearly everyone is comfortable and satisfied. "We are successful and doing things just about right," becomes the organizational theme, and even the Young Turks in the faculty find little to complain about. Some persons within and outside the college, however, begin to mumble about complacency and to worry about the loss of spirit and excitement compared with the old days. Meanwhile, the college's environment has not held still but has changed in ways that present new problems and new opportunities. The college may reach a stage where it is considerably out of joint, with resources diminishing and unfulfilled demands accumulating. Then the firmness of its institutionalization becomes a problem. The central authorities can either let the organization remain fixed—likely their hands will be tied—or attempt to break the chains of custom and strike out on new ways.

To break with the old is a painful process, generally requiring a sweeping out or swamping of the old personnel. Many schools and colleges are unable to make a major change until confronted by crisis—near bankruptcy or an exodus of staff or an explosive split among key personnel. Crisis is the common condition under which old enterprises are reborn, allowed once more to begin anew with a sense of starting down an uncharted road.

The technological age, with its rapid speed of change, presses hard on most organizations for flexible adaptation and innovation. It dictates that the fixing of organization character through processes of institutionalization will be a problem confronted more frequently by more administrators. The dilemma can be acute: to do a job well requires a strong commitment of personnel and resources, a distinctive effort along a particular line of work; but to make such a commitment is to tie one's hands somewhat for the future. If no distinctive effort is made on the present task, however, in order to maintain flexibility, then the job at hand may be performed inadequately. Combining competence in the present with flexibility for the future taxes managerial inventiveness, especially in agencies that have staffs fixed under tenure or civil service. A rapidly changing environment shortens the time between present competence and future potential incapability.

IDEOLOGY AND IMAGE

Schools and colleges have official ideologies that attempt to state, in the language of uplift and idealism, what is distinctive about their own aims and methods.[9] Such doctrines are an important technique for infusing behavior with long-run meaning and purpose. In spelling out a broad rationale for daily work, an organizational ideology helps to convince the personnel that their efforts are worthwhile, contributing to a valued, common end. The ideology offers the outsider an appealing definition of the organization: "service to the community," "the training of our nation's leadership," "we are a community college," "we train the character as well as the minds of young people."

Such conceptions, often vigorously and continuously voiced, are in part the verbal blankets that cover and warm the cold bed of administrative acts. They may at times be advanced cynically, largely to manipulate loyalties and shape impressions. But successful doctrines are more than that, even when put forward deliberately by an insecure organization to strengthen its appeal and gain support. Take the concept of "service to our state" that many state universities develop as their central ideal. To be effective, this service ideology cannot be restricted to speeches, catalogues, and appeals for money. Some members of the staff will come to feel that acts should live up to the stated ideal, that the university should indeed engage in a wide variety of specific services. Those in a position externally to enforce demands upon the university, the state legislature or an association of farmers, will not be content with empty

[9] This discussion draws upon Philip Selznick, *Leadership in Administration* (Evanston, Illinois: Row, Peterson and Co., 1957), pp. 151–152.

verbal statements but will want the words redeemed in practice, from generous admission of the state's youth to research useful for the state's major industries. The service ideology then comes to color many aspects of university policy, affecting standards of admission, the scope of the curriculum, and the direction of research. One does not "serve" a butter-producing state by research on oleomargarine!

Administrators sometimes use official ideologies to change an organization. A college known for commuting students and teacher education decides it would like to become a residential liberal-arts college. Hardly before opening a dormitory or making any change in the curriculum, the administration begins to speak of the college as residential and liberal-arts, claiming the status to which it aspires. This "claiming in advance" may speed up the desired evolution through changing public impressions, attracting different kinds of students and faculty, encouraging curricular changes. Doctrines used in this fashion may outrun reality to the point where they appear pretentious as well as premature, but when strongly held they provide new guidelines by which to steer and speed change.

Administrative doctrines in education also change as the values of the community change, especially in agencies closely linked to the public. When many parents are interested primarily in the social and emotional development of their children, the case in the United States in recent decades, the public schools are encouraged to adopt a "life-adjustment" philosophy. This outlook in the schools, impelled in part by a philosophy of education developed within the field, found resonance in many neighborhoods. If John Dewey had not lived he would have had to be invented, it has been said, for the schools needed a philosophy that would "fit" the new demands being made upon them—to prepare the young for a world where psychology had come of age, the school population was increasingly diverse in background and ability, and work increasingly demanded the skills of selling, trading, manipulating, and persuading. Now, after sputnik, the public temper has swung back toward the older emphasis on intellectual development, and the schools find the adjustment doctrine an embarrassment.

In many communities, as the "hard" attitude of what was formerly a minority of teachers and parents finds wider support among parents, school administrators come to think otherwise than they once did, and we find them talking the language of special programs for the gifted, tightened standards, foreign languages in the elementary school. Sometimes the talk is pure talk, but often it reflects and impels internal change, even a marked change in some cases. Doctrine and practice in dependent schools, unless heavily institutionalized, change, with some lag, as people's beliefs about the roles of education wax and wane.

In brief, administrative doctrines bear on practice: (a) they rationalize current actions; (b) they unintentionally cause new expectations to arise that must then be met; (c) they are used intentionally to change the character of an organization; (d) they often reflect current environmental pressures, especially in organizations that depend on a broad social base.

Related to an organization's formal statements of its orientation are the impressions held of it by the public. Images of organizations have been little explored outside of consumer research, but images play an increasingly important role in the relations of organizations with their environment. Men act according to the way they perceive, and they act toward organizations on the basis of their impressions of them. Public impressions are important social facts, whether they are accurate or not. They are becoming more important to more organizations since in a complex society impressions gained at some distance increasingly substitute for direct, close contact.

The "organizational portrait" carried in the minds of outsiders looms particularly large in the lives of organizations that have voluntary clienteles which must be renewed from time to time. In these cases, the attracting of clients must be repeated over and over again. Such is the case of colleges. Students can choose among colleges in ways they cannot in the lower grades, where choice is limited mainly to the neighborhood public school and the one or two available private or parochial schools. Colleges also cannot compel students to enroll, where the public schools have compulsory attendance, up to a certain age. In this situation of choice, students, their parents, and other advisors "know" colleges according to what they have heard about them. Public knowledge has it that one college has high standards, another low; one is "Ivy," another a streetcar college; one is pure liberal arts, another a trade school; one a place for the dedicated intellectual, another a place for the beer-drinking, party boy. Such images underplay the diversity present on any campus, and often distort the actual case, but what they offer is a summary, a stereotype, of the campus as a whole—one that guides the choice of schools in many cases.

Self-selection of colleges on the basis of their public images often sets limits within which the colleges make their formal selection.[10] The admissions officer out on a recruiting drive can sometimes change a person's mind, or inform him when he knows little about the college, but admissions personnel find their work constrained by the impressions that have long proceeded them into the countryside. The

10 An extended discussion of this topic can be found in Burton R. Clark, "College Image and Student Selection," in *Selection and Educational Differentiation* (Berkeley: Field Service Center and Center for the Study of Higher Education, 1960), pp. 155–168.

effects of image on selection are strong for small, distinctive schools that claim unique character. They exist in lesser degree for large comprehensive colleges which, if not distinctive in any significant way, are seen by outsiders as members of a class of colleges—"it's a state university," or "you know what a teachers college is like."

Through their effect on recruitment, public images of a college play a key part in an on-going cycle of effects between reputation and student quality. A student body of high academic ability contributes to a public image of institutional quality which draws good students to the college in succeeding years. This interaction of reputation and operational quality occurs similarly for colleges of average and low caliber. Public images thus often have the function of maintaining the institution as it is. Images contribute to a rolling equilibrium by recruiting members similar to those who are lost through graduation: like attracts like through public impressions.

Such is not always the case: images can also lead to a snowballing effect of getting worse or getting better. As the reputation of a college *spreads,* a "positive" image can lead to an upward cycle of attracting better and better students. Similarly, an institution with a widening reputation of mediocrity may find itself in a down cycle, attracting fewer good students and an increased number of poorer ones.

Whether these snowballing effects occur, instead of images maintaining the *status quo,* depends largely on the general state of higher education at the time. When the quantity of students is relatively fixed, most colleges are not on the move and their images tend to conserve them as they are; but when the supply of students is undergoing change, some colleges are in motion, attempting to take advantage of new opportunities or to avoid new disasters.

The situation now found in the United States of rapidly expanding numbers of students has put colleges on the move, many to become much bigger, some to become much better. In this context, rapid upward cycles are possible; and colleges of low to modest reputation that attempt to "sit still" are likely to find themselves in a worsening position. Status among colleges is relative, and public images of one depend considerably on how it looks compared to others. Thus when higher education is stirring, many colleges must scramble to see that the interaction between reputation and organization character leads to a "virtuous" rather than to a "vicious" cycle. The pressures of the technological age on colleges and universities dictate close attention to reputation; even the gaining of research contracts from the government is heavily influenced by overall image.

When we turn to the role played by public images in elementary and secondary education, attention goes less to the self-selection of students and more to financial and moral backing. *Private* elementary and secondary schools, of course, depend considerably on a special reputation to attract students; but since student enrollment is largely provided for the public schools by geographic area, their images function for them primarily in other ways. The support of various community groups, as discussed in Chapter 4, must be maintained; hence, it matters greatly whether these groups have the impression the schools are doing a "good job" and whether their loyalties are enlisted on the basis that the schools are "our schools."

The strongest elements in the public image of American public schools apparently are the views that they are democratic institutions and integral parts of local communities. They are seen as taking in all youth and reflecting local values. On the first point there is little difficulty, since universal education in the lower grades is a fact, firmly grounding the correlated public image. But much controversy arises around the values contained in the school's program. While school authorities continue to reassert the image that local values are faithfully adhered to, public impressions are shaken as some cosmopolitan or advanced outlooks are brought into the schools by new teachers; or as particular community groups are satisfied to the dissatisfaction of others. The public schools, it is little wonder, seek usually to cultivate broad, diverse public images—almost deliberately ambiguous images—in order to appear as all things to all men, and to rationalize their internal heterogeneity.

In brief, public images of educational organizations play an expanding role as society and education become larger and more complex. Organizational anonymity, like personal anonymity, grows in the technological society; more organizations are perceived or "known" at a distance, if at all. Mental portraits increasingly substitute for direct experience, especially for schools and colleges that draw on other than a local constituency, mediating many contacts with outside groups. Images have strong effect when students can choose their school, for then self-selection helps to determine the student body; and behind self-selection lie the images assigned to different schools by various segments of the population. Knowing this, we can better understand why some colleges pay so much attention to their public impressions; why the catalogue of a college so often portrays the campus as the nearest thing to an earthly paradise—ideally situated on a hill overlooking a beautiful valley, combining rural charm with urban convenience, peopled by scholars and dedicated youth of almost cinematic sex appeal.

Chapter 6

Student Culture in College[1]

STUDENTS HAVE always resisted to some degree the authority of the teacher and the learning he attempts to impart. Such resistance has been strong and systematic in American society, deriving from attitudes developed in the home and neighborhood and reinforced in the age groups of the young. Schools and colleges themselves contain subworlds that orient students through their own continuing traditions. Some of these worlds are all that the teacher could ask, with the members seriously pursuing intellectual interests and academic tasks, as well as otherwise supporting the school. But neither in the lower grades nor in college have the norms of academia typically dominated the students; rather nonintellectual and anti-intellectual orientations have prevailed. In this and the following chapter we turn to these students' worlds and look at student orientations and their causes. Here we consider student culture in college; in Chapter 7, student culture in high school.

In viewing student culture, many alternatives present

1 This chapter is based largely on work done jointly by the author and Martin A. Trow, as reported in "Determinants of College Student Subculture," in Theodore M. Newcomb and Everett K. Wilson (eds.), *The Study of College Peer Groups* (forthcoming). I am especially indebted to Trow for the typology of student subcultures.

themselves: we could, for instance, inquire into dating and mating practices. We shall largely bypass the romantic, however, to focus on the development of the mind, seeking to determine the outcome of students' orientations and informal life for the purposes most citizens and educators see as central to the schools. What are the social conditions within schools and colleges of academic achievement? What causes students to be supportive of, indifferent to, or hostile toward the formal purposes of education?

TYPES OF SUBCULTURES

Let us consider some of the orientations toward a college education which are represented on American campuses, and which may be in competition on any one campus. These orientations are held by individual students and they are important elements of student subcultures, or subsystems, where they appear as group norms, shared notions of what constitutes right action and attitude toward a range of experiences confronted in college. In many colleges these subcultures are the prime forces, more important than the classroom in the development of attitudes and values of students.

The Collegiate Subculture

The most widely held stereotype of college life in America pictures the "collegiate subculture," a world of football, fraternities and sororities, dates, cars and drinking, and campus fun. The leading symbols of this subculture are the star athlete, the homecoming queen, and the fraternity dance. A good deal of student life on many campuses revolves around this subculture; it both provides substance for the stereotypes of movies and cartoons and models itself on those stereotypes.

The collegiate subculture has been a strong if not the dominant governor of student life ever since the 1890's. In the period 1880–1910, faculties lost much of the control they previously had over student activities. In this golden age of American history, the philosophy of the gentlemen's C developed and the "side shows" of the campus were elaborated. Membership in fraternities rose from 72,000 to 270,000 in the 25 years after 1890; social clubs emerged to set the social pecking order of many campuses; and football became a fever. College came more and more to be what the undergraduate made it, and in his raccoon coat he chose to make it the life of Joe College.

Today, the fraternities and sororities set the patterns of the collegiate way of life. The activities within their own houses most fully epitomize this subculture; fraternity members also engage heavily in the extracurricular activities of the campus, more than do the independents, and their participation extends their influence. In a recent study of what college students think,[2] fraternity members pointed to the support given the extracurricular activities by the fraternity system:

When we have shape-up sessions they tell you, "You're not going out for enough activities. Better get on it."

Our house is an athletic house. We have the lettermen and we always try to get the fellows who'll make lettermen. We take as pledge-class those who are interested in sports and who look like good bets. And we put the pressure on. We have to keep up our reputation.

Our house is BMOH (Big Man on the Hill). That is, we try to get the wheels. We pledge the ones who look as if they could make it.

I'll tell you frankly, we're a party house. Just out for a good time. We don't rush men to go out for things. I'd say we're the only house on the hill that doesn't.

Many nonfraternal dormitories attempt to model themselves largely after this style of life—from candlelight and song to

2 Rose K. Goldsen, *et al.*, *What College Students Think* (Princeton: D. Van Nostrand Co., Inc., 1960), p. 66.

parade floats and panty raids. The Joe College style, tempered by a latter-day coolness and sophistication, is still the most visible model and often virtually the only model available for new dormitory groups to emulate.

Teachers and courses and grades are in this picture, but somewhat dimly in the background. The fraternities have to make their grade point average, students have to hit the books periodically if they are to get their diplomas, gestures have to be made to the adult world of courses and grades which provide the justification for the collegiate round. As one fraternity man reported:[3]

> Lots of pledges come in with the idea that fraternity life means all fun and no studying. We quickly educate them. Not that we want grinds—no—we try to get them to maintain a respectable average. Nothing very glittering, of course, just respectable.
>
> We try to keep our house's grades up to standard. There's plenty of help for the brothers who fall behind. We have files of old examinations in almost every course that they can use in studying. We even assign certain men to tutor any brothers who need help. They don't have to get super grades. After all, when you get out of college nobody asks what your grades were. Just maintain a decent average.

In content, this system of values and activities is not hostile to the college, to which, in fact it generates strong loyalties and attachments. It is, however, indifferent and resistant to serious demands emanating from the faculty, or parts of it, for an involvement with ideas and issues over and above that required to gain the diploma. One battle cry of the collegiate student is: I have no intention of letting my studies interfere with my college education!

The collegiate subculture is characteristically upper- and upper-middle-class—it takes money and leisure to pursue the busy round of social activities—and flourishes on the resident campuses of big state universities. Commuting stu-

[3] Goldsen, *What College Students Think,* p. 73.

dents, part-time work, intense vocational interests, an urban location, all work against the full flowering of a collegiate subculture; as do student aspirations for graduate or professional school, or more generally, serious intellectual or professional interests on the part of students and faculty.

The Vocational Subculture

The collegiate subculture is made weak on some American campuses, and its influence diminished on others, by the countervailing forces of student poverty and vocationalism. In the state and city colleges, for example, which recruit the ambitious sons and daughters of working-class and lower-middle-class homes, there is simply not enough time or money to support the expensive frivolities of the collegiate subculture. To these students, many of them married, most of them working between 10 and 40 hours a week, college is largely off-the-job training, an organization of courses and credits leading to a diploma and a better job than they could otherwise command. When asked what the principal goal of a college education should be, they will answer "provide vocational training."

The Cornell study of student opinion on eleven campuses (Goldsen, *et al.*) showed that 68 per cent of the working-class students, 58 per cent of the middle-class students, and 49 per cent of the upper-class students, chose this as the primary objective. These figures show both a difference by social class *and* a large amount of acceptance of this educational goal at all class levels. Students who are immediately and narrowly inclined toward job preparation[4] appear in largest numbers in state colleges and technical schools, but they also bulk large at the state universities

[4] Virtually all students are vocationally inclined in one form or another. We speak here of an inclination so direct that it causes the student to conceive of his undergraduate years as primarily a prejob training.

and even in many private colleges that are publicly identified as liberal-arts colleges. Vocational motivation can be combined with the collegiate life, of course, especially for those with money. Vocationalism has its purest expression among those who pull themselves through, financially, by the skin of their teeth.

The vocational students usually have little attachment to the college where they pick up ten credits one semester, six in another, fifteen in the next, according to what they can afford in time and money. For them, college is an adjunct of the world of jobs, and like the participants in the collegiate subculture they are resistant to intellectual demands beyond what is required to pass the courses. To many of these hard-driven students, ideas and scholarship are as much a luxury and distraction as are sports and fraternities. If the symbol of the collegiate subculture is the football weekend, the symbol of this vocationally oriented subculture is the student placement office.

The vocational subculture is likely to have little social unity. Its members interact less with one another than do those caught up in the collegiate subculture; out-of-class relations are diminished, sometimes entirely absent, as students bolt for the streetcar or the parking lot after class. Any ties among students are likely to be clusters of two and three people formed around the major—nursing, engineering, business administration, or whatever it might be. In the extreme, the vocational subculture is supported by an atomized aggregation of students who labor under similar conditions of commuting and poverty, and are similarly oriented toward college as primarily a center of prejob training. Such subcultures are today a major element of almost every public institution of higher education, and can be found in many private colleges and universities as well.

The Academic Subculture

Present on every college campus, dominant on some while marginal and almost invisible on others, is the subculture of "serious students," the academic subculture. The essence of this system of values is its identification with the intellectual concerns of the serious faculty members. These are the students who work hard, get the best grades, but also talk about their course work outside of class and let the world of ideas and knowledge reach them. They are "greasy grinds" in the eyes of the collegiate crowd. Where participants in the collegiate subculture pursue fun, and the job-oriented pursue skills and a diploma, these students pursue knowledge; their symbols are the library and laboratory and seminar. If the faculty members who embody these values also represent the college as a whole, then this academic subculture is both identified with the college and involved in learning. For these students, their attachment to the college is to the institution which supports intellectual values and opportunities for learning; the emotional tie is through the faculty and through campus friends of similar mind and temper. This is the climate encouraged at the academically strongest colleges; and, when colleges aim to upgrade themselves, it is the students already oriented in this direction whom they seek to recruit.

Increasingly, the products of this subculture look forward to graduate work. It is not surprising that they identify strongly with the faculty and seek to take on scholarly and scientific habits as part of their socialization to future professional roles. These students are often oriented toward vocations, but not so immediately or narrowly as those who hold the consumer-vocational values described above. When asked what goal of college education is most important to them, students of the academic subculture chose "a basic general education and appreciation of ideas" more often than "provide vocational training." In any case, it is not necessary to decide whether they are concerned with their studies more for the sake of learning than because of their career ambitions. The distinctive qualities of this group are (a) they are seriously pursuing ideas beyond the minimum required for passing and graduation, and (b) they identify themselves with their college and its faculty.

The Nonconformist Subculture

It is in this latter respect, identification with the college, that "nonconformist," "intellectual," "radical," "alienated," "bohemian" students differ most sharply from their serious academic classmates. Some kind of nonconformist subculture exists in many of the best small liberal-arts colleges and in a niche of the undergraduate world on the large university and state-college campuses. These students are often deeply "concerned," in part with the ideas they encounter in the classroom, but more largely with issues current in the art, literature, and politics of the wider adult society. To a greater degree than the academically oriented, these students use off-campus groups and currents of thought as points of reference over against the official college. Often critical of the "establishment," they seek to be independent.

The distinctive quality of this student style is a rather aggressive nonconformism, which usually includes a critical detachment from the college they attend and a general hostility to the college administration. The forms this style takes vary from campus to campus, but where it exists it has a visibility and influence far beyond its usually tiny, fluid membership. Its significance lies in offering a home, an alternative, to the rebellious student seeking a distinctive identity in keeping with his own temperament and experience; in a sense it provides some *intellectual* substance to the idealism and rebelliousness generated in adolescence in some parts of American society. Where the preceding three types of students pursue fun, a diploma, and knowledge, respectively, the nonconformist students pursue an identity, not as a by-product but as the primary and often self-conscious aim of their education. They adopt a distinctive style—of dress, speech, attitude—that in itself partially represents the identity they seek. Their most notable symbols recently have been beards and bare feet, and they are the great unwashed in the eyes of their more conforming classmates.

These four types of subcultures emerge analytically from the combination of two factors: (a) the degree to which students are involved with ideas, and (b) the extent to which students identify with their college:

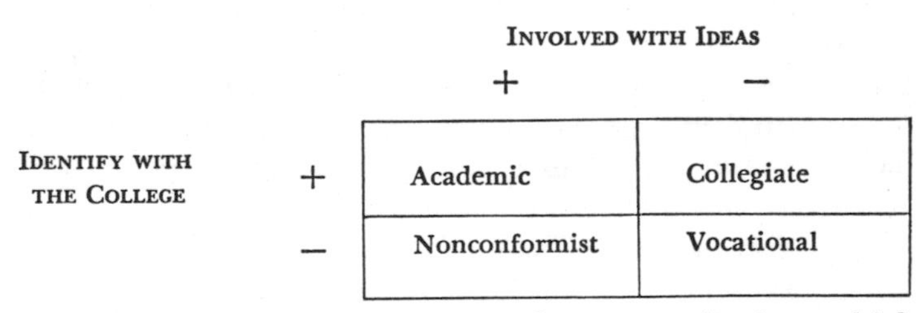

		Involved with Ideas +	Involved with Ideas −
Identify with the College	+	Academic	Collegiate
	−	Nonconformist	Vocational

These subcultures are systems of norms and values which overlap and flow into one another on any campus. They vary in strength in different types of colleges; they are reflected in individuals in various blends.[5] The question is: What determines their relative weight? One set of determiners lies in the resources that students possess—material, moral, intellectual, emotional—when they enter college. Their resources are largely determined by the kinds of life experience they have had, and these are shaped by the

[5] Also, as broad abstractions, these four "subcultures" oversimplify; and, as pure types, they picture the extreme in each case. The subcultures that flourish on any one college campus may blend elements from several types—the collegiate and the academic, for instance—and may contain other important elements not discussed here. In short, four analytical categories do not exhaust reality.

statuses they and their parents hold in the larger society. Other conditions determining the strength and balance of the student subcultures are found in the colleges themselves: their historical development, their climate of values, their faculty and administrative structure, and the campus environment thus provided for student life. We will first examine briefly some features of student background and then take up more extensively the college itself.

THE SOCIETY AS DETERMINANT

Among the broad forces affecting student subcultures are the values regarding higher education held in different parts of the population—notions of what a college is and ought to be. These values are influenced by changing requirements of the occupational structure, which in turn reflect the changing character of a society's major institutions. We reviewed in Chapter 2 the growth of large-scale enterprise, the concomitant growth of technical, managerial, and professional occupations, and the trend toward longer schooling. More students now than in past decades find that bureaucratic career lines dominate the postcollege horizon, and more plan to pursue postgraduate studies. At Yale, for example, the proportion going on to graduate or professional school changed from about 20 per cent in 1920 to about 50 per cent in 1950 and over 75 per cent in 1960.[6] The students going on know that deans and graduate faculties will be reviewing their undergraduate records; the job interviewers from corporations in growing numbers also show a close interest in the transcripts which record college performance.

The sobering effect of these anticipated scrutinies on campus activities and relationships is still escaped by some students. The boy who envisions a place for himself in his

[6] *The New York Times,* June 5, 1960.

father's automobile agency or other small business can throw himself into the fun of the collegiate subculture with a lighter heart than the boy whose record will be examined by the corporate recruiter or graduate-school dean. But the number of students who can afford to ignore the record is diminishing.

As a result of this situation, and of other tendencies in the greater society and the college, the subculture of big-time sports and fraternity weekends that has long provided the dominant image of college life is now in decline. "As academic pressures are stepped up, students have less time to rehearse cancan numbers for variety shows, hunt down floodlights to illuminate fifty-foot homecoming signs, and fashion castles out of tin foil for floats. The result: any number of traditional extracurricular activities are being scrapped."[7] Those who attempt to meet the stronger academic demands while keeping up the old collegiate routine are promising candidates for mononucleosis.

This diminishing of the collegiate subculture has been called "creeping asceticism" by a Princeton man. Clearly, the rapid academic upgrading of leading private colleges in the last decade has seriously undermined the collegiate subculture on these campuses. The fraternities on many campuses, public and private, are moving away from the "rah-rah" life; this evolution has gone so far on a few state-university campuses that the prestige of a fraternity rests on members making the highest possible grade average. While the collegiate subculture is in no danger of extinction, especially on its state-university preserves, the sober demands of the technological revolution, the Cold War, and large organization are having the effect of strengthening the academic and the vocational subcultures, while reducing the prestige and appeal of the collegiate.

7 "Is Apathy on the Way Out?" *Mademoiselle,* May, 1960.

The vocational subculture is also encouraged by the extension of opportunity for higher education to lower social strata. We have indicated that the sons and daughters of the working class and the lower middle class who now go to college in increasing numbers often see college in instrumental terms, as the place where they can gain the skills and diplomas that will earn them good jobs. When these students go, as so many of them do, to large campuses that lack a strong intellectual tradition, then the vocational subculture flourishes. Upper-middle-class students, on the other hand, can afford the luxury of an interest in ideas somewhat more often, as they also can afford the luxury of the collegiate subculture and its fun morality. Which way they go depends on the intellectual climate in their homes, their own academic skills, their occupational aspirations, and the kind of college they enter.

Thus such social forces as the bureaucratization of organization and the democratization of education work to modify where the college population comes from and where the students go after graduation. Origins and destinies, in turn, influence what the students seek in college and how they use their college years—and thus affect the student subcultures. Broadly, lower social origins and modest aspirations for job security, especially where the Bachelor's degree will be enough, predispose students to take a vocational stance toward their college studies; higher origins and aspirations for the intellectual occupations and professions incline some students toward the academic subculture.

This picture oversimplifies, but it helps to link broad trends in the general society to the distribution of student subcultures on American campuses and how this distribution is likely to change. Insofar as skills and formal knowledge grow in importance—as they are—and as more and more students of lower social origins go to college—as they do—the vocational and academic orientations grow at the expense of the collegiate.

THE COLLEGE AS DETERMINANT

We now turn to the campus context in which student groups arise, persist, and change, to inquire into organizational reasons why student subcultures assume particular contents. What are some of the organizational conditions that promote student commitment, indifference, or hostility to intellectual effort? Here we shall extend the organizational analysis of Chapter 5 by showing how major features of a college affect the student realm.

Purpose of the College

Student subcultures are located within larger systems that vary widely in purpose, for American colleges are up to quite different things. At one time most of the colleges were alike in being an arm of a church and were internally unified by their religious purpose. But as they were secularized in the nineteenth century, the colleges became more diverse, many of them shed religious control, and they lost their internal unity. The intrusion of science in the curriculum also broke the fixed classical pattern of study. The advent of the state university in the last half of the nineteenth century greatly accelerated the diversifying and fragmenting of purpose, and the trend toward diversity between and within colleges has continued in the twentieth century.

The most important division in purpose in the middle of the twentieth century seems no longer to lie between the secular and the sacred, but between the single-purpose colleges intent on providing a liberal education and the multipurpose campuses that serve diverse interests. Most colleges that restrict their effort largely to the liberal arts are private and four-year;[8] the comprehensive, service institutions are predominantly public, and include as major forms the state university, the four-year state college, and the two-year junior college. Although the comprehensive enterprises dominate the American scene in student numbers, the liberal-arts centers possess an older tradition and stand high in public esteem.

In the colleges committed to liberal education, the academic and collegiate orientations have long competed for the time and energy of the student, with the vocational and the nonconformist largely excluded. Students have readily identified themselves with these colleges; the conflict has come over whether they would primarily study or play, be seriously interested in the traditional curriculum or develop their character through sports, women, and leisure. The academic intentions of these colleges in the past were often diluted by contrary student impulses and compromised by necessity.

Liberal-arts colleges have been enormously competitive; like businesses, many have been pushed to the wall by shortages of patrons and money. Out of 516 colleges established in 16 states before the Civil War, only 104, or 19 per cent, survived. In Ohio, the survivors were 17 out of 43; in Missouri, 8 out of 85; in Texas, only 2 out of 40. "Physically, the great continental settlement of the United States in the pre-Civil War era was carried out over the graves of pioneers; intellectually, over the bones of dead colleges."[9] Liberal-arts colleges throughout the nineteenth century, both religious and secular, faced not only the competition of their *bona fide* neighbors but also were perpetually

[8] This is not to say the reverse, that all private colleges are genuine liberal-arts colleges. Many that are liberal-arts in name are heavily vocational; others are primarily centers of religious indoctrination.

[9] Hofstadter, in Richard Hofstadter and Walter P. Metzger, *The Development of Academic Freedom in the United States* (New York: Columbia University Press, 1955), pp. 211–212.

plagued by the competition of fly-by-night colleges. After 1870, when the fixed classical curriculum gave way to optional curricula and student choice of courses, the colleges especially had to vie with one another in being attractive to students. In this competition, in short, most of the colleges prepared to offer youth what it wanted. College came more and more to be what the undergraduate made it as student choice took over, and the expectations and controls of the authorities were adjusted to what the market would tolerate.

Students came ready to prolong adolescent play and participate in the emerging collegiate subculture; the authority of officials over their play was checked by the need to hold their limited clientele if there were to be a college at all. For this reason, among others, the collegiate subculture has predominated in the liberal-arts college during most of the last 75 to 100 years other than (a) where a stern religiosity has been maintained, or (b) the college has been able to select and hold an especially serious segment of the college-going population. For a college to approach the ideal of the secular liberal-arts college it is necessary to obtain the kinds of students and patrons who will support the intellectual goals over the competing collegiate interests. A few colleges have built such social bases through heroic effort. For most colleges, however, containment of the collegiate subculture has depended on the state of the market, on such a high demand for entry into college that the selection of serious, high-ability students becomes a genuine alternative.

The universities and colleges committed to servicing the needs of cities, states, and other broad publics have long had vocational subcultures contending and mixing with the collegiate and the academic, especially in recent decades. Vocational values in the student body have been encouraged by the willingness of the college itself to meet the training requirements of specific fields of work. The changing nature of our occupations, especially the professionalization previously remarked, affects college programs and student values:[10]

> The chief characteristic of man's work in our time is that all occupations tend to become professions. And these professions, following the example of medicine and law in past centuries, tend to become academic subjects. That is, the practices become codified, they are written up in textbooks, courses are given, specialties proliferate, and degrees multiply. Work and study fade into each other and are deemed equivalent. Young men of business toil at a Ph.D. in marketing, real estate operators write theses, personnel managers take and learn to give tests, accountants, diplomats, writers of advertising copy are taught in universities. In short, every worldly youth is poring over a book in hopes of passing into an office. That great aim is expressed by the verb: *to qualify.*

In 1958 the three big vocational fields, business, education, and engineering, accounted for almost half (48 per cent) of all the Bachelor's and first professional degrees awarded by American colleges and universities. In the same year, the number of Bachelor's degrees awarded in business alone outnumbered the degrees in English, history, the physical sciences, mathematics, and all modern foreign languages combined.[11]

Thus if we ask why large numbers of students are vocationally oriented in certain state colleges and universities, a part of the answer is that these enterprises themselves are strongly and directly committed to occupational-professional training. Students would need to deviate widely from their college environment if they were to become involved in

[10] Jacques Barzun, "Where are the Disciples?" *Antioch Review,* Vol. 20 (Spring, 1960), pp. 5–14.

[11] *A Fact Book on Higher Education* (Washington, D.C.: American Council on Education, n.d.).

academic subcultures while majoring in such fields as accounting and marketing. The purposes and practices of the service college are a basic condition of student vocationalism.

The broad curriculum of the comprehensive college also contains some easy as well as practical offerings. Any college, but especially the large university, is a congeries of hard and soft fields; the soft majors reduce the academic pressure on students, lightening the work load for large numbers and allowing some to remain in college who otherwise would fail. The softer majors have been important curricular props to the collegiate subculture. The physical-education major for athletes and the home-economics program for the beauty queen are simply extreme cases of a general phenomenon, where the curriculum provides special educational loci for those primarily oriented to the collegiate subculture, as well as those oriented to vocational consumership. Soft majors and low standards in sectors of the comprehensive campus amount to a mass democratic version of the older tradition of the "gentlemen's C."

Administrative Interests

How do the interests of college administrators bear on student subcultures? Like management elsewhere, one interest lies in the orderly conduct of internal affairs. College managers in this country are charged with regulating systems in which hundreds of young men and women are simultaneously clients, participants, and wards; as a result, the proper ordering of students looms large in their affairs. Administrators also bear the brunt of demands made by outsiders, from parental complaint about the care and feeding of a particular student to the often vigorous efforts of major interest groups, such as the alumni or local businessmen, to shape the outlook of the college. The administration is also responsible for college finances and the recruitment of students. In short, it needs to know how to placate a public, find a donor, or cultivate a constituency.

The interests of the administration, and segments of the faculty, in financial support, student supply, internal order, and public approval, other things aside, have favored "conservative" student subcultures in the majority of colleges—subcultures that contain perspectives rather than stimulate them, subcultures of custodial care rather than of intellectual ferment. Collegiate subcultures are ordinarily seen as frustrations of academic purpose that college staffs, administrators and faculty alike, have long labored to overcome. But these collegiate subcultures have certain conveniences: they are routine, predictable, and acceptable to important constituencies; and they are not only condoned but officially supported by administrators and influential segments of the faculty on many campuses.

Consider student government in this regard. A collegiate student government is not dangerous administratively, since it avoids controversial ideas and political action. Its main interests are social and it serves administrative needs in helping to monitor student social activities. The surveillance of students' morals that is expected of college administrations by outsiders is a time-consuming task, one that in the first instance is delegated to an administrative unit, usually the dean of students' office, that stands apart from the faculty. In turn, the routine work of policing student life is further delegated to the student council, the interfraternity council, the individual student house; the making and enforcing of rules at this level is supervised and coordinated through an officialdom of assistant deans, housemothers, and hall advisors. When such student organizations are primarily oriented toward the routine social problems of the student community, they can serve as a grass-roots arm of the official control system.

At most colleges in the United States, student government

is either explicitly or implicitly considered by officials to be an integral part of the administration. One university that makes an explicit definition states: "Student governments are established by the University for the purpose of conducting student affairs on the campuses." The governments have their power through a "delegation of University administrative authority." This means on controversial issues that: "The student government, as any other integral part of the University administration, must also refrain from taking positions on such issues." The collegiate and vocationally oriented students are more likely to accept this definition than are those who are intellectually inclined. The vocationals are not interested, the collegiates care only that their social life not be too greatly hampered; academics and nonconformists, interested in ideas, may or may not be interested in student government, but when they are they tend to relate it to outside issues, hence involve it in "politics."

The tendency of liberal intellectual students to turn a student government into a political unit, taking stands on controversial issues, sharply conflicts with the desire of administrators to use it as an administrative unit, one that works only on campus and within prescribed areas of nonpolitical activity. The kind of student government most threatening to administration is one entailing *serious* political involvement, as is so often found in Europe and other parts of the world, for then a subsystem of the college will take stands on issues and enter into alliances that irritate segments of the outside community, including those which are sources of financial and moral support.

Powerful traditions and outside groups also work to convince college administrations—and faculties—that collegiate subcultures have their justification. The collegiate life has long prepared students socially for business and the professions; it has been supported by alumni associations, national fraternal organizations, and spectator publics; and it has been the style of life expected of "kids" in college. Academic, nonconformist, and vocational subcultures, in contrast, have not had such widespread social and cultural supports. At the same time, internally, the collegiate subculture has been a reasonably well-ordered system of adolescent play and social development, with problems of control taking the form of sanctions against disreputable social acts that come to public view. A tradition that is publicly supported and internally orderly is not easily laid aside; unless powerful counterforces enter, there will be good reasons to condone it.

Administrative interest in internal order and external equilibrium has also supported the big-time sports aspect of the collegiate subculture. A big intercollegiate sports program centering around football serves in a number of ways. For one thing, it organizes and channels the energies and high spirits of young men in reasonably orderly and nonviolent ways. The early history of American colleges, before the advent of organized sports, was full of student violence, directed at each other, at the faculty, the institution, and the "townies."[12] Brawls, riots, even knifings and shootings, were common; the policing of student life, the sheer maintenance of order, was a major and onerous task of the faculties and administrators. Intramural sports drain off some of the high spirits and physical aggressiveness; intercollegiate sports do that and more: they encourage strong feelings of local patriotism, of identification with the institution over against "the enemy," and thus focus aggressive feelings outward, away from the college and its staff, at the same time that they confine it within certain rules of the game. Moreover, the powerful identifications thus promoted become the basis of continuing ties between the institution

[12] Ernest Earnest, *Academic Procession* (Indianapolis: Bobbs-Merrill, 1953), pp. 102–106.

and its alumni. For many alumni, the football team is the most important continuing link to alma mater and reinforcement for their college loyalties—a link for which many colleges have been unable to find an intellectual substitute. Loyal and active alumni are a primary source of funds for private colleges, and of both funds and political support for public colleges and universities. If this is so, it takes strong alternative sources of support, or a sports program running heavily in the red, or strong purposes in conflict with big-time sports, to cause administrators to reduce an already established big-time sports program.

We have become so accustomed to the main extracurricular features of colleges and universities that it becomes difficult to see clearly what an unusual element they constitute in an educational institution. The extracurricular staff is strongly linked to outside groups and is often a separate state within the university; the responsibilities of the athletic director orient him toward alumni and the sports gate. Much of the extracurricular is public relations, and is covered in the sports section and social pages of the newspaper rather than as educational news. Since the extracurricular activities hook into the mass media and the entertainment world, the activities take on some of their coloration—the star system, for example. Many universities are known to the broad public more through the noted coach and the star athlete than through the president and the combined faculty.

In sum, a student government that restricts itself to student social life and a sports program that excites large numbers of students and outsiders is likely to find favor with administrators whose roles insist that they reduce student disorderliness and seek support among nonintellectual groups externally. When intercollegiate sports first began, the reduction of student disorder was the principal basis for administrative support of organized games. But as these sports became spectator sports, public relations became the most important source of the encouragement the collegiate subculture has received from many administrators. This support is probably most vigorous and enthusiastic when, additionally, the college officials share some of the sentiments of the alumni—their distaste for political radicalism, intellectuality, beards and bare feet.

The most important counterforce today to collegiate adaptation by the administration and the faculty is the greatly increased number of recruits. Many colleges are moving into a relatively permanent condition of student glut, a situation that diminishes their dependence on traditional constituencies and gives them greater freedom to change. Before 1945, even the elite colleges of the country were generally constrained by limited applications. Prestige colleges before World War II usually had at best only three contenders for every two places; in 1959 they averaged about four applicants per place. Amherst, for example, had 371 applicants for 232 openings in 1941, a ratio of 1.6 to one, but in 1959 was able to choose among 1,677 applicants to fill 259 openings, or 6.5 to one. Princeton had 925 applicants for 644 seats in 1941 (1.4 to one); 3,213 for 757 in 1959 (4.2 to one).[13] Princeton officials have reported that from 1921 to 1941 the college essentially had no choice, never refusing admission "to boys with good character testimonials and adequate scholastic preparation."[14] In contrast, the colleges of modest to high reputation are today in an economy of abundance that permits selection for high aptitude and seriousness and a stiffening of the requirements for completion.

Colleges all down the line are in the position of being able

[13] Lawrence Bloomgarden, "Our Changing Elite Colleges," *Commentary,* Vol. 29 (February, 1960), pp. 150–154.

[14] W. Jacobs, "Need More Diversity," *Princeton Alumni Weekly,* (February 7, 1958), p. 11.

to take a tougher line in selection and retention, if they wish to do so. Colleges in this situation of plenty are encouraged to use academic aptitude and achievement as *the* selection criteria, for a number of reasons: college staffs prefer intelligent students; there is increased interest nationally in utilizing talent; and these criteria seem legitimate and fair in light of democratic belief in equality of opportunity. By widening administrative discretion in selecting and retaining students, heavy demand leaves administrators freer to respond to their own inclinations toward quality, to faculty desires for a tougher tone, and to public calls for the pursuit of excellence. In addition, the national temper since World War II has encouraged college officials to become impatient with the traditional "rah-rah" form of collegiate subculture, which increasingly is seen as a foolish luxury that the seriousness of international tension no longer allows colleges to afford. "Buckle down Winsocki," becomes simply "buckle down." The collegiate subculture has also lost some of its appeal as a mechanism for controlling student energies, as the academically and vocationally oriented students of today increasingly discipline themselves.

Faculty Orientations

In order to perform effectively, a college usually needs diverse kinds of work performed by its faculty; these include the teaching and advising of students, a hand in administration, and scholarly study or research. Colleges vary in what efforts they reward most heavily, with four-year colleges largely rewarding attention to the student and universities rewarding orientation to one's discipline or profession. The kind of professor idealized in the small liberal-arts college may be the teacher-scholar, the teacher-counselor-friend, or just plain teacher, but in any case the norm emphasizes teaching and points to the student; in these colleges, the undergraduate is what the whole show is largely about. But the university, on the other hand, is involved in many other operations, being primarily a center of research, scholarship, and professional training. Undergraduate teaching has relatively low standing compared to the other operations, and close attention to the education of the individual undergraduate is not generally a prominent part of the professor model, as it is viewed from within the ranks. There are few logs with a teacher at one end and a student at the other in the undergraduate sector of large universities.

The faculty incentive system thus bears sharply on student subcultures. The interests of faculty members vary from the single purpose of shaping the undergraduate student to a complex of interests in which the student plays a small part. At one extreme there is the teacher who deeply involves himself in the lives of students, seeing them frequently and informally in diverse situations and being on call at any hour for advice and support. For such locally oriented teachers, "their" college is a way of life, for their families as well as for themselves. Here faculty interests encourage an interpenetration of faculty and student subcultures. At the other extreme is the professor who teaches as little as possible and then is off to interests that separate him from students, often but not always the pursuit of research and scholarly writing. These interests reflect an orientation to the cosmopolitan world of scholarship, science, and distant peers, and a career pattern of movement from college to college.[15] Such interests tend to reduce faculty-student relations to formal interaction in the classroom. Cosmopolitan interests are an important source of the

[15] Alvin W. Gouldner, "Cosmopolitans and Locals: Toward an Analysis of Latent Social Roles," Parts I and II, *Administrative Science Quarterly*, Vol. 2 (December, 1957, and March, 1958), pp. 281–306 and 444–480.

schism between faculty and student subcultures typically found in the university. In pulling the faculty away from the students, these professional interests promote autonomous student subcultures whose content is little affected by the faculty. These separate worlds of the students are shaped largely by their own interests. These may be intellectual, as is often the case around European universities, with serious students modeling themselves after the distant, professionally committed faculty. In this country, however, the interests have been strongly collegiate and vocational, and the autonomy of the student subculture blunts contrary influences from the faculty.

In the strain between professionalism and localism in faculty interests, between an orientation to a far-flung discipline and a commitment to the local college and student, some faculty members work out a compromise whereby they have many avenues of contact with students while sustaining a professionally rewarding career. A few such men are found in the better small colleges, and are afforded high status because they are both professionally competent and locally committed. They are also found in the large universities, where they receive somewhat less acclaim since involvement with undergraduates is less esteemed. In general, however, most faculty members do not balance these interests in a rough parity, but come down heavily on interests rewarded by the organization and promising for the career. The faculties of small colleges tend to be strongholds of personal, particular relations with students; university staffs, centers of impersonal relations and universal criteria. The one generally produces some faculty understanding and penetration of student life; the other is based on and reinforces social distance between faculty and students. In case this account seems unduly romantic about small colleges, however, it should be pointed out that many small colleges appear to be societies of containment, where weak faculties go along with adolescent play in return for obedience to traditional belief and morality.

The trends in higher education of an advanced technological age are furthering the differentiation between those who attend closely to students and those who do not, within faculties and between them. As the ideal of the expert ascends over the ideal of the cultivated man, liberal-arts colleges as well as universities move toward the specialist-professor and the prespecialist student. The training of students as experts requires little attention to their life outside the classroom and laboratory; and the specialist type of faculty man cares less about student life and its influence on character than the older faculty type who was, or thought he was, a cultivated man.

Size and Complexity

The trend in Western society toward increasing size and complexity in formal organization is apparent in American higher education: a large college before the Civil War had 600 students and most were much smaller, while today central campuses of state universities run to 20,000 and over. Large scale in college organization is permanently with us, campuses of over several thousand students accommodating the vast majority of college students. For the form and content of student life, no other trend means as much.

In large organizations that work on people rather than on products, thousands of individuals must be routinely admitted, classified, treated, and ejected. This is generally done by routinizing procedures and processing people in batches; on the large campus, impersonal batching is reflected in the registration line, the objective test, and the mass graduation. With increasing size, the faculty member also usually relates to more students in the classroom than ever before but interacts less with the individual student outside the classroom. Unless the new techniques of the televised appearance and the taped lecture are carefully handled, students need a special appointment or even a trip out of town in order to meet the man. Mass handling, in turn, discourages serious concern with ideas on the part of most students. As the anonymous student in the large class has long known, the class work that becomes routinized can be completed without serious thought—"copy it down and feed it back." We can hypothesize that large scale in colleges best fits a vocational-consumer usage, and primarily promotes vocational subcultures.

The tendency for increasing size to weaken social ties, turning groups into aggregations, in itself leads toward the atomized vocational subcultures. Conversely, vocationalism encourages growth in size and complexity. Business associations, professional bodies, and other interest groups that see the college as a training center encourage colleges to proliferate occupational curricula; parents and students mindful of upward mobility seek broad admission and occupational preparation in a host of fields. Occupational training in a complex, technological society is efficiently handled by large enterprises tooled to train large numbers in diverse fields.

If increasing scale primarily promotes vocational subcultures, it secondarily supports the continuation of collegiate subcultures, this principally through weakening the connections between the academic and the social. Large scale tends to separate work from nonwork, teaching and learning from what goes on outside the lecture hall. Student life is left free to develop aside from the academic structures, its content filled in by student interests. Thus, size of institution and professional faculty interests work toward the same outcome in this regard.

As previously noted, the interests of most American college students are not strongly intellectual, for they are products of a society and an earlier training in which intellectual values are marginal rather than central. Many of those who are most intellectually inclined seek the small schools that have a liberal-arts image. Those finding their way to the large institutions have predominantly a vocational interest, with an additional or alternative inclination to have fun, college-style, before work and marriage. The collegiate world, in its less "rah-rah" forms, also continues to receive some administrative support in the very large places for the help it gives in solving the problems of student housing and social activity. Too, the collegiate way of life also helps to soften the harsh contours of vocationalism, offering some leisurely play around the edges of the campus, and making the large college appear more like its smaller prestigeful predecessors.

The scale of the college and the presence or absence of housing facilities may well be the most important determinants of where colleges fall along a continuum from community to bureaucracy. At the extreme of community, approached principally in the small residential campus, the interaction of students, faculty, and administration is intense and informal; judgments are particular to the person, as faculty and students respond to one another as personalities—"she's bright but erratic, and would profit from work with . . ." The individual is known across the system; the death of a student or professor is a campus event. Importantly, social and academic activity are integrated. Here the faculty has some chance to shape student culture and educate liberally through personal influence and example. But for occupational training in a complex society, the small, intimate academic communities are unspecialized, expensive, and thought by many to be inappropriately oriented.

The bureaucratic end of the continuum is reached chiefly through large size and off-campus living. Here interaction is formal and segmented, universal criteria are used throughout the system, to judge impersonally and objectively, and academic activity is separated from the social. Teaching and studying are jobs, the personality of the student is little involved, and death is an announcement in the newspaper. Such conditions are not favorable for liberal education but rather for occupational training; the college can offer expert instruction and service in a large number of fields.

Before the advent of the university in the last quarter of the nineteenth century, the American college apparently approximated a community: "Students sat in the same classes together, met daily in chapel for instruction and reproof, shared common study hours in a common dormitory, and grumblingly observed—or surreptitiously violated —the same code of behavior . . ."[16] With common experience and unitary code, student life tended toward the primary relations characteristic of a natural community. This, together with close supervision by faculty and administration, insured some interaction of the academic and the social, with the interaction leading to violent reaction as well as to peaceful integration and control. Whatever else they may or may not have been, such tightly knit colleges appear to have been character-shaping settings. But the increasing scale of organization after 1875 worked to transform colleges from communities to bureaucracies, removing the student from prolonged, extensive contact with individual faculty and putting him more into a succession of briefer contacts with a large, specialized staff. Direct personal control of the faculty member over the student, in the dormitory as well as the classroom, has gradually given way to indirect, impersonal control of a bureaucratic staff;

16 G. P. Schmidt, *The Liberal Arts College* (New Brunswick, N.J.: Rutgers University Press, 1957), p. 194.

for example, the dean of students' office regulating study and play in the dormitory.

Sheer size, while important, is not an unequivocal determinant, however. The *absolute* size of colleges and universities can be misleading, for the effect of size on interpersonal relations and student culture changes markedly with the nature of the *organization substructure*. Harvard's house system clearly "reduces" its size, since a student belongs to a relatively small house as well as to the university as a whole; and some state universities are psychologically and socially smaller than others of similar size because of the way that campus subunits ("colleges," "houses") substructure an otherwise loose aggregation. Some substructures provide groups small enough to encourage networks of face-to-face relationships and to prevent the "we-they" dichotomy between the students and the faculty that inheres in large scale. They offer systems of action that are more easily identified and comprehended, and this can be quite important to the adolescent not long removed from the high school and the family. At the same time that the student participates in the smaller sector, the large campus as a whole may also offer a cosmopolitan environment in which he can explore a wide range of experiences.

Most huge universities have developed little substructure along these or other lines. The faculties have not been markedly interested, their attention diverted by other commitments, while college managements and outside supporters have held "logics" of economy and efficiency that hold back dormitory construction and the decentralizing of a campus into distinctive subunits. Paradoxically, many small colleges worry about the consequences of size every time they contemplate expanding by one or two hundred students, for they are concerned that the existing character of the campus, especially the closeness of personal relations, will be altered.

One answer offered by small colleges to the problem of how to grow and yet stay small is a federation of colleges—essentially a multiplication of small, distinct units rather than the continued growth of one. The five colleges of the Pomona-Claremont complex in California are one example; another is Wesleyan University in Connecticut, which is attempting a reorganization that will allow the enterprise as a whole to grow larger, while newly established "colleges" involve the student in smaller systems of activity focused on a set of related disciplines. All large universities have units called colleges, but in most cases these are largely paper assignments for students. We can say that substructures are real when they have real consequences, changing the nature of involvement. A set of subcolleges on a comprehensive campus may enable students and faculty to keep one another in view and share some academic interests, important conditions of academic student subculture where collegiate fun and vocationalism come naturally. Dormitories and fraternities may also possibly serve in this way.

Another aspect of college scale is rate of growth, and this is especially important as the public colleges of the nation move into a period of rapid expansion. Slow growth permits the assimilation of the new into the old; for example, new faculty members may be acculturated, slowly and undeliberately, to the special values and customs of a college. Rapid growth, on the other hand, reduces the likelihood that traditional character will absorb and control the new elements. New faculty come along so fast that there is not time for the old staff to orient them; administrative energies are pre-empted by the problems of growth, such as recruiting personnel and expanding facilities to accommodate annually an increase in enrollment of 500 to 1,000. The existing balance of student subcultures is also seriously modified. The student subcultures that are disrupted are commonly either primarily academic or collegiate; the outcome of rapid growth in either case is predictably an increase in the vocational-consumer use of college, centering for faculty and students alike on the means of career achievement in the general society.

Selection and Retention

We may ask of a college: What does it take to get in, survive, and get out in good standing? The answers are very different across the landscape of American higher education, for selectivity varies from none to severe and the standards of performance range from subliminal to savage. These differences affect the strength and balance of the student subcultures. Relatively high academic selectivity tends to make the academic subculture dominant. Such selection at least brings students with the potential for difficult study and vigorous intellectual life; to boot, the highly selective college may also scan the faces and records of its applicants for marks of serious attitude. In contrast, the unselective college will normally attract a large number of students whose limited ability restricts the possibility of their grappling with complicated issues and ideas. These are boys and girls who also in their previous schooling have not been encouraged toward academic values by the rewards of high performance.

Thus sharp selection adds greatly to the power of the official staff in shaping student subcultures so that they embody academic values. *Restraint by recruitment* is perhaps the most important means of control by college officials over the values and practices of students; conversely, little or no selection greatly reduces the general influence of the official establishment. The extremes of selection are now found in the public junior college, where open-door admission permits students of all levels of ability and achievement to enter, and in the several dozen elite private colleges and universities where applicants heavily outnumber entrants and most students are in the upper 10 per cent of college students in ability.

The length of time that students in good standing spend in a single college also varies. In the elite private colleges, 75 to 90 per cent of the students typically sustain four continuous years and graduate. In state universities, 40 to 60 per cent generally survive, and some of these students are in and out, taking five to eight years. State colleges, with their working students, have even more movement in and out and sometimes only 20 per cent or less of the entering students are continuously enrolled over four years. In junior colleges, mortality and movement are very heavy, and the typical length of stay is between one and one and a half years.

The length of uninterrupted time on the various campuses undoubtedly affects the content and viability of student subcultures. Where students remain in the same college for four years, their relationships with each other and the faculty have that much time to grow and ripen. If this uninterrupted time is combined with certain other conditions, especially small-scale, on-campus living and faculty involvement, it very likely means four years of community-like participation. It is no wonder, under these conditions, that life-long attachments and identifications are often formed. At the other extreme, relationships are fleeting, and are further attenuated by the realization that one's self and one's friends are here today and gone tomorrow to another college, marriage, or a job. Colleges of short duration and high dropout rate take on some of the atmosphere of a distribution center, resembling in some degree the Army's replacement depots, in which people are classified, sorted, and moved out. A short span of time virtually forecloses the possibility of strong academic subcultures, weakens collegiate subcultures, but encourages no-nonsense pursuit of job preparation.

The impact of performance standards on student orientations can also be quite striking. As we suggested earlier, low standards of work in a college clear the way for participation in the collegiate life. Conversely, it is a truism that high standards make hard work a condition of remaining in the system, and thus make it probable that the demands of the curriculum will predominate over any tendency of students to restrict output. We should not allow this simple fact of academic life to be obscured by elaborate analyses. Faculties possess the means, in the quality and amount of work they require, to weaken seriously the competition of the side lines and side shows about which they habitually complain. But, of course, raising standards is more easily said than done. There must be sufficient supply of students, as earlier established, and the staff has to be ready to ride out the stress excited among students, parents, and other interested parties when a "tough line" is taken. A secure college finds such a step easier than an insecure college, although heroic commitment has sometimes served in lieu of security in colleges without much financial or moral support.

We now come to a point of reconciling two levels of phenomena—the society and the organization—in their shaping of the ways of life of the college student. We earlier suggested certain general relationships between the social origins of students and their orientation in college; for example, that students from working-class and lower-middle-class origins are more vocationally oriented and less culturally sophisticated than are students from upper-middle-class business and professional homes. But this is a general correlation, not an ironbound law. Now, most colleges in effect comb through the vast pool of potential students and pull out individuals of particular orientations and interests. This is done deliberately through official screening, and it comes about also through the self-recruitment of students in line with their images of various colleges—the party boy to the "country-club" college, the brain to the "tough" school, and so on. The effect of selection and self-recruitment for many colleges is to draw *similar* students out of the *different* backgrounds. Thus, at some of the leading private colleges, the small minority of students from lower-class origins are not very distinguishable in their habits and orientations from the majority of students who are of high social origins. Conversely, at some state colleges that are heavy on the vocational, the upper-middle-class students are roughly similar in orientation to the students of lower- and lower-middle-class backgrounds. The general tendency is this: among the students within any one college, the effects of selection, through self-recruitment and screening, reduce and sometimes wash out the differences in attitude that are correlated with social origins in the student population at large. Thus a relationship that holds for students as a whole may be only weakly found, if at all, within individual colleges, especially the smaller ones.

This is not to say that the societal determinants are unimportant. The general society's broad currents of attitudes and values are reflected in the array and diversity of colleges; social changes cause new types of colleges to be raised to prominence and older types to adapt, decline, or fight a rear-guard action. The broad currents also dictate the dominant orientation of entering students and the relative number holding various values. But the individual colleges within the vast array still have their own character and image, and instead of reflecting the balance of student interests found nationally, they draw a slice of those interests. For some that are choosy, the slice is very thin; for others of broader appetite, the slice may go halfway around the pie. But in these varying degrees, the colleges have the power to shape the distribution of student orientations on their own campuses.

Thus we have two levels of social phenomena at which different determinants predominate in the shaping of student culture. Across the society, broad traditions and trends largely determine the orientations of students, the nature and strength of their subcultures. But at the level of the individual school, the characteristics of the college enter the picture and the college's own character sets the terms of existence for the student subcultures.

From among the many characteristics of colleges that shape student life, we have selected and reviewed a few of the important: the purpose of the college, the interests of the administration, the orientations of the faculty, the college's size and complexity, and its policy of student selection and retention. Many other characteristics deserve analysis and discussion. The organization of the extracurricular activities was barely mentioned, yet it matters considerably how the extracurricular is handled and related to the curriculum. Who controls the sports? How does the dean of students' office work? Too, the physical and intellectual autonomy of the campus plays a role, for geographic isolation produces intense student life, and most campuses dominated by vigorous academic subcultures have the sense of being a cultural island unto themselves, even in the midst of a metropolitan area. The organized setting that shapes student culture is a many-sided thing.

THE TRIUMPH OF VOCATIONALISM

In the battle of student subcultures, the vocational tends toward dominance, growing stronger at the expense of the collegiate and the academic (the nonconformist is too small to enter into contention in other than a few colleges). The strength of the trend toward vocationalism is sharply etched in the following excerpt from William H. Whyte's *The Organization Man.*

VOCATIONALISM IN COLLEGE [17]

While it is hardly news that the U.S. inclines to the vocational, the magnitude of the swing has been greater than is generally recognized. Only three out of every ten college graduates are now majoring in anything that could be called a fundamental discipline—in the liberal arts *or* in the sciences. Figures also indicate that this trend has been gathering force for a long time and that it is not to be explained away as a freak of current supply and demand or a hang-over from the disruptions of World War II.

In 1954-55, 183,602 men were graduated. Let's take *all* of the men majoring in mathematics, *all* of the men majoring in the physical sciences, *all* of the men majoring in the biological sciences, *all* of the men majoring in the liberal arts, *all* of the men majoring in the basic social sciences. Together they come to 48,999—26.6 per cent of the total.

The rest? Most were studying to be technicians: 22,527 were in engineering (12.3 per cent); 7,052 (3.8 per cent) were in agriculture; 14,871 (8.1 per cent) were in education. The largest single group of all: the 35,564 (19.4 per cent) in business and commerce—*more than all of the men* in the basic sciences and the liberal arts put together. (And more than all the men in law and medicine and religion: 26,412.)

These figures bring out a very important point. The conflict is not, as some embattled humanists believe, between the sciences and the liberal arts. The conflict is between the fundamental and the applied.

In the last thirty years the number of men majoring in business has swelled almost in direct ratio as those in the humanities

[17] Adapted and abridged from William H. Whyte, Jr., *The Organization Man* (Garden City, New York: Doubleday & Co., Inc., Doubleday Anchor Books, 1957), pp. 86–94. *The Organization Man* was published originally by Simon and Schuster, Inc., New York, 1956.

majors have declined, and since 1940 the rate of increase has been growing steeper. Between 1940 and 1950 the number of business students doubled. By 1955, they had become the largest single undergraduate group—more than the majors in mathematics, all the natural sciences, all the physical sciences, all the biological sciences, and English put together.

Something has had to give and it has been fundamental education. The great increase in business education has not been channeled into graduate schools of business administration which, like those of Harvard and the University of Chicago, require a basic education as a prerequisite. The increase has been in the undergraduate "schools of commerce," and the students who are enrolling in them include many who ten years ago would very likely have majored in economics or politics or history.

Not only have the business schools been diverting more and more men away from basic studies, they have been subtly changing the climate of the whole campus. It is often the business school of the college that sets the dominant tone, and those students who major in the humanities are on the defensive, not to mention their professors. In a remarkably frank appraisal of the situation at the University of Pennsylvania, *The Daily Pennsylvanian* (January 14, 1955) had this to say about the effect of the business school on the rest of the campus:

> The first and most important destructive influence at Pennsylvania of the atmosphere important for the nourishment of the humane arts is the Wharton School of Finance and Commerce. Justly famed for the excellent business training which it offers, and for which it grants an academic degree, the Wharton School by the sheer force of its reputation and undergraduate appeal has given to undergraduate social and extracurricular life an atmosphere which, while it is seldom anti-intellectual, is usually nonintellectual, and which tends to discourage the popularity of those interests which ordinarily occupy the time of the students of other universities where the school of liberal arts is the main impetus for student activity.
>
> An undergraduate body where half the members have

> definite educational interests of a material, nonacademic nature is bound to create an atmosphere that reflects something less than enthusiasm for the theoretical sciences and the liberal arts. This is especially so when those members are frequently people of particular intelligence who are adept at pointing out to their fellow students the apparent flaws of an education seemingly for "nothing at all," and whose idea of what they are in the philistine habit of calling "culture" is an elementary course in the fine arts or history, judiciously chosen for its adaptability to the most inconsiderable demands of a thorough business school.

Some forces behind this growing vocationalism—professionalism, occupationalism, technicalism, or whatever else we may wish to call it—are recapitulated here to establish better their mutually re-enforcing effects.

1. *Expansion of higher occupations.* The expansion of higher education is in large part a response to the growth of professional, managerial, and technical occupations which require advanced training. As a result of this change in the occupational structure, and also contributing to it, the growth in the undergraduate college population in recent years has been largely in fields of applied study, such as business administration, engineering, and education.

2. *Education as the means of mobility.* Formal education has been the chief ladder of mobility for aspiring lower- and lower-middle-class people in America for many decades. Their movement toward college continues the secular trend toward greater education which saw the growth of nearly universal secondary education in the thirty years between 1910 and 1940. People of lower social origins now increasingly see college as the prerequisite for the economic and social advancement of their children, and these perceptions are reflected in the rapidly growing college enrollments. As an instrument for the achievement of higher status, col-

lege is defined as a way of getting the training and diplomas which are needed for the better-paying jobs.

3. *Responsive character of public colleges.* This rapid expansion of college attendance among job-oriented young people of lower social origins has taken place largely in the public colleges. These colleges are inexpensive, generous in admission, and often conveniently located; they are responsive to state and local demands and willingly provide training for the expanding array of occupations that require advanced skills. Comprehensively organized, they take on many characteristics of a large service enterprise. Their commitment to liberal education is only partial.

4. *Bureaucratization of academic organization.* The comprehensive colleges are people-processing institutions, whose administrative staffs must deal with and organize the scattered activities of large numbers of students enrolled in a variety of programs. Relations between teachers and students under these conditions are typically in the mass, fleeting, and impersonal. Additionally, in the university, teachers involve themselves less with students because they are busy with research, professional activity, and off-campus service. Impersonal relationships between students and faculty members, and between students, fit vocational education, which aims to transmit technical information efficiently.

5. *Withdrawal of student involvement.* An increasing proportion of college students enroll in nonresidential colleges. Living at home and holding part-time or full-time jobs, students visit the college campus to attend class or use the library; they drop in and out of college, some finishing in six to eight years while many do not finish at all. In brief, the student role is narrowed to course work and squeezed in among other roles that are oriented off campus.

All these forces, which are on the rise in American higher education, reduce the impact of college on the student in the older academic sense and support vocationalism. Increasingly, students with narrow vocational interests enroll in colleges where faculties and administrators neither are able nor strongly motivated to modify those interests. That the vocational trend is not taking place solely in the United States we saw in Chapter 2. There we emphasized that the recent immense advances of science, organization, and industry exert pressures on higher education, in every industrial society, to become "the training institutions for the skilled manpower required by a complex technology."[18] It will be recalled that the USSR has gone furthest in making education an arm of the state and the economy; but that even in England, where the aristocratic tradition of the cultivated man is strong, the years since World War II have seen a greater emphasis on vocational and professional studies.

This trend means that a different kind of cultural conflict is emerging *in* colleges compared with the past. The great contest on American campuses over the past fifty years has been between the academic and the collegiate subcultures, with the faculty upholding intellectual values, and the majority of students successfully opposing them with their own nonintellectual or anti-intellectual interests. Increasingly, however, the struggle is between the vocational and academic subcultures, with the cleavage more nearly vertical—proponents of each set of values found in the faculty as well as in the student body.

Both the vocational and the academic orientations are "adult" in a way that the collegiate subculture is not; while collegiate practices were widely condoned by college au-

18 A. H. Halsey, "The Changing Functions of Universities in Advanced Industrial Societies," *Harvard Educational Review,* Vol. 30 (Spring, 1960), p. 120.

thorities, comparatively few adults in college were prepared to defend them as an adequate definition of the college experience. In contrast, the vocational orientation as the *primary* orientation to college is held in very respectable quarters, finds expression in books on educational philosophy, and has many spokesmen both among college teachers and administrators. The collegiate life was not "serious," but vocationalism is. It borrows many of the traditional symbols of academia: pictures of students listening to a lecture or hard at work in a library can as easily be signs of vocational training as of liberal education. The engineer's slide rule swinging from the belt in its brown case perhaps most distinctively symbolizes the vocational subculture—a picture, incidentally, not anathema to most faculty members today.

The new conflict between vocational and academic values—new only in extent—is not as dramatic as the old one between the collegiate and the academic subcultures; the symbols are less clear and the cleavage is not so sharply drawn along the lines of academic status and rank. But the outcomes of the conflict mean much for students' experiences in college and for the nature and functions of higher education. In practice, we undoubtedly will see the conflict result in various combinations of the academic and the vocational subcultures. The difference will lie in whether they are combined in generous proportions or blended by adding a drop of the one to a heavy dose of the other.

Chapter 7

Student Culture in High School

WHAT TYPES of student culture loom large in the American high school? Current answers are no more than educated guesses, for high schools are diverse and research has covered only part of the ground. First, a system of values akin to the collegiate subculture, which we shall call "the fun subculture," is strong and nearly universal. Second, scholastic orientations also are present, although rarely to the degree teachers and other adults would like and often playing second fiddle to the fun subculture. Third, many schools are plagued with disaffected, rebellious youths whose orientations comprise a delinquent subculture. This orientation looms large in schools of the lower-class sections of large cities but in varying form and strength it is found nearly everywhere, even in the small town and the elite suburb. It does not have an analogue in colleges; its leaders drop out of school as soon as they can—or are bounced out by the staff as soon as *that* can be arranged—and hence may not graduate from high school, let alone enter college. On the other hand, the rebellious intellectuals found in small numbers in colleges are nearly absent from the high school; apparently at high-school age they have not yet attached their rebellion or their quest for identity to the world of ideas. Finally, the college subculture of vocationalism has at best a weak parallel in high school; the vocational fields in high school have low status and are in decline, since occupational training of any stature is being pushed into the post-high-school years. High schools train for some occupations but student subcultures are little formed around this function.

Thus we hypothesize three major types of student subculture in the high school—the fun subculture, the academic, the delinquent—of which the first two have some parallel in college and the last is unique. We will examine the fun subculture first and in some detail, for it has been described in several studies that tell us much about the social habits of the high school. It has had great vitality in many places ever since the secondary school became more than college preparation for the few. Whether it is increasing or declining in strength is debatable, as we shall shortly see. Secondly, we take up the academic, and here we are on our own, for no one has bothered to report on how high-school students support one another in serious work. The academic outlook shows signs of new strength in many neighborhoods and schools. Thirdly, we consider the delinquent subculture, the home of extreme rebelliousness in the high school, and again we will note signs of increased strength. The over-all picture is confusing.

THE FUN SUBCULTURE

During the last thirty years, several sociologists have analyzed the beliefs and practices of high-school students and drawn a picture showing sports, cars, dating, and beauty queens in the center, with course work, books, and the life of the mind dimly located around the edges. This picture is partly exaggeration, a result of focusing on a dramatic type and ignoring prosaic student activities. But the exaggeration need not destroy the main point: American high-school students throughout much of the twentieth century have been strongly influenced if not dominated by values and practices that range from nonintellectual to anti-intellectual and subvert the formal purposes of the school. This conclusion is drawn from Willard Waller's *The Sociology of Teaching* (1932), A. B. Hollingshead's *Elmtown's Youth* (1949), C. Wayne Gordon's *The Social System of the High School* (1957), and James S. Coleman's *The Adolescent Society* (1961). Coleman's account of "the social life of the teen-ager and its impact on education" is the most up-to-date, and we can best present the fun subculture by drawing heavily upon his work. Largely by means of questionnaires, Coleman studied nine public high schools (and two private high schools not reported here) in 1957–58 located in cities and towns of different size and social composition in northern Illinois. He described a set of norms and values that he termed "the adolescent culture." Since we wish to describe three types of adolescent orientation, we will use the term "fun" for what Coleman calls the adolescent and treat his findings as only part of the picture.

NORMS AND VALUES IN THE ADOLESCENT CULTURE [1]

The values of the adolescent subcultures in these schools were studied in several ways, including questions asked of each student. One question asked: "What does it take to get to be a member of the leading crowd?" The major categories of response are tabulated in Table 3, for boys and girls separately.

[1] Abridged from James S. Coleman, "Academic Achievement and the Structure of Competition," *Harvard Educational Review*, Vol. 29 (Fall, 1959), pp. 330–351. Coleman's work is reported in full in *The Adolescent Society* (New York: The Free Press of Glencoe, 1961). The table number is Coleman's.

TABLE 3—CRITERIA FOR MEMBERSHIP IN THE LEADING CROWD, AS PERCEIVED BY BOYS AND GIRLS

Criterion for Membership in the Leading Crowd*	Boys† ($N = 4{,}021$)	Girls† ($N = 4{,}135$)
Good personality, being friendly	26.6	48.7
Good looks, beauty	14.3	28.9
Having nice clothes	9.0	27.4
Good reputation	17.9	25.9
Having money	7.7	14.2
Good grades, being smart	11.9	11.6
Being an athlete (boys only)	16.3	—
Having a car (boys only)	10.7	—

* Only categories which were mentioned 10 per cent of the time or more are included.

† Percentages add to more than 100 per cent because some students responded with more than one criterion. Boys responded as to boys, girls as to girls.

Consider first the girls' responses, at the right of the table. Most striking in these responses is the great importance of "having a good personality" or "being friendly." Not only is this mentioned most often over-all, but it is mentioned most often in seven of the nine schools. The importance of having a good personality or, what is a little different, "being friendly" or "being nice to the other kids," in these adolescent cultures is something which adults often fail to realize. Adults often forget how "person-oriented" children are: they have not yet moved into the world of cold impersonality in which many adults live. This is probably due to the limits on their range of contacts—for in the limited world of a grade school, a boy or girl *can* respond to his classmates as persons, with a sincerity which becomes impossible as one's range of contacts grows. One of the transitions for some children comes, in fact, as they enter high school and find that they move from classroom to classroom and have different classmates in each class.

After "a good personality" come a wide range of attributes and activities. A flavor of them is indicated by the collection of responses listed below—some hostile to the leading crowd (and in their hostility, often seeing it as immoral), others friendly to it (and in their friendliness, attributing positive virtues to it).

(What does it take to get into the leading crowd in this school?)
"Wear just the right things, nice hair, good grooming, and have a wholesome personality."
"Money, clothes, flashy appearance, date older boys, fairly good grades."
"Be a sex fiend—dress real sharp—have own car and money—smoke and drink—go steady with a popular boy."
"Have pleasant personality, good manners, dress nicely, be clean, don't swear, be loads of fun."
"A nice personality, dress nice without over-doing it."
"Hang out at ——'s. Don't be too smart. Flirt with boys. Be cooperative on dates."

Among these various attributes, the table shows some mention of "good looks" to be second to "personality" in frequency. Having nice clothes, or being well-dressed, is also important in most of the schools, as the responses above suggest. What it means to be well-dressed differs sharply in a well-to-do suburb and in a working-class school, of course. Nevertheless, whether it is the number of cashmere sweaters a girl owns, or simply having neat, clean, pastel frocks, the matter of "having good clothes" is an important one in the value systems to which these girls pay heed.

In part, the importance of having good clothes appears to derive from its use as a symbol of family status and general opulence. But in some part, it appears to derive from the same source that gives importance to "good looks": these items are crucial in making a girl attractive to boys. Thus in this respect the values of the girls' culture are molded by the presence of boys—and by the fact that success with boys is itself of overriding importance in these cultures.

Another element in the constellation of attributes required if one is to be in the leading crowd is indicated by the class of responses labelled "having a good reputation." In all these schools, this item was often mentioned (though in each school, a disgruntled minority saw the leading crowd as composed of girls with bad reputations and immoral habits). A girl's "reputation" is a crucial matter among adolescents. A girl is caught in a dilemma, a dilemma suggested by the importance of good looks on the one hand, and a good reputation on the other. A girl must be successful with the boys, says the culture, but in doing so she must maintain her reputation. In some schools, the limits defining a good reputation are stricter than others—but in all the schools, the limits are there, and they define what is "good" and what is "bad." The definitions are partly based on behavior with boys, but they also include drinking, smoking, and other less tangible matters—something about the way a girl handles herself, quite apart from what she actually *does*.

Another criterion by which a girl gets into the leading crowd or fails to get in is expressed by a girl who responded simply, "Money, fancy clothes, good house, new cars, etc. (the best)."

These qualities are all of a piece: they express the fact that being born into the right family is a great help to a girl in getting into the leading crowd. It is expressed differently in different schools and by different girls, sometimes as "parents having money," sometimes as "coming from the right neighborhood," sometimes as "expensive clothes." . . .

Another criterion for being in the leading crowd is scholastic success. According to these girls, good grades, or "being smart" or "intelligent," has something to do with membership in the leading crowd. Not much, to be sure—it is mentioned less than 12 per cent of the time, and far less often than the attributes of personality, good looks, clothes, and the like. Doing well in school apparently counts for something, though. It is surprising that it does not count for more, because in some situations, the "stars," "heroes," and objects of adulation are those who best achieve the goals of the institution. For example, in the movie industry the leading crowd is composed of those who have achieved the top roles—they are by consensus the "stars." Or in a graduate school, the "leading crowd" of students ordinarily consists of the bright students who excel in their studies. Not so for these high school girls. The leading crowd seems to be defined primarily in terms of *social* success: their personality, beauty, clothes—and in communities where social success is tied closely to family background, their money and family are important, too.

For the boys, a somewhat different set of attributes is important for membership in the leading crowd. The responses below give some idea of the things mentioned.

"A good athlete, pretty good looking, common sense, sense of humor."

"Money, cars and the right connections and a good personality."

"Be a good athlete. Have a good personality. Be in everything you can. Don't drink or smoke. Don't go with bad girls."

"Athletic ability sure helps."

"Prove you rebel the police officers. Dress sharply. Go out with sharp Freshman girls. Ignore Senior girls."

"Good in athletics; "wheel" type; not too intelligent."

By categories of response, Table 3 shows that "a good personality" is important for the boys, but of less prominence than it is for the girls. Being "good-looking," having good clothes, and having a good reputation are similarly of decreased importance. Good looks in particular are less important for the boys than for the girls. Similarly for the items which have to do with parents' social position—having money, coming from the right neighborhood, and the like.

What then are the criteria which are more important for boys than for girls? The most obvious is, as the table indicates, athletics. The role of athletics as an entree into the leading crowd appears to be extremely important. Of the things that a boy can do, of the things he can *achieve,* athletic success seems the clearest and most direct way to gain membership in the leading crowd. Having good grades, or doing well academically, appears to be a much less safe path to the leading crowd than does athletics (and sometimes it is a path away, as the final quotation listed above suggests).

An item which is of considerable importance for the boys, as indicated in Table 3, is a *car*—just having a car, according to some boys, or having a *nice* car, according to others. But whichever it is, a car appears to be of considerable importance in being part of the "inner circle" in these schools. In four of the five small-town schools—but in none of the larger schools—a car was mentioned more often than academic achievement. When this is coupled with the fact that these responses include not only juniors and seniors, but also freshmen and sophomores, who are too young to drive, the place of cars in these adolescent cultures looms even larger.

Several other questions in the questionnaire present the same general picture that this "leading crowd" question reveals: social success with the opposite sex (to which good looks, a good reputation, good clothes, and a car contribute), athletic achievement for boys, a few school activities such as cheerleading for girls, being willing to "have a good time" for both boys and girls, are the attributes and activities which are highly valued among teenagers. Far less important to the adolescent community are the activities which school is ostensibly designed for: scholastic achievement, leadership of academic clubs, and the like. For example, the question: "If you could be remembered here at school for one of the three things below, which one would you want it to be: brilliant student, star athlete, or most popular?" Boys responded star athlete over 40 per cent of the time, and brilliant student less than 30 per cent of the time. This despite the fact that the boy is asked how he would like to be remembered *in school,* an institution explicitly designed to train students, not athletes.

It is clear from all these data that the interests of teen-agers are not focused around studies, and that scholastic achievement is at most of minor importance in giving status or prestige to an adolescent in the eyes of other adolescents. This is perhaps to be expected in some areas, where parents place little emphasis on education. Yet the most striking result from these questions was the fact that the values current in the well-to-do suburban school were no more oriented to scholastic success than those in the small-town schools or the working-class school.

There were differences in the value climates, but not at all in expected directions. And the differences were dwarfed by the similarities. For example, in every school, more boys wanted to be remembered as a star athlete than as a brilliant student. And in six of the nine schools, "good looks" was first, second, or third in importance as a criterion for being in the leading crowd of girls. Having good grades almost always occupied roughly the same place for girls. It was seventh in seven schools, fifth in one, and eighth in one. That is, in eight schools, it ranked below some of the less frequently mentioned items not included in Table 3. For boys, the average was higher, and the variation was the greater: it was fifth in three schools, sixth in two, third in one, fourth in one, seventh in one, and eighth in one. In all schools athletic achievement held a high place for the boys (it was first, second, or third in six of the nine schools).

In short, despite wide differences in parental background, type of community, and type of school, there was little difference in the standards of prestige, the activities which confer status, and the values which focus attention and interest. In particular, good grades and academic achievement had relatively low status in all schools. . . .

In fact, there is a good deal of evidence that special effort toward scholastic success is *negatively* valued in most teen-age groups. Scholastic success may, in the minor way indicated by the data above, add to a student's status among his fellows; but the success must be gained without special efforts, without doing anything beyond the required work. For example, along with nine public schools, the research mentioned above included a private university laboratory school whose average IQ level is probably surpassed by few schools in the country. This school should be an extreme example of the academically inclined school. It is, and many students individually pursue their studies with intensive effort. Yet student leaders of the school reported that the "thing to do" to be part of the crowd was to get reasonably good grades *without* expending special efforts in doing so. In other words, even at this extremely scholastically oriented school, there are group norms in the direction of holding down effort. How effective they are at this high school is unimportant. The important point is that despite the academic inclinations and background of the students, there is a norm against working too hard on one's studies.

Other observers who have studied the fun subculture have testified to its strength. C. Wayne Gordon studied a midwestern high school intensively in 1950 and reported a similar if not stronger glorification of athletics and social activities coupled with a low regard for serious work. Gordon tells (see Table 7.1) about the activities that make

TABLE 7.1—ACTIVITIES OF A BIG WHEEL IN HIGH SCHOOL

Activity	Grade level
Major office in Student Assembly	12
Social Committee	12
Assembly Committee	12
Guidance Council Chairman	12
Guidance Team	11
Choir	9, 10, 11, 12
Boys' Octet	11, 12
Double Octet	12
Junior Rotarians	12
Rifle Club	12
Pep Club	12
Radio Club	9
Varsity Football	11
"B" Basketball	9
Baseball	10, 11, 12
Intramural Tennis	11, 12
Intramural Basketball	11, 12
Intramural Track	12
Representative to National Youth Conference	11
Representative to Boys' State	11
Yearbook Staff	12
Yearbook Queen Escort	12

a boy a "big wheel" in high school, and anyone who has read a high-school yearbook in recent years might remember similar four-year records.[2]

Prestige and influence in the student body went to those who distinguished themselves before the school, and this possibility lies not in the classroom but in the activities. The pinnacle of success for girls in Gordon's high school

[2] C. Wayne Gordon, *The Social System of the High School* (Glencoe, Illinois: The Free Press, 1957), pp. 63–64.

was in being queen of the yearbook or a member of her court. "The Queen was crowned in a public ceremony called the Yearbook Coronation, the major social function of the school year." The queen was selected "by a school-wide vote from a slate of nine condidates nominated by the senior boys. The eight candidates who were not chosen Queen served as Maids of the Queen's Court."

The girls worked as hard to make the Coronation Court as boys did to make the basketball team. One girl reported: "In your senior year, if you're half-way popular at all, everyone thinks that you think that you're going to be on the Court. You live with that coronation ordeal from the time you're a freshman until the time it comes in your senior year." Said another: "In my sophomore year when I came to Wabash, one of the first things that I noticed was the girls in my class and their desire to be on the Court. The first day at school I heard a discussion of who in 1951 would be on the Coronation Court. Various girls were named, so I thought I was as likely a candidate as any of them. So a girl friend and I set out to be popular." This school tradition rewarded good looks, popularity, and service, placing these above scholastic achievement. In the model held up to adolescent girls, intellect occupied a minor place.

Determinants of the Fun Subculture

Various interests of the school, the community, and the adolescent support the fun subculture. For the school staff, parts of the fun subculture function as a means of control. As in college, many extracurricular activities are sanctioned outlets for adolescent energies or substitutes for tabooed activities.[3] Athletics play a special role; they have been

[3] Willard Waller, *The Sociology of Teaching* (New York: John Wiley & Sons, Inc., 1932), p. 112.

used to hold the interest and channel the energy of some of the poorer students, often ones near delinquency. Extracurricular activities are part of the "holding power" of the modern public school, making it attractive to students who otherwise would be bored or disaffected.

The adolescent activities promote school cohesion, with interscholastic competition and rivalry uniting the entire school into a "we" against the competitor. This cohesive thrust serves many school interests, notably the maintenance of morale and discipline:[4]

> It is perhaps as a means of unifying the entire school group that athletics seems most useful. . . . There is a tendency for the school population to split up into its hostile segments of teachers and students and to be fragmented by cliques among both groups. The division of students into groups prevents a collective morale from arising and thereby complicates administration; the split between students and teachers is even more serious, for these two groups tend to become definite conflict groups, and conflict group tensions are the very antithesis of discipline. This condition athletics alleviates. Athletic games furnish a dramatic spectacle of the struggle of picked men against the common enemy, and this is a powerful factor in building up a group spirit which includes students of all kinds and degrees and unifies the teachers and the taught.

Such school spirit also "makes" alumni, as in college, leading to identification and support after graduation.

Another function of the fun subculture for school administration is public relations with the local community. School men everywhere can testify to the strong interests generated in their community by sports and the more glamorous of the other extracurricular activities. A town is unlikely to wax enthusiastic about the school's stamp club; but marching bands, annual festivals, and big games draw spectators and partisans. Community interest is the founda-

[4] Waller, *The Sociology of Teaching,* pp. 115–116.

tion on which much of the fun subculture rests. The local community typically "participates" in the extracurricular in ways it cannot—or has not—in the curricular.

Colleges also influence the norms and values of the high school. The collegiate life of higher education acts as a model, defining certain activities as prestigeful and fun. The social activities of the high school prepare students to enter the college's social whirl. The high school, and even the junior high school, train for college sports, just as colleges now train for the professional leagues. There is a downward influence in football, for example, that ranges from style of offense to equipment and tape. The "pre-professional" training of players in high school, often by coaches who are satellites of a college coach, occurs throughout the country, pushing amateur athletics toward Big Sports. Once upon a time in many towns, the biggest structure was a church; later it was the school house. Today in the case of the high-school "big time," it is the basketball pavilion or football stadium that will hold all of the townspeople, along with a good share of the surrounding populace. The high school as a sports enterprise offers "its" area the same kind of spirit generated in larger populations by major universities.

The fun subculture in high school also receives sustenance from a general adolescent culture that extends across the nation. This youth culture has growing support from institutions which operate apart from the parent, the church, and the school in shaping the young; the young are hooked into the mass media and their adjuncts, from nursery-level television programs to the movie to the disk jockey and jukebox. These means of communication leap over other forms of social contact in affecting the style and content of the general youth culture. Their effectiveness is shown in the national crazes that race through the homes and haunts of the teen-agers. The rapidity of communication and adaptation within the subworld of the young can be baffling to their elders, and is another point of tension between the generations.

A national youth culture, while most evident in America, emerges everywhere in technological societies. The adolescent is less of a child than he used to be because he has earlier independence from family regimen; but he is also less of an adult because of the longer delay in becoming a member of the work force and hence of the adult world.[5] He has an in-between new status—"the teen-ager." He and his friends are also given many of the means which can make them a quasi-separate stratum—money, cars, freedom in dating, entertainment designed especially for them. As the adolescent becomes a special kind of man, with distinctive needs, practices, and resources, the mass media and other businesses learn to serve and shape him, making the teen-ager into an industry. In brief, the youth culture develops facilities and ways of its own, and it is supported by interinstitutional ties to the worlds of business and mass entertainment.

The fun subculture that appears *within* the high school, then, is part of more pervasive orientations held by many youngsters whether they are at home, in the school, or in the corner drugstore. The school can adjust to these orientations, or set its face against them and seek to change them, or keep them out of the school as much as possible. But for many students, these orientations are part of the mental equipment developed in prior experience and nurtured through the numerous contacts they have with the large society.

[5] Earl Raab and Gertrude J. Selznick, *Major Social Problems* (Evanston, Illinois: Row, Peterson and Co., 1959), p. 34.

THE ACADEMIC SUBCULTURE

Subcultures of "serious students" also exist in high school. There are schools where students are more oriented to their studies and to the academic extracurricular activities than to anything else. The larger high schools have a pluralistic climate of values that allows those who are intellectually inclined to group together. These students' ideals, their mutual support, and their partial anonymity and insulation within a large student body protect them from the control of those who would ridicule them, tag them as "grinds" or "curve-raisers." This subgroup has a structure of rewards in which top prestige goes to the student who performs brilliantly in the chemistry laboratory or receives high grades in the toughest subjects.

Although Coleman emphasized the fun subculture in his study, his findings revealed academic values. When boys were asked how they would like to be remembered in school —as star athlete, brilliant student, or most popular—they responded brilliant student about 30 per cent of the time. In several of the schools, the per cent choosing "brilliant student" was only a few points less than the proportion saying "star athlete"—this despite the pull of the schools "leading crowd" toward athletics. The number of students who would prefer to be remembered as brilliant students ranged from about 25 to 40 per cent in these schools. Whether these students clustered together and assigned status primarily on the basis of academic values was not determined by Coleman; his analysis did not go into the question of the variety of subcultures within the schools. Many a boy, of course, would like to be remembered as an athlete *and* a good student—or as the perfect adolescent who is at once handsome, popular, athletic, and studious.

A study made in 1952 of the values of 2,500 ninth- and tenth-grade students in eight New Jersey towns found high value placed on academic work.[6] The students responded to a series of twenty vignettes (in a questionnaire) which described characteristics and skills and activities of high-school boys and girls; for example, one vignette emphasized popularity, another centered on working hard to be a success. The students responded to the vignettes on the basis of "do I want to be just like them?" Being a good student ranked high: favored by 79 per cent of the students, it was outranked only by "popular" (85 per cent) and "friendly" (82 per cent) and was more highly valued than "good time with the gang" (73 per cent) and "athlete" (71 per cent). The students did not take their peer group as the measure of all things. The students were affected by their friends' expectations of having fun with the gang, but they also cared about their parents' wishes that they achieve in school.

The students also were asked to respond to the vignettes on the basis of "would this help me later on when I am through school?" The result? Being a good student and working hard to achieve success moved up on a par with friendliness and popularity, while the valuation placed on having a good time decreased. When the adolescent looks ahead to being a member of the adult world, the researchers inferred, he drops his close affinity to his current peer group and his values come close to those of his parents.

The interesting question is: What is the trend in the strength of the academic orientation in high school? Despite the apparently growing independence and influence of the fun subculture of sports and popularity, the balance may be swinging away from it. The evidence is meager either

[6] The information about this study is taken from Matilda W. Riley, John W. Riley, Jr., and Mary E. Moore, "Adolescent Values and the Riesman Typology: An Empirical Analysis," in Seymour M. Lipset and Leo Lowenthal (eds.), *Culture and Social Character: The Work of David Riesman Reviewed* (New York: The Free Press of Glencoe, 1961), pp. 370–386.

way; since no studies have compared students of one era with those of another, we lack reliable information about whether the schools are now more or less dominated by the fun-subculture orientation than they were ten, twenty, or thirty years ago. Clearly, however, serious study in the high school has come back into fashion, among students as well as among the adults—parents and teachers—who influence them. Whether or not brilliant students outnumber athletes in most schools' leading crowd, increasing numbers of students probably perceive the tightening connection between education and career. Rising college ambition spreads seriousness; the tightening of college standards puts on pressure; school authorities are making courses tougher and adding to the homework. State, national, and private scholarship plans for college, now developing rapidly, dramatize the academic and provide additional incentive for seriousness. More adults are more serious about the whole matter, and this concern is bound to carry through to adolescents.

Coleman found, though it did not support his main theme, that more high-school students are oriented to the approval or disapproval of their parents than to the influence of their closest friend. When asked whose disapproval would be most difficult to accept, in the case of joining a club in school: 53.8 per cent of the boys answered parents' disapproval; 3.5 per cent, teacher's; 42.7 per cent, friend's; the answers of the girls were about the same (52.9, 2.7, and 43.4 per cent). Even in the "leading crowd," with its inclinations toward play, 50 per cent of the boys and of the girls said that parents' disapproval would be hardest to take.[7]

School authorities and teachers, too, with their change in

[7] James S. Coleman, *The Adolescent Society* (New York: The Free Press of Glencoe, 1961), pp. 5–6.

outlook, are modifying the outlook of the young. Martin Mayer in his book *The Schools* describes cases in which schools have developed a dominant educational spirit, even when their students came from culturally deprived backgrounds. The best-known effort is the Higher Horizons program in New York City, which began with one school in 1954 and has expanded to over sixty elementary and junior high schools in the slums. The program tackles self-image and motivation through means that range from a trip to the Metropolitan Opera to the awarding of a Leader badge for reading twelve books. The New York City effort does not stand by itself. Consider Central High School in Kansas City:[8]

Kansas City was one of the first school systems to integrate in response to the Supreme Court decision in the Brown case. Central High School had been all-white; now, rapidly, it became half Negro, a proportion still increasing. Courageously—with the complete backing of the Negro community—Kansas City's leaders decided that the standards of their old schools would not slide. Anything wrong with the home environment was to be kept out of the school. Social events would not be curtailed, but the emphasis would be shifted into competition within the school—competition for grades (pictures of everybody who gets straight "E's" for Excellent are posted in the hallways), for constructions in the shops, for athletic excellence, for student government jobs.

In its last years as an all-white school, Central never sent more than 15 per cent of its graduates to college, and only four or five Central kids won scholarships in an average year. Now, despite the great drop in socio-economic level, 150 out of 350 graduates go on to college, 50 of them with scholarships. "From the moment they step in the door," says James Boyd, an able, charming, open young man who became Central's principal in 1959, "our Miss Schaller [guidance counselor] hits at them that if they work hard, they can get scholarships." In recent years, Central has sent

[8] Martin Mayer, *The Schools* (New York: Harper & Brothers, 1961), pp. 120–122.

its Negro graduates to Yale, Vassar, Smith, Oberlin, Northwestern and Chicago, among others.

Miss Schaller comments mildly, "It's been a big help in integrating—the fact that these Negro children feel they can go to college. At first, the teachers were afraid of the stress on college—they were worried it would cut enrollment in the commercial courses. But when we had 50 people on that stage to receive scholarships, they burst with pride. We put a big stress on accomplishment—any accomplishment—everything helps. We have a boy who's a runner, and the other day he won the cross-country championship. It pulled up his scholarship, and now, I notice, he's singing in the chorus, too."

No one should think of Central as a beautiful garden where all the plants grow: the place is full of problems that never go away. Forty-odd per cent of the graduates go to college (which means more than 30 per cent of the entrants: Central does not have a severe drop-out problem). But except for the scholarship group—and not all of them—only a fraction will finish college. Integration is successful within the school (at assemblies one does not see whites and Negroes sitting singly together, but groups of five or six alternate throughout the room), but Miss Schaller knows only a handful of cases where a white child has visited a Negro home, or vice versa. Meanwhile, the socio-economic level of the school continues to descend.

Like most successful people in schools, Miss Schaller uses the technique that works. She is a plump, handsome woman with gray-brown hair, and she began her teaching career in 1928 in an elementary school, moving on to secondary science teaching in 1938. But behind the motherly appearance lies a tough mind and a contempt for weakness: she is sentimental about what the kids *do,* not about what they *are*. Guidance as she practices it looks very firmly toward the future. "We had a top performer," she says, "who wanted to be a carpenter. He said, 'What's wrong with being a carpenter?' I said, 'Nothing—but *you* ought to go to college.' Well, he went into service, where they spotted his ability and put him to teaching. He was top student of seven thousand at the University of Nebraska, and now he's doing graduate work in engineering at Stanford."

Kansas City's main office is more than a little worried that too much is being asked of the students at Central, though everyone is overcome by admiration for Miss Schaller, and the Negro parents threaten to raise the political devil if anything is done to make Central more like the city's other lower-class schools. Principal Boyd is concerned that many of his teachers "are not fully aware of the environmental conditions," and he may regard as more fixed than it is the "AQ—or Attitude Quotient," as he calls it, with which the kids come to school. But Boyd was principal of Kansas City's Manual High Vocational before he came to Central, and he is sick and tired of supervising the operations of a dumping ground. The difference between Central and the typical slum high school is not something an observer can miss: the casual atmosphere in the halls, the easy jokes in the classroom, the almost complete absence of fear, the relative rarity of apathy.

The New York City and Kansas City cases indicate ways that school authorities throw their weight behind the academic subculture, and make it viable and attractive even in the settings where it is the weakest. The students' perspective changes on what is rational for themselves. Collectively restricting effort has long been seen as rational by most students, since it holds down the demands of the school to a level easily maintained by the majority. But on grounds of college and career, the devaluation of the academic is not rational, and significant numbers of high-school students in some cities and towns are shifting their judgment accordingly.

THE DELINQUENT SUBCULTURE

A third major orientation in the high school is concerned neither with having fun in the organized activities nor with study and the classroom, but rather with avoiding or rebelling against the whole enterprise. This orientation, the delinquent subculture, actually takes many different forms, varying styles that can be loosely classified together. "Delinquency," legally or morally defined, varies from a single, mild breach of acceptable behavior, which would include most youngsters, to the professional criminal who escapes being labeled as such only because he has not lived long enough.

Most students who are seriously delinquent want to get out of the school. They see no connection between school and future status, if they think about long-run goals at all, or believe that the cards are stacked against them. They have a general hostility toward adults and most of the other students. These rebellious youths do not merely evade rules in high school, they *flout* them, and in so doing they challenge the authority of the teacher and the school official. In this negativistic subsociety, there is "an element of active spite and malice, contempt and ridicule, challenge and defiance,"[9] that could only come from a deep disaffection. These students create a severe problem of discipline that exists in only mild degree in the case of the other students, detracting the teacher's attention from teaching and making the maintenance of order the first consideration. Surprisingly, this subculture extends down to the first grade in some schools, when it is connected to a general neighborhood orientation of negativism, hedonism, and violence. At its worst, in a slum area of Chicago for example, the elementary school or the secondary school is a place where violence is always in the air:[10]

A young white teacher walked into her new classroom and was greeted with the comment, "Another damn white one." Another was "rushed" at her desk by the entire class when she tried to be

[9] Albert K. Cohen, *Delinquent Boys* (Glencoe, Illinois: The Free Press, 1955), p. 28.

[10] Miriam Wagenschein, "Reality Shock" (Master's thesis, University of Chicago, 1950), pp. 58–59, as reported in Howard S. Becker, "Social Class and Teacher-Pupil Relationships," in Blaine E. Mercer and Edwin R. Carr (eds.), *Education and the Social Order* (New York: Rinehart & Co., Inc., 1957), p. 279.

extremely strict with them. Teachers report having been bitten, tripped, and pushed on the stairs. Another gave an account of a second grader throwing a milk bottle at the teacher and of a first grader having such a temper tantrum that it took the principal and two policemen to get him out of the room. In another school, following a fight on the playground, the principal took thirty-two razor blades from children in a first grade room. Some teachers indicated fear that they might be attacked by irate persons in the neighborhoods in which they teach. Other teachers report that their pupils carry long pieces of glass and have been known to threaten other pupils with them, while others jab each other with hypodermic needles. One boy got angry with his teacher and knocked in the fender of her car.

In the slum school, the symbol of the delinquent subculture is the switchblade. Students caught up in this subculture of violence and physical aggression learn little and are generally considered the "incorrigibles" or "unteachables" by the authorities. They are in school but not of it; their function there is to disrupt and the function of the school is custodial.

The increased concern in recent years about delinquency stems in part from the lower-class hoodlums in the slums of the big cities who have made the streets unsafe and the school into a blackboard jungle. The concern is also generated by the apparent spread of delinquent behavior to other areas and social strata. Delinquency appears no longer localized on the other side of the tracks, down where the poor people live, but is found throughout the community of adolescents, in most neighborhoods and schools. Stealing cars, extorting money from younger children, fighting in gangs after a basketball game, breaking up house parties—these are acts characteristic of middle- as well as lower-class boys. This spread is a baffling phenomenon and reliable explanations are hard to come by.

Several factors shed some light on the growth of a delinquent subculture *within* the high school. For one, the modern comprehensive high school with compulsory attendance up to a certain age (14, 15, or 16) embraces all of the young. Young people are in the high school now whose counterparts twenty or forty years ago would not have been there. Not long ago, youngsters who became violent or had to be disciplined too often were simply expelled; now they are kept in the school. Also, in the past, a large proportion of the lower-class boys and girls did not reach high school. As the high school increasingly retained them, lower-class norms of behavior were brought into the school. These norms are more approving of physical aggression; the lower-class more than the middle-class neighborhood typically sanctions, or does not strongly proscribe, the direct acting out of hostility. In their selection, colleges largely screen out these norms, but in their compulsory attendance, high schools pull them in. From the modern secondary school's wide coverage alone, we should expect a greater tendency toward delinquent acts compared to the days when only the "good boys" were in attendance.

This absorption of the violent students and the more permissive lower-class norms converges in the high school with a broader American tradition that masculinity is demonstrated by toughness. Any accenting of physical aggression on the part of some boys is not easily rejected by the others; norms against fighting, stealing cars, and so forth may be controlling, but the absorption may also go the other way. "Masculinity" in the eyes of teen-agers can easily become dependent on the willingness to stand up to a fight or race a car or "make" a girl. In this serious game of who is tough and who is not, there is a tendency to raise the stakes; and if a sizable segment of the school has the habit of carrying knives, for example, then there is pressure on the youths in the school to define toughness in such terms, let alone to protect themselves.

The extreme of the emphasis on toughness is found in the traditions of the fighting gang:[11]

> The role-model in the conflict pattern of lower-class culture is the "bopper" who swaggers with his gang, fights with weapons to win a wary respect from other gangs, and compels a fearful deference from the conventional adult world by his unpredictable and destructive assaults on persons and property. To other gang members, however, the key qualities of the bopper are those of the successful warrior. His performance must reveal a willingness to defend his personal integrity and the honor of the gang. He must do this with great courage and displays of fearlessness in the face of personal danger.
>
> The immediate aim in the world of fighting gangs is to acquire a reputation for toughness and destructive violence. A "rep" assures not only respectful behavior from peers and threatened adults but also admiration for the physical strength and masculinity which it symbolizes. It represents a way of securing access to the scarce resources for adolescent pleasure and opportunity in underprivileged areas.

The growing strength of delinquent orientation in the high school also partly results from the growing autonomy of the adolescent subworld. The formidable youth culture pulls the young out of the grasp of adult supervision and control; as was mentioned earlier, the family is less controlling than previously, as are the neighborhood and the church. The cry of the parents of a delinquent commonly is: He's a good boy at home, but we can't control what goes on out there in the streets. The agents of community control are increasingly the formally designated officials—the police, the judge, the teacher. Close, informal social control by adults, in short, lessens, and the quasi-autonomous society of adolescents answers mainly to its own needs and impulses. This "society" does not face the problem of responsible

[11] Richard A. Cloward and Lloyd E. Ohlin, *Delinquency and Opportunity* (New York: The Free Press of Glencoe, 1960), p. 24.

government, of stable arrangements for the raising of the young, and the other basic requirements that lead in larger societies to the establishment of stable institutions. However poorly we understand the adolescent world, we know that its requirements for social order are somewhat different from those of adult society. Left alone, it develops some deviant or quasi-deviant traditions that are "irresponsible" by the standards of adult society. The fun subculture is irresponsible in mild form and in tolerated ways; the delinquent subculture is a more extreme expression of irresponsibility.

Among adolescents, deep rebellion that turns into a delinquent orientation within and outside the school has other supports. One is the blockage of opportunity faced by many who come from backgrounds that deprive them of the resources they need but who pick up the ethic of achievement. They have the goal of success but not the legitimate means of achieving it. Blocked, they may respond in various ways —retreating into apathy, or rebelling and adopting "illegitimate" means of gaining status and making money. Delinquent rebellion is also supported by the prospect of meaningless work, faced by many from lower social origins whose future is work in the factory or the gas station. Worse than this prospect is the likelihood, faced by others, of no work at all.

There is also the lack of function felt by adolescents who physically are adults but are not yet at work and are denied other adult rights and responsibilities. Various social forces are at work in making some adolescents vulnerable to delinquent orientations and prone to anti-social behavior. The technological age apparently strengthens many of these forces: the lengthening of education postpones entrance into adult roles; the rising educational threshold of good jobs outstrips the capability of many students, whether their limitation is determined by native endowment or environmental restriction; and the unskilled eighteen year old has nowhere to go.

We have presented the possibility that three orientations —the orientation to sports and fun, the orientation to serious study, the orientation to delinquent behavior—are all growing stronger in the American high school. What is the balance? That the adolescent world as a whole is growing stronger, we have little doubt. Within this world, there is much differentiation, and it may be that the "big wheel," the brilliant student, and the hood will each become a stronger, more distinctive model for adolescent behavior.

The diversity in American communities and schools allows—and encourages—diversity in the orientations of the young. They, too, live in a pluralistic society in which an unending tug of war takes place between forces that would cast them in a single mold and other forces that induce them to be unlike one another. What we will probably see, of course, is various blends of these types. The most common mixed type will likely combine study and elements of the fun subculture—the student who works harder and is more serious about his books than was his counterpart ten or twenty years ago, but who also finds rewards and gratifications in the precollegiate dens of escape, fantasy, and play. Rising college ambition coupled with academic reform in the high school apparently will reduce the dominance the precollegiate norms and values have had in so many schools, blunting and blending them with the academic.

Another common mixed type is the student who is marginal to all three orientations. A large proportion of adolescents are not serious students, are not involved in the whirl of activities, and are not delinquents. The pure type here is the almost faceless student who never speaks up, goes unnoticed during the school hours, and vanishes after the last bell—drifting through school unengaged by any adolescent values. Such routinized adolescents, overlooked in a typology of adolescent subcultures, are perhaps best characterized by the quality of their participation—their apathy and low affect, their withdrawal and avoidance. The apathetic adolescent is capable of only minor play, minor study—or minor delinquency.

Adolescents in high school, then, even more than adults and more than older students in college are unlikely to respond to the changing world with a single voice. They will proceed in a multitude of directions, pushed and pulled by various forces, and responding in a cacophony of voices that will grate on adult ears. For while some high-school students perceive the growing connections between education and adult life, the bearing of present activity on future status is less clear and directly compelling for 14- to 17-year-old students than for those in college. For some, the problems of self-identity consume all energy. For some, now is the time to goof off, for tomorrow we become adults. For some, the inclination grows to strike out against an incomprehensible, unfeeling world. In the advanced society, especially American society, adolescence has been a troublesome time in the life cycle. The future promises a deepening of complications that will be reflected in the subcultures of youth and the problems of education in the high school.

Chapter 8

The Educational Process and the Expert Society

THE SOCIOLOGY of education flings a wide net, since education has ties to the other major institutions and is itself a complicated enterprise. Education connects intimately with culture, social class, politics, and the economy, to minorities, religion, government, and the family. Education has impulses set in motion and sustained by its own traditions, its forms of control and organization, the nature of the persons who work at it and receive it. In focusing on education in the United States in the mid-twentieth century, we have covered some connections and impulses that are important in their own right in shaping men and society; for example, the effects of residential segregation on the education of the Negro. Within this coverage, we have, in addition, pointed to the developments in American education that result from accelerating technology, expanding population, and growing international obligations. In some instances, the effect of the major social trends is strong and apparent, as in the growth of university research; in others, the influence of the modern trends is not strong or perhaps simply not so apparent, as in the interaction of teacher and pupil in the elementary school.

Our findings demand some regrouping and summarizing. Thus far we have spread the discussion of elementary-secondary education and higher education in chapters on education and culture, the education of minorities, the structure of control, and the like. Here we summarize by first pulling together some effects of the primary social trends on elementary-secondary education and then reviewing the effects on higher education.

This done, we turn to three phenomena, each fundamental to our age, that are fraught with problems for education. The first is the trend toward mass processing of people inherent in large organization in a large society. We glanced briefly at this matter in considering the formalization of organizational practices (Chapter 5) and in the discussion of impersonality on the large campus (Chapter 6). Here we consider more generally the bearing of mass processing on education. The second phenomenon, again one appearing in the earlier chapters, is the acceleration of social change in modern times. Rapid change runs as an undercurrent of disturbance through most modern institutions. The rapidly changing environment beats hard upon education, disturbing traditional functioning, and we wish to highlight this phenomenon and some of its implications. Finally, we return to the problem of the preparation of experts. The global contest between democratic and totalitarian powers that lays its shadow over all human affairs affects education, as we have repeatedly emphasized, by inducing the sense of national need for technologists. But modern societies need technically trained men who are more than technicians to assist the new underdeveloped nations, and the quality of thinking of the technologists will do much to determine the quality of human affairs at home. We close on a theme sounded in the Introduction: the technological age raises the problem of cultivating educated experts.

ELEMENTARY AND SECONDARY EDUCATION

We pointed in Chapter 1 to a decline in moral training in the schools. In this subtle matter, facts are few; but the *public* schools in a large, complex society, for important reasons, will move away from the narrow transmitting of fixed moralities and will particularly avoid religious doctrine. The public schools strive for a value neutrality in order to serve, and avoid controversy with, groups of differing views who send their children to the schools and contribute to their support. To advocate a specific moral or religious point of view is to take sides, making some groups unhappy and putting the schools in the untenable position of teaching what is heresy to families of other persuasion. The accommodation of the schools to plural interests moves them toward the common denominator, a classroom morality that encourages the child to understand and tolerate different points of view. Moral indoctrination also lessens in the schools as teachers come increasingly from diverse cultural backgrounds, and as they themselves, like most other adults, become unsure about the proper role of the school in instilling morality amidst cultural diversity.

The diminishing of moral training stems partly from its displacement by other interests and tasks, notably the greater concern over the last forty to fifty years with developing sociability in the young. This tendency connects with the growing necessity, in a world of large organizations and proliferating services, for many individuals to develop the skills of influencing people. It also relates to the growing importance of peer groups in the lives of the young, especially in the adolescent years, which makes getting along with others seem important. The doctrines and practices of progressive education have encouraged a concern with the social, as part of the well-rounded development of the child. The students who terminate their education at the secondary level, many educators feel, should be taught skills of interpersonal relations and given rudimentary training in civic participation and tolerance. Thus, under many impulses, the schools have moved toward sociability. One outcome of the shift from morality to sociability is a change in the nature of teacher authority. The stern, openly dominating figure has given way in many schools to a friendly appearing adult whose control is muted and exerted more by indirect manipulation.

One of the effects of accelerating technological development and deepening world tension is to blunt the interest in social relations and move toward knowledge. The schools are now under public pressure to turn to a no-nonsense teaching of reading, arithmetic, science, history, and languages. Impelling need for trained men urges the schools to speed the education of the talented children, leaving the social aside. The trend toward "hardness" in the schools is not a return to moral indoctrination, but rather to the primacy of transmitting knowledge. Much of the renewed emphasis on subject matter centers on natural science in which spectacular leaps in knowledge have been made. It is the scientist and engineer that most critics have in mind when they think of a national need for educational reform. This tougher attitude about book learning is also encouraged by the greater proportion of students going on to college. Many parents who would have been unwilling a decade or two ago to have their children face a hard taskmaster are now asking that teachers take sterner measures to prepare the student for college. Thus a fundamental dilemma of the modern school is how to reconcile a vigorous, forceful teaching of the hard subjects with the institutionalized emphasis on friendliness and sociability that continues to receive support from the home and the community. These institutional contradictions will undoubtedly lead to new adaptations, as teachers and administrators struggle to produce a tolerable compromise.

In Chapter 2 we referred to the extending of elementary and secondary education to an ever larger share of the population. This has been a primary trend in American education for some time, impelled by democratic ideals and by the movements against illiteracy and child labor, as well as by the rising educational threshold of work on which we concentrated in our account. The schools incorporate all the young in the early grades; virtually everyone completes elementary school, and a high proportion, increasing year by year, complete high school. Compared with the past, this trend prolongs schooling for the young of various social classes. Differentials in educational attainment between lower, middle, and higher classes continue, but the differentials move upward in the educational ladder and there are no longer sharp cleavages at any level between the education available to one class and to another. This lack of cleavage is different from the situation obtaining until 1880–1900, when higher education was for the few (2 to 4 per cent), secondary education was college preparatory, and most lower- and middle-class youth proceeded no further than the first six to eight grades. The technological age speeds the trend toward universal completion of high school, as it presses for higher levels of cultural and technical competence.

Within the diversity of the American scene, however, trouble spots are growing in education because powerful social forces block the move of lower-class youth toward the necessary competence. One growing trouble results as urbanization and discrimination together concentrate lower-class minority families, especially Negroes, in ever larger residential heaps. The concentration produces the special problem of the segregated or nearly segregated slum school that is repugnant to parents, students, and teachers alike—

the latter often finding it the Siberia to which they are banished as new recruits. The slum school looms large as a deepening social problem. In coping with it, administrators and teachers make adaptations that vary from banging heads against the wall to instituting elaborate and expensive projects for motivating the unmotivated and making intelligent the unintelligent. In its requirements for work, the expert society complicates the problem of the adequate preparation of the youths who are raised in an educationally wrong neighborhood. The necessity that they acquire some skill is again calling the attention of authorities to the strengthening of the vocational track in the high school, in order to do *something* for them. But in vocational capability as well as in cultural competence, the slum school remains an open question. Such schools may "catch up," or their belated adjustments may lag further and further behind the fast-changing requirements of the age.

Besides the changes in their cultural and social tasks, the public schools also face the effects of their own growing scale. With some lag, the schools are paralleling the movement in other institutions toward bureaucratic organization as they grow in size and complexity. The one-room schoolhouse lingers on the scene, as a rear-guard action in rural areas, but its days are numbered. The movement to consolidate small districts and build larger schools, especially at the secondary level, proceeds rapidly. Schools grow bigger because of the economies of larger size in servicing concentrated populations, and because the tasks of the schools have multiplied and their work made more complicated and specialized. To many authorities, the small school appears an anachronism, ineffectual for the specialized training and cultural preparation needed today. James B. Conant, in his influential study of the American high school, portrayed high schools with graduating classes of less than one hundred students as "too small to allow a diversified curriculum except at exorbitant expense," and hence as "one of the serious obstacles to good secondary education throughout most of the United States."[1]

With the larger schools and their diversified curricula come more specialized teaching, more administration, and more staff specialists. The student comes in contact with more adults, but each for a briefer time; he is more tested, counseled, and scheduled. The teacher finds his control over the student diminished, as guidance becomes an official duty of others and as lower layers of administration direct the traffic of student affairs and conduct. At the same time, the diversified school is generally a beehive of activities, and teachers, although now more specialized in the classroom, have their attention and time pulled toward more matters outside the classroom. In brief, internal organization and the proper utilization of personnel become ever more important—important to the morale and satisfaction of the personnel, important to the caliber of the education received by the young.

Along with the growing scale, and the bureaucratization and professionalization of the schools, we also noted in Chapter 4 some centralization of authority, with authority drifting upwards from the local districts to state systems to the federal government. But this trend is mild, resisted mightily by the engrained sentiment of local control and the firmly rooted structure of decentralized authority. To be effective, efforts to influence education nationally still require wholesale persuasion of board members and school administrators—by reaching their minds through books and speeches or reaching their organizational pocketbooks through the dispensing of funds for buildings or programs. We will see more federal legislation and money, and hence

[1] James B. Conant, *The American High School Today* (New York: McGraw-Hill Book Company, Inc., 1959), p. 77.

a growing federal influence, but there is no national ministry in the offing, and local discretion will continue to be decisive. The problem is not one of federal dominance, but of the timeliness and appropriateness of local responses to increasingly *national* needs and problems. The decentralization or centralization of authority is thus in itself an important aspect of the adaptation of education to societal change in the modern era.

Lastly, the public schools are affected by the seemingly growing differentiation of an adolescent society and its composite of subcultures. The fun subculture of good, clean play is encouraged by the mass media and the easy availability of cars. It has been supported by the growth in modern society of the status of teen-ager, the near-adult without responsibility. But this subworld of fun is squeezed by the growing connection between education and work; some of its fellow travelers have recently been seen in the company of serious students and even its hard-core members probably will crack more books in the future. Academic orientations, in short, are given new vigor by the requirements of higher education and career, and by the temper of serious times. We noted, however, that delinquent orientations are also apparently spreading and growing stronger. Dominant in some schools, marginal in others, the delinquent subculture appears on the scene nearly everywhere as a major alternative orientation or "solution" for the adolescent. In brief, there is occurring a differentiation of adolescent styles, symbolized broadly by the three idealized types of the star athlete, the brilliant student, and the hood. With its partial detachment and its leeway for irresponsibility, the adolescent world is capable of producing its own responses, including its own deviations, to the technological age. It is affected but not completely controlled by the changing requirements of adult life.

HIGHER EDUCATION

The expert society changes the appearance and substance of higher education by altering its functions and its orientations, its organization and its unity. The relation of higher education to the general culture changes markedly as the university expands its research and its role in preparing researchers, and thus becomes evermore the creator as well as preserver and transmitter of knowledge. The university becomes a most active cultural and social force as its institutes and laboratories make it the producer of scientific ideas that transform work and society. The trend toward this active role has been underway since the last half of the nineteenth century; the years since 1945 have seen the trend rapidly accelerating.

So, too, is the relation of higher education to social class and personal attainment undergoing a transformation. When college was for the few, it helped to preserve the existing class and status alignments rather than to alter them. But now, increasingly, higher education is for all. The expert society needs more college-trained men and democratic doctrine encourages mass entry to college. As education becomes linked more closely to career and as an increasing proportion of the young gain access to college, the college becomes the common carrier, the vehicle, of upward social mobility for those from middle- and lower-class backgrounds. As *the* means for acquiring higher status, as well as of maintaining the high status obtained by some parents, the college encroaches upon the traditional strength of social class and family in determining the fate of the young.

With higher education's new and widening roles in modern society come changes in its structure and organization. Higher education is ever more differentiated, from trade schools devoted to handwork to liberal-arts colleges cast in a classical mold, from the intimate residential campus of several hundred to the impersonal, streetcar college aggregating twenty thousand students. Some colleges, based on specific clienteles and rooted in special traditions, stubbornly resist modern trends; others, linked to broad publics and devoted to general service, are immensely adaptive. The diversity notably contains: (a) *elite colleges,* largely oriented to the prestigeful liberal arts, but a few with a strong scientific-technological base; (b) *service institutions,* large colleges and universities that give Bachelor's and higher degrees and offer a wide array of occupational curricula as well as the liberal arts; and (c) *screening centers,* two-year colleges that classify and distribute students, sending some to the Bachelor-degree centers, keeping others away from the extended programs, and providing short-term training. The growth in enrollment takes place almost entirely in the service institutions and the screening centers, and the trends of the expert society promise to broaden even more this large place in higher education.

The growth in size and complexity of colleges, we also noted, extends and deepens the problems of administration. Colleges face from within the growing need for experts; even small places find themselves adding to the staff year by year men to specialize in admissions, purchasing, public relations, fund raising, and development. A central problem amidst the growing internal complexity is the distribution of authority. Administrations and faculties contend for authority, with each other and with the board of control. With increasing societal pressure and growing administration, authority is made a more critical issue than in most other institutions, for board influence and administrative control run up against the community-of-scholars conception of professors, their strong belief in freedom of inquiry and expression.

Lastly, we noted the existence of many student orientations in college and denoted four as the collegiate, the academic, the vocational, and the nonconformist. The collegiate, long dominant, is under assault from the academic and the vocational. The impulses of the expert society turn some students from play to serious study; they propel a larger number of students toward a vocational definition of their undergraduate years. The trend toward the vocational in the balance of the student subcultures is linked to the growing role of colleges as the producers of trained men, from physicists to medical laboratory technicians.

Thus many changes in higher education point to a growing vocationalism—more occupational curricula, more students directly preparing for work. Specialization in college education, as in work, is the underlying trend. The undergraduate college of the university as well as its graduate and professional schools prepares students for a growing assortment of advanced occupations. The traditional four-year liberal-arts curriculum is under double assault from preparation for work and preparation in a particular discipline for graduate study. The ubiquitous "general education program" is the counterattack of liberal-arts professors (themselves increasingly specialized) against the growing forces of the applied specialists.

MASS PROCESSING

According to all the signs, schools and colleges will be larger in the future, perhaps in some cases growing to a size not yet imagined. They will also be more complicated in structure and administration. The increase in scale, now upon us, cannot help but affect the educational experience. As suggested in Chapter 6, organizations that service or work upon a large number of persons commonly establish impersonal, objective procedures and often process persons in batches. When a single organization handles thousands of persons every day, the situation is unfavorable for prolonged personal contact and the organization generally finds it cannot "afford" an individualized approach.

There is no reason to think that most educational organizations growing in scale will escape the trend toward the impersonal. The health services of a state college in 1961 reported giving physical examinations to four thousand entering freshmen in a two-week period, at one point processing a thousand in a day. The quality of the relationship to student under such circumstances must take on some of the coloration of a military induction center or a civilian unemployment office. The long lines for registration that weave in and out of doors and down the street are now a common feature of education—as is the remedy for these long lines of using the IBM card and the mails as the means of contact between the college and the student. That large student bodies will be handled by various means of mass processing is already evidenced in large colleges and universities in the large lecture hall and the anonymous graduation, as well as in the registration line. Mass processing implies distant and fleeting relations, between students and teachers, and to a lesser degree among the students themselves.

The drift toward mass treatment extends the age-old problems: How do different relations among teachers and students affect the quality of the educational experience? How do the years spent in the confines of the educational establishment affect the mind and character of the young? Students, like other humans, are influenced deeply by (a) close personal contact and (b) membership in a group or organization that excites involvement and elicits identification. The most significant interactions in the formation of personality are emotional. "When interaction has emotional import, it reaches most deeply and has a more lasting effect on the core of personality."[2] Significant interaction generally results from persisting face-to-face contact; at all ages, and especially for the young, personal contact seems the primary condition of influence. Organizations also seem to promote their influence when they are able to make membership an exciting rather than a routine matter. Excitement, identification, a sense of belonging to a *different* organization—these are means by which some high schools and colleges reach and shape their students.

In schools and colleges where personal contact is weak and membership lacks excitement, we may expect that broad effects of education on the mind and character of students will be weak. There is little doubt that historical facts, technical data, and even broad concepts can be taught in the mass by highly impersonal means—the lecture hall of a thousand students. But there is ample doubt, on grounds of the psychological and social conditions of influence, whether mass processing can develop in students the broader understandings necessary for civilized men in a complicated civilization. Independent judgment, humane sensibility, an understanding and appreciation of subtle human affairs have long been taught, if at all, by the close interaction of a teacher and a small group of pupils or disciples. These central attributes of educated persons seemingly require prolonged influence by capable adults who are close enough to the student to act as model and mentor; or, to require a situation where the involvement of students in their work drives them, through mutual stimulation, to higher levels of understanding and greater maturity of judgment. Students can educate one another, but only when they are frequently accessible to one another.

Can the conditions of close contact and meaningful membership be cultivated in large schools and colleges? They

[2] Leonard Broom and Philip Selznick, *Sociology* (Evanston, Illinois: Row, Peterson and Co., 1958), p. 90.

apparently can to a large degree, through the subdividing of the whole into parts to which these conditions more readily attach. As indicated in Chapter 6, some colleges attempt to remain small as they admit more students by apportioning their students to a cluster of discrete units. The units remain small and personal, while the over-all framework grows larger and more impersonal. Too, the public schools have long committed themselves, more than the large colleges, to small size and personal attention. In a sense, the public schools have always extensively substructured—breaking down the district into small neighborhood schools and subdividing the school by grade level and homeroom.

Over all, however, the trend is away from substructuring. The public schools, especially the high schools, are grouping students in larger aggregates, and the college campuses that are growing by leaps and bounds are little inclined to subdivide their student bodies. When officials think about substructuring, they consider it expensive. It does not seem important, compared with the problems of providing enough classrooms and bedrooms. Efficiency in preparing the young for the modern age, most authorities argue, depends largely on quality of facilities and personnel, and large size is the way of gaining the higher quality.

Educational television, in this matter, has many pros and cons. The televised lecture or demonstration can reach large numbers of students economically; such programs generally have excellent teachers and hence represent an efficient use of scarce talent; the televised performance is often a dramatic demonstration, utilizing techniques too expensive for the individual classroom, and hence can better excite and stir students; and educational TV in the classroom can have the side effect of invigorating the classroom teacher, through the intrusion of the knowledge, methods, and personality of the televised instructor. Educational TV is apparently effective in transmitting technical information, explaining concepts through dramatic demonstration, and presenting adult models of considerable personal appeal.

Many schools and colleges experimenting with televised instruction also attempt to combine it with classroom instruction in ways that will maintain a close, two-way interaction between students and teachers. In the main, however, classroom television furthers the drift toward mass processing in education. It removes the person giving the instruction from the classroom and interposes the studio and machine between the student and the teacher. Impersonality in education is extended, and fixed by the technical investment. The effects of televised instruction in this direction will be strong in the school systems and colleges where dollars or teachers are in drastic shortage, for then the temptation will be strongest to substitute the machine *for* the teacher, rather than to use it as an aide or surround it with personal contact.

RAPID CHANGE

It is slowly dawning on mid-twentieth-century man that his world is different from his predecessors' in the rapidity of social change. Especially in technology—rocketry is a startling example—the new develops at an exponential rate. In industry, methods of production and distribution succeed one another in quick succession and organizational structures are revamped time and again to fit changing methods or to meet changing conditions. Change is also dramatically rapid in international relations, where new nations, volatile in impulse, become in a brief span of years industrialized powers of sufficient potency to affect the course of world history—even perhaps the survival of mankind.

Such changes constitute a massive pressure on an educational institution to re-examine its nature and synthesize anew, over and over and over again. American schools and colleges are under pressure to be up-to-date with the latest knowledge, but also to retain the best of the past. Many groups, from national foundations to local chambers of commerce, press them to revamp and extend. We may expect, in societies caught in accelerating change, a growing consciousness that the lessons of the past are not sufficient, a questioning of whether they are good enough. Rapid change places the burden of proof on the "tried and true" to justify its place, to show its relevance. In the stable society, the education of the son can be safely modeled after the education of the father. But rapid change raises the problem of obsolescence—in curriculum, teacher, plant, administrative structure, and parental perspective—in education as it does outside of education in technique and product. What has been done before is made problematic; it may be right but people are less sure it is.

With the environment changing and the habits of today potentially inadequate for tomorrow, the need deepens in educational organizations for a posture of flexibility—the leeway and capability to make changes when appropriate. This need is strong in the public schools and colleges, challenged by their broad constituencies to assume additional tasks, to adapt to the new, to diversify to please the host of supporters. Private establishments also find they must offer adaptive responses; for example, to expand in number or to commit themselves more rigorously to excellence for a few. Compared to virtually all of the past, the future will call for greater adaptability within education as a whole and within many of its specific organizations.

Yet the institutionalization of thought and behavior that takes place in organization insures always a certain resistance to change. Organizations whose character was cast in the mold of the past are generally conservative. In a crisis, they may be transformed by the infusion of new personnel; but matured organizations are usually well anchored and devoted to the manner in which they were raised. The more radical adaptations are generally left to new organizations. This tendency, together with such other reasons as the growing volume of educational tasks, promotes a greater division of labor among and within schools and colleges. In the pluralistic society of the future, we will see more different kinds of schools and colleges, with some remaining primarily the carriers of the older programs and styles while others will be the vehicles for the introduction of new combinations and radically new formulations. The substantial educational systems of industry and the military are cases in point. The educational institution will become more dispersed and disparate, resembling a crazy quilt patched with materials of varied hue and size.

It helps in understanding the impact of modern social trends to realize how different education was only a century ago. Before the Civil War, education was relatively detached from the problems of the dominant economic and political institutions. In an age of educational simplicity, schools and colleges were relatively passive, residing apart from the main stream of state and national affairs. This sequestered condition was altered between the Civil War and the turn of the century, attendant upon the country's industrialization and growth into a large nation. As indicated in the earlier chapters, education, especially higher education, then gradually became, in the twentieth century, more closely and intricately linked to the economy. It is inherent in a technological society that education becomes evermore involved, never again to be an innocent institution. The future promises more ties between education and other institutions that are constantly being reconstituted by the effects of technology and their own dynamics of expansion and change.

The problem of leadership in education at the broadest level, as in other institutions, is to understand what is happening, and foresee what is about to happen, fast enough to engage the will, to counter drift with design by building organizations and fashioning programs that steer change in desired directions. Matters are changing sufficiently fast in many sectors of society that to guess the future is barely to keep up with the present. "The rate of change has increased so much that our imagination can't keep up. There is *bound* to be more social change, affecting more people, in the next decade than in any before. There is *bound* to be more change again, in the 1970's."[3] After technology, rapid change is the elementary social fact of the times.

TECHNICAL BARBARISM

Education also is drawn into the main stream of society as it is mobilized as a national resource, a tendency now widely promoted by the rivalry of nations, especially the bitter contest between democratic and totalitarian powers. Totalitarian regimes, by their nature, amalgamate education to the dominant political institution and attempt to shape its development in line with the needs of party control and national purpose. The international struggle against such regimes also pushes democratic nations toward an instrumental conception of education, as demonstrated in the United States by the heightened concern after sputnik with education's contribution to national strength. In the democratic nations, however, with their relatively plural structure, national need is but one of many ends, for local interests are brought to bear and the educational organiza-

[3] C. P. Snow, *The Two Cultures and the Scientific Revolution* (Cambridge, England: Cambridge University Press, 1959), p. 40.

tions themselves have some autonomy in deciding what they will do. Compared with totalitarian countries, education in democracies is not so readily mobilized for national purpose, but the efforts to mobilize it do move it toward the status of national agent.

The democratic-totalitarian contest extends the part played by education in the relationship of industrial societies to the underdeveloped countries of the world. The pre-industrial nations—Indonesia, India, Egypt, Ghana—desire strongly to accelerate their own development, and in one way or another industrialized they will be. The prime way to industrialize rapidly is to borrow men, knowledge, equipment, and technique from the technologically advanced nations, which means turning to the democratic or Communist powers or both. This creates a greater need in the major advanced societies to export scientists, engineers, and technicians to the underdeveloped areas to help them with their modernization and in the process to convince them that rapid industrialization can be accomplished within a preferred political framework. But the thousands of trained men needed for this work must be more than specialists if their effort is not to boomerang. They ought to be "trained scientists and engineers adaptable enough to devote themselves to a foreign country's industrialization for at least ten years out of their lives. . . . These men, whom we don't yet possess, need to be trained not only in scientific but in human terms. They could not do their job if they did not shrug off every trace of paternalism."[4] The educational problem is how to prepare in large numbers the engineers and scientists who are more than specialists—trained "in human terms"—and who will devote part of their lives to working abroad in underdeveloped areas.

The requirements for adequately assisting under-

[4] Snow, *The Two Cultures,* p. 45.

developed countries are one segment of a larger problem: What are the social and organizational conditions for preparing educated experts? To train men technically, we now know, is relatively simple. The difficulty lies in finding the inclination, the time, and the ways to combine the technical training, simultaneously or in sequence, with an education in the basic sciences, the humanities, and the social sciences. Various attempts are being made in the high school, the undergraduate college, the graduate school—even in the corporation—to bring the cultural disciplines and the social sciences, plus a broad scientific understanding, into the technical programs or to place the specialized training in a liberal-arts setting. Yet the underlying trend is for marked specialization and separation of fields of knowledge, making it ever more difficult to attain an adequate combination of depth and breadth, of "education" and "training."

The problem of the expert raised by the democratic-totalitarian struggle and the needs of underdeveloped societies is thus finally the large issue of the possibilities of educating men for cultural maturity and social responsibility in a technological age. Can the educational enterprise develop the capability to educate broadly as the curriculum turns toward technical thought and men train for specialized occupations? Historic functions may be lost or weakened as an institution necessarily becomes absorbed in a new function. The basic trends of a technological society move the perspectives of the technical man toward the center of educational affairs, while edging the style and the knowledge of the nontechnical generalist toward the periphery. As a society veers toward expertise, the cultural strains highlighted by the old distinctions between the cultivated man and the expert, the pure and the applied, are made severe. The efforts to bring liberal education to the expert constitute a social response to the strain, an attempt to avoid a barbarism of men acute in technical judgment but myopic in social affairs, politics, and cultural understanding. The future of the expert society challenges education to close a gap that in the natural course of affairs will ever widen.

Index